Global Shaping and
its Alternatives

Global Shaping and its Alternatives

edited by

Yıldız Atasoy
Simon Fraser University

and

William K. Carroll
University of Victoria

Garamond Press
Aurora, Ontario

Printed and bound in Canada

Published 2003 in Canada by Garamond Press Ltd,
63 Mahogany Court, Aurora, Ontario L4G 6M8

Published 2003 in the United States of America by Kumarian Press Inc.,
1294 Blue Hills Ave., Bloomfield, Connecticut 06002

Cover photo courtesy Y. Atasoy

National Library of Canada Cataloguing in Publication

Global shaping and its alternatives / by Yildiz Atasoy and
William K. Carroll, editors

Includes bibliographical references and index.
ISBN 1-55193-043-9

1. Globalization. 2. Globalization—Social aspects.
3. International economic relations. I. Atasoy, Yildiz, 1961-
II. Carroll, William K.

JZ1318.G5589 2003   303.48'2   C2002-
905394-3

Garamond Press gratefully acknowledges the support of the Department of Canadian Heritage, Government of Canada, for its publishing programme, the Canadian Studies Bureau of the same department for support of special projects, and the Vice-President, Research, of the University of Victoria for support of this specific work..

Contents

Contributors

Yıldız Atasoy received her Ph.D in sociology from the University of Toronto. She is an Assistant Professor in the Department of Sociology and Anthropology at Simon Fraser University, Burnaby, British Columbia, specializing in transnational political economy, political sociology, and gender relations.

William K. Carroll is Professor of Sociology at the University of Victoria, British Columbia, where he participates in the Interdisciplinary Graduate Program in Contemporary Social and Political Thought. He is currently Sociology Editor of the *Canadian Review of Sociology and Anthropology*.

Robert Chernomas is an Associate Professor in the Department of Economics at the University of Manitoba.

Elaine Coburn is currently competing her Ph.D at Stanford University in California, researching the emerging resistance to globalization.

Jean-Luc Chodkiewicz received his Ph.D in anthropology from Columbia University. He is an Associate Professor in the Anthropology Department at the University of Manitoba and President of the Society for Applied Anthropology in Manitoba.

Ann Denis is Professor and Chair in the Department of Sociology at the University of Ottawa.

Vanaja Dhruvarajan is Professor of Sociology, retd., from the University of Winnipeg, and former President of the Canadian Sociology and Anthropology Association.

Helen O'Neill, Ph.D (Economics, McGill) is Director of the Centre for Development Studies in the National University of Ireland, Dublin (University College Dublin).

Ardeshir Sepehri is Associate Professor of Economics at the University of Manitoba.

Preface

Vanaja Dhruvarajan

This book originates from a colloquium titled "Globalization, Societies and Cultures" which was held during the Congress 2000 in Edmonton, Alberta.

The colloquium was sponsored by the Humanities and Social Sciences Federation of Canada (HSSFC), the organizer of the Congress, which also provided financial and organizational support. The then president Dr. Louise Forsyth gave strong moral support and encouragement for the colloquium and Mr. Paul Ledwell, the director of the Congress took care of many administrative details and provided help to organize the colloquium. This colloquium was the second one on the theme of Globalization sponsored by the HSSFC. The first one held during the Congress 1999 was titled "Globalization and the Nation State" and focussed on understanding the structures of Globalization and the role of Canadian state in that context. This particular colloquium was considered a sequel to the previous one with a focus on critical appraisal and suggestion of alternate paradigms.

Globalization, Societies and Cultures, was one of the three major themes chosen for the Congress 2000 by the HSSFC Board of Directors. The procedure is that for each Congress, the member associations are asked to submit the themes and three out of the many submissions are chosen for a given Congress. I proposed this theme which was titled "Globalization, Discourse of Inevitability and a search for Alternate Paradigms" as president of the Canadian Sociology and Anthropology Association (CSAA) with the backing of the Women's Caucus of the Association. This theme was chosen with some modification in the title, which I understand was for the sake of simplicity in presentation, but the objective was not altered.

I was motivated to propose this theme because I was profoundly disturbed by the many negative impacts of corporate sponsored globalization currently underway. I was particularly appalled by the general lack of critical evaluation of this project; there was an implicit faith that this is the only right way, and no other alternatives were considered. A discourse of inevitability is constructed and widely disseminated. Reminiscent of dictates of religious fundamentalism, this project is implemented with faith and commitment by developing a language of its own and developing its own methods of assessments of success. No critical reflection of the process or the outcome is entertained. If fault lines are identified and negative outcomes are impossible to deny, the diagnosis is that the project is not implemented with enough diligence, faith and efficiency. Therefore, more of the same is prescribed. This is done when the increase in the disparity between the rich and the poor, erosion of powers of democratically elected governments, destruction/depletion/pollution of environment and spread of ethnic violence are occurring all around us. In spite of these negative outcomes, evident for everyone who cared to see, the often repeated slogans are "this is the only way," "in the long run the tide will raise all boats," "we must stay the course," and so on. If one persists on pointing out that the negative outcomes are endemic to the process and not an accidental short-term outcome, one is called a globophobe, a protectionist and a Luddite. The intent is to dissuade everyone from considering that there are alternatives.

The fact is that there are alternate paradigms, but they are all marginalized, discredited, stigmatized, and trivialized. The hegemonic status enjoyed by the neoliberal paradigm has made it difficult for any other paradigm to get enough exposure to be considered a viable alternative. Among the alternatives we can include the ecology movement, post-colonial thought, feminist movements, re-localization movements. Those who are involved in the ecology movement have shown how living in harmony with nature is the best way. Environment is not something that is out there but it is part of us. If we harm the environment, we harm ourselves. Imposing a paradigm of unlimited growth on a planet with finite resources is nothing but courting disaster. Those who are working within the area of post-colonial thought make us aware of multiple ways of life successfully practiced for generations in different cultures. They point out that imposition of a way of life that commodifies all aspects of human life and natural resources will virtually destroy all these cultures. Feminists have been arguing that the philosophical foundations of the globalization paradigm have the effect of producing dehumanized societies obsessed with consumerism. Emotional and spiritual needs of people are ignored to the detriment of the welfare of all. Organization of social life must be guided by a holistic approach that pays attention to material, spiritual and emotional needs of all people. There are those who argue that the needs of communities are best satisfied when powers to make decisions about all aspects of social life reside within local rather than global arena. Bureaucracies residing in the distant global centres cannot respond to the needs of people in different localities with varied histories, cultures and consequently different hopes and aspirations. The attempts to impose a monoculture and homogenize all institutional structures will be tantamount to dehumanization and cloning. In order to be able to lead an enriching creative life, people should be empowered to choose their own way of life and be in control of their own destiny. There are many such alternatives coming from multiple sources.

The events of the last two decades have cast in doubt the hopes and aspirations of people who thought that they had emerged victorious after casting off the yoke of colonial rule and imperialistic control. Fond hopes of feminist and anti-racism movements worldwide of ridding us of sexism and racism are being shattered. The old bondages are taking new forms, as corporate colonialism becomes the order of the day. Thus, there are many continuities in the nature of oppression and exploitation as the new economic regimes are built on existing patriarchal, racist, colonial and imperial foundations. But the globalization currently underway also differs from the old forms of oppression and domination. Significant among them is its speed and reach. The awesome power the centralized global economic institutions can wield with the help of new technology and sophisticated organizational structure is frightening. Governments across the globe are being forced to cede the power of governance to these global bureaucracies, while the people have nowhere to turn to protect their interests. But, the carefully crafted discourse constructs this project as having been naturally evolved and freely chosen as the only alternative to serve the needs of humanity.

The objectives of this colloquium were to deconstruct the discourse of inevitability by demystifying the project. Making the process of the project's implementation transparent establishes that it has neither evolved naturally, nor do the people have a choice to exercise their options. The discussions and dialogues also were meant to show how the negative outcomes of this project are intrinsic to it rather than short-term effects, which eventually will correct themselves. Such revelations establish that 'the tide of economic growth and prosperity does not raise all boats'. By delineating alternate paradigms the slogan 'there is no other way', was intended to be proved a myth. The hopes and expectations were that these efforts along with many such efforts underway will help provide conditions conducive for the spread of counter-hegemonic movements that eventually discredit the project of corporate sponsored globalization and deprive it of the hegemonic status it currently enjoys. History is full of examples in which struggles against structures of oppression and domination, apparently insurmountable, have been successful. This has been possible when people get rid of their apathy, feel empowered rather than alienated, and participate enthusiastically in the movements for change. But the future is uncertain, as there are always unforeseen factors. It is under these circumstances that I am inspired by the exhortations of the Geetha, the Hindu religious sacred scripture—"Do your duty because it is the right thing to do. You do not have control over the outcome but only on your own actions." So the struggles must continue…

Part I Sociology of Globalization

Chapter One

Explaining Globalization

by Yıldız Atasoy

Today it is rare to read a book, a journal article or a news item without encountering the word "globalization." Scholars, politicians, policy-makers and the general public are all concerned with the meaning of globalization. It seems that the word "globalization" is frequently used to mean major transformations in the global system under the influence of what Polanyi (1944) called the "self-regulating market." For example, the authors of *The Case Against the Global Economy* (Mander and Goldstein, 1996) discuss various issues concerning globalization from several perspectives, but with a specific reference to the market. They all agree that there is something fundamentally different about "globalization." According to these authors "globalization" involves the most fundamental redesign of the planet's political and economic arrangements since the Industrial Revolution.

Although many agree that globalization refers to profound transformations world-wide, some scholars argue that the term "globalization" is fundamentally misleading and amorphous (Strange, 1996; Carroll, this volume) and what the word refers to is not new (Panitch, 1996; Wallerstein, 1999; Arrighi, 1999). According to Carroll (this volume), it represents a new phase of imperialism – ultra-imperialism.

Many books and journal articles written in the field define globalization as a self-consolidating homogeneous "thing" created and regulated by the "invisible hand" of the market economy. These studies are also concerned with the adverse consequences of a market economy for human life and the natural environment. They suggest ways to counter globalization by taking steps towards reconfiguring our lives within the local communities (Mander and Goldstein, 1996). But, little scholarly attempt has been made to problematize the transformative power of the "self-regulating market," even though many agree that globalization involves integration into the globalized world markets through commodity chains (Hoogvelt, 1987).

Some scholars define "it" as the reorganization of production and international trade to the integration of financial markets (Mittelman, 1996). Others approach it as "internationalization" generated by shifting price-cost relations in the service of increasing national competitiveness (Keohane and Milner, 1996). These studies sometimes invoke ideas about a "new international division of labour" (Frobel et al., 1980) and "global market integration" (Cox, 1996). What is common to all these definitions is the notion of "time-space compression" (Harvey, 1989) in which the unprecedented speed of transactions affect global political economy in unprecedented ways. This is a process which is also greatly facilitated by improvements in technology and communications (Menzier, 1998)

McMichael (2000) suggests that the word "globalization" points to a qualitatively new phenomenon pertaining to a process that broadens and deepens the rule of capitalist market economy everywhere. The global economy reshapes the conditions under which states make economic policy (McMichael, 1996: 33). This cannot be understood as a quantitative expansion of older trends related to international trade, financial expansion or any other inter-national transactions. The behaviour of market forces does not aggregate into a whole. It is the changes in the state structure and actions that produce a coherent outcome at the aggregate level. Focusing on issues related to economic development and mechanisms of debt management, McMichael (2000) conceptualizes globalization as a project dictated by a private-public coalition of global managers on states. The debt regime of the 1980s institutionalized the power and authority of global management within the very organization and behaviour of states. Although there is no agreement on the role of states (Arrighi, 1999; Weis, 1998; Sassen, 1996), through this project national states and cultures become subordinated (Friedmann, 2000) or accessories (Carroll, this volume) to the market economy and its structure of class domination.

In addition to market economic integration and subordination of states, there is also growing interest in the globalization of culture. The advocates of this dimension of globalization argue that we are moving toward greater global integration as Western cultural values based on individualism, rationality and progress gain primacy over the particularizing tendencies of traditional/local cultures. "Cosmopolitanism" (Tomlinson, 1999; Cheah and Robbins, 1998) and "McDonaldization" (Ritzer, 2000) are among the catchwords.

While not denying the importance of any of these ideas, this book is not an attempt to define globalization. But there are important insights that we draw from McMichael's analysis of the globalization project. First, the idea that it is impossible to understand globalization unless strategies of capital accumulation are examined under changing power relations of capitalism. Drawing from Arrighi (1994), Friedmann (1998) and McMichael (2000), we understand globalization as an expression of the changing world historical dynamics of political economy, including development strategies, class interests, the state and geopolitics (Chernomas and Sepehri, this volume; Atasoy, this volume). Second, we maintain that the notion of globalization is deeply saturated with an ideology which asserts the "inevitability" of market integration and subordination of states to the requirements of market capitalism (Carroll, this volume). Drawing from Polanyi (1944) we maintain that markets exist by virtue of state-made rules and state-enforced agreements that create and sustain the illusion that they are self-regulating (Atasoy, this volume). This makes us suspicious of the notion that the processes of globalization are at work unchecked.

We question the notion of "inevitability" attributed to global market integration, and build on the idea that markets are political creations. Polanyi (1944) insists that there is nothing inevitable or natural in the historical changes that gave way to market capitalism. State policies are fundamentally constituted by political choices made by state managers in response to domestic and international political and ideological/cultural pressures (Block, 1986). After all, it was the decision of state authorities to restructure state organs and institutionalize the power of the financial, transnational corporate elite and the managers of the multilateral institutions for the global debt crisis management (McMichael, 1996). Local cultural values, political practices and historical legacies are very much part of developing policies and the making of political choices (Atasoy, this volume). In line with this argument, we argue that it is also possible to develop alternative projects.

Drawing primarily upon feminist perspectives, we analyse the politics of alternatives to the global market integration and explore ways of constructing a political basis for broader political alliances and empowering victims of market capitalism. This is also a significant attempt to build a bridge between debates on the economic and cultural dimensions of globalization.

This book offers a unique opportunity to make conceptual connections between market capitalism, politics of alternatives, and the cultural elaboration of social change. It argues that there is a need for an alternative explanatory framework of the shaping of globalization – one which rejects a fatalistic stance by problematizing the inevitability of it. Without understanding how the global shaping is taking place and how it affects human life across the globe, there can be no transformational possibility for humanizing our conditions of existence.

Part II, *Economic Shaping of Globalization*, offers an overview of changes in the dynamics of the world economy, states, state system, and capital accumulation. We examine the rival economic strategies within a global economy by looking at the politics of various capital groups across the globe. Specifically, there is a growing number of business groups, industrialists and financiers who are actively shaping market-oriented economic growth projects around the world. An analysis of their activities provides a meaningful understanding of global political economy. Here we incorporate macro level changes in the world economy and state system into the emergent politics of community-based alternatives.

Chapter 2, *Is Globalization a Reality, a Tendency or a Rationale for Neoliberal Economic Policies?*, analyses the rise of the current economic orthodoxy by focusing on the debt crisis and the world economic changes which took place after the mid-1970s. Globalization, viewed as "internationalization," is defined in terms of the cross-border flows of money, investment, goods and services and the growing world market integration. Although Robert Chernomas and Ardeshir Sepehri argue that the turning point in the "internationalization" of the economy was a shift in government policy from a concern with the welfare of its citizens to a fight with inflation, deficits/debt and costs of social-civilian spending, they suggest that current globalization does not present new dynamics in the present organization of the world economy. To show this, the authors organize their analysis around the following categories:

1. The extent of internationalization as measured by the share of foreign direct investments (FDI) and the exports-imports ratio in GNPs across the globe and within geographic trading blocs.
2. The shift in the state-policy and changing dynamics of decision making process as dictated by such multilateral organizations as the WTO.

Chapter 3, *Undoing the End of History: Canada-Centred Reflections on the Challenge of Globalization*, challenges the ideology, promoted by conservative theorists and advocates of a free market economy, which claims that there is no alternative to global economic integration, suggesting that global expansion of market forces is inevitable and uncontested. Bill Carroll complements the argument advanced in Chapter 2, which looks at the quantitative expansion involved in the cross-border flows of goods, money and investments, to argue that key aspects of global transformations are not new at all. What is "qualitatively" new at a new juncture in the long history of capital accumulation, according to Carroll, is an "ultra-imperialism" which subordinates states to the laws of market expansion of capital. What is most convincingly different about globalization at present is that it presents ultra-imperialism as inevitable, natural and universal. Carroll argues that globalization is deeply imbued with an ideology which "de-historicizes" capital accumulation by veiling humans from ever-widening inequalities and political and class interests, by naturalizing human subjectification to capital and securing popular "consent" for market domination as common sense. He locates the agency that might undo this "end of history" in the emergence of a democratizing globalization-from-below.

Chapter 4, *Explaining Local-Global Nexus: Muslim Politics in Turkey*, illustrates the locally specific politico-cultural meaning of global shaping. Yıldız Atasoy examines the conjunction of global and local within a broad historical context of market economic expansion from 1839 to 2000, focusing on the interplay between secular and Islamist trajectories of social change in Turkey. The analysis is based on a theory of social change that employs a form of comparison linking the global relations of capital accumulation (including changing patterns of trade, investment and labour migration), military alliances and transnational dynamics of Islamist political movements to the political and discursive tensions of national politics. This perspective bridges the economic and cultural dimensions of globalization, problematizing the dichotomous conception of universality attached to Western cultural arrangements, on the one hand, and the particularism and "traditionalism" attached to local cultural projects on the other. Islamists in Turkey combine Muslim values with strategies of capital accumulation. This may be seen as an attempt to reposition Islamist capitalists within the global economy as a competitive class, conversely, this may also be interpreted as a case of an anti-Western resistance movement against the Western dominance in the global market economy. Either way, Atasoy argues that globalization is not just the cross-border flows of trade and investment, but also involves substantial political/ cultural transformations within states as well as within the military-strategic alliances of the state system.

Part III, *Global Politics: The Role of Non-Governmental and Governmental International Organizations*, offers an overview of the role of international institutions in generating a political space for action beyond the regulatory framework of nation-states. We are not concerned here with a discussion of state "sovereignty"; but, rather, explore the possibility of conceptualizing "globalization" without taking the state as a primary analytical tool. We advance a "globalization" perspective by examining the operation of international and nongovernmental organizations which operate with considerable autonomy from states.

Chapter 5, *Globalization, Competitiveness and Human Security: Revisited*, discusses the consequences of globalization and economic competitiveness among national states for human well-being throughout the world. Helen O'Neill defines "competitiveness" as a state design to make national economic space "attractive" for foreign investment. Globalization, on the other hand, is conceptualized as both quantitative and qualitative changes in the world economy. It consists of processes of cross-border flows of money, goods, investment as well as the regional/global integration of corporations around "production/commodity chains." Focusing on various dimensions of "human security," a relatively new concept introduced by the United Nations in 1994, O'Neill suggests that citizens of both "North" and "South" may share similar human insecurities, resulting from globalization, around such issues as food safety and un/availability of food, threat of unemployment, homelessness, breakdown of the family, and widening income inequalities. Although she argues that a global economy left to the unregulated market could be devastating, she is optimistic that corporations could be made socially responsible. O'Neill attributes a regulatory and managerial role to various international organizations concerned with development and poverty eradication in order to make "globalization" work for all. This involves promoting "human security" among national governments and incorporating policy alternatives negotiated within the international organizations into the national policies of the states. This may constrain the autonomous capacity of the nation-states to make policy, but points to the beneficial possibilities of a carefully managed global economy for ensuring "security" for humankind.

Chapter 6, *Capitalism, Class and Collective Action: Emerging Conflicts and Contradictions*, is concerned with the contradictory character of the political shaping of globalization, Elaine Coburn departs from Helen O'Neill's optimism. Rather than expressing a preoccupation with a global political management and more regulation, she is concerned with organizing alternative ways of living, looking at the role of transnational NGO-led social movements in countering economic liberalization and integration programs of international organizations. She suggests that the tension between capital accumulation (economic globalization) and NGO movements designed for greater democratization (political globalization) produces an outcome which is qualitatively different, yet whose shape is unknown. In contrast to a singular understanding of globalization which hypothesizes that market forces are turning the world into a homogeneous totality, this chapter explores the possibility of articulating differences and transnational political movements in the contradictory character of political shaping of globalization. By focussing on the Multilateral Agreement on Investment (MAI) and its political undoing, this analysis poses a challenge to the ideological conservatism which considers the globalization project of capital inevitable.

Part IV, *Politics of Alternatives*, examines four case studies on consequences and structural constraints of contemporary globalization. Their empirical focus is on the unfolding history of economic integration of states into the global economy and the implications for women's lives.

These chapters offer a sense that neoliberal globalization is not an inevitable outcome, and that the locally-embedded politics of organizing alternative ways of living still matter.

Chapter 7, *Women and Globalization in the Economic North and South*, suggests that globalization needs to be seen as a gendered phenomenon. Ann Denis studies women working the CARIBCAN and NAFTA free trade zones by focusing on Commonwealth Caribbean, particularly Barbados, and Canada. After comparing corporate strategies of structural adjustment of economies and work to the globalized markets, she asks how this affects the daily lives of women working in the unpaid reproductive sphere of the non-market economy and the paid productive sphere of the market economy. She suggests that globalizing women's work in both spheres of the economy creates conditions for further appropriation of women, in the form of "sexage," which sets "inescapable constraints" on women's choices. Nevertheless, building on the optimism generated by the long history of feminist struggles, Denis sees women as active agents in shaping their own lives, rather than passive victims. Women create alternatives, either to help them cope with the adverse effects of global appropriation, or to resist it through building on the global feminist networks.

In Chapter 8, *Two Faces of Globalization in Mexico: Maquiladoras and Zapatistas,* Jean-Luc Chodkiewicz analyses the introduction of new work practices within maquiladoras in Mexico after the economic crisis of the 1970s. This chapter takes us to a critical understanding of the impact of neoliberal policies on women producing commodities, in the maquiladoras, to be consumed in the NAFTA nexus of global consumption. Chodkiewicz shows how restructured work places and work place practices are built on "old" gender ideologies and offers an indigenous local strategy of resistance drawn from the example of the Zapatista movement, itself a response to the neoliberal agricultural policy of a government which subordinated local food production to U.S. agribusiness interests.

In Chapter 9, *Feminism and Resistance to Globalization of Capitalism*, Vanaja Dhruvarajan offers a provocative discussion for the re-evaluation of women's experiences in a globalized market economy by focusing on women's practical needs and daily life requirements. She emphasizes that women's experiences within globalization differ across nations. Therefore, it is imperative that coalitions across gender, race/ethnicity, nationality and class be forged under the unifying theme of an emerging feminist paradigm, emphasizing the intersecting and interlocking relations of gender, race/ethnicity and class in striving for a just and caring world.

In the concluding afterword, *September 11 and the Reorganization of the World Economy*, the focus is on the reorganization of the world economy in the immediate aftermath of the September 11th attacks on the World Trade Center and Pentagon, and the American declaration of war on al Qaeda and Taliban regime in Afghanistan. Yıldız Atasoy analyses the conjunctural articulation of political-military, cultural-ideological and economic forces. She reaffirms the book's argument that globalization is not an inevitable process but a deliberately designed political project. If it is a project designed by political and economic elites to reorganize the world economy and the state system, then it is also possible to develop alternative counter projects.

References

Arrighi, G. (1999). "Globalization and Historical Macrosociology" in *Sociology for the Twenty-First Century* (ed. J. Abu-Lughod). Chicago: University of Chicago Press, pp: 117-133.

(1994). *The Long Twentieth Century.* London: Verso.

Block, F. (1986). "Political Choice and the Multiple 'Logics' of Capital" in *Theory and Society* 15: 175-192.

Cheah, P and B. Robbins (eds.). (1998). *Cosmopolitics: Thinking and Feeling beyond the Nation.* Minneapolis: University of Minnesota Press.

Cox, R. (1996). "A Perspective on Globalization" in *Globalization: Critical Reflections* (ed. J. Mittelmann). Boulder, CO: Lynne Reinner Publishers, pp. 21-30.

Friedmann. H. (2000). "What on Earth Is the Modern World System? Foodgetting and Territory in the Modern Era and Beyond" in *Journal of World System Research, Special Issue: Festchrift for Immanual Wallerstein - Part I*, VI, 2, Summer/Fall, pp. 48-515.

(1998). "Warsaw Pact Socialism: Detente and the Disintegration of the Soviet Bloc" in *Rethinking the Cold War* (ed. A. Hunter). Philadelphia: Temple University Press.

Froebel, F., J. Heinrichs, and O. Kreye. (1981). *The New International Division of Labour.* Cambridge: Cambridge University Press.

Harvey, D. (1989). *The Condition of Postmodernity.* Oxford: Basil Blackwell.

Hoogvelt, M. A. (1987). *The Third World in Global Development.* London: Macmillan.

Keohane, R. and H. Milner (eds.). *Internationalization and Domestic Politics.* Cambridge: University of Cambridge Press.

Mander, J. and E. Goldstein. *The Case Against the Global Economy and For a Turn Toward the Local.* San Francisco: Sierra Club Books.

Menzier, H. (1998). *Whose Brave New World? The Information Highway and the New Economy.* Toronto: Between the Lines.

Mittelmann, J. (1996). *Globalization: Critical Reflections.* Boulder, CO: Lynne Reinner Publishers.

McMichael, P. (2000). *Development and Social Change, 2nd ed.* Thousand Oaks, California: Pine Forge.

(1996). "Globalization: Myths and Realities" in *Rural Sociology* 61(1): 25-55.

Panitch, L. (1996). "Rethinking the Role of the State", in *Globalization: Critical Reflections* (ed. J. Mittelmann). Boulder, CO: Lynne Reinner Publishers, pp. 83-113.

Ritzer, G. (2000). *The McDonaldization of Society.* Thousand Oaks, California: Pine Forge Press.

Sassen, S. (1996). *Losing Control?* New York: Columbia University Press.

Strange, S. (1996). *The Retreat of the State: The Diffusion of Power in the World Economy.* New York: Cambridge University Press.

Polanyi, K. (1944). *The Great Transformation.* Boston: Beacon Press.

Tomlinson, J. (1999). *Globalization and Culture.* Chicago: University of Chicago Press.

Wallerstein, I. (1999). "States? Sovereignty? The Dilemmas of Capitalists in an Age of Transition", in State Sovereignty and the "Endless" Accumulation of Capital" in *States and Sovereignty in the Global Economy* (eds. David A. Smith, D. J. Solinger, and S. C. Topic). London: Routledge, pp.20-33.

Weis, L. (1998). *The Myth of the Powerless State.* Ithaca: Cornell University Press.

Part II Economic Shaping
of Globalization

Is Globalization a Reality, a Tendency, or a Rationale for Neoliberal Economic Policies?

by Robert Chernomas and Ardeshir Sepehri

The Great Stagnation-
Historical Context for Globalization

In the decade of the 1960s the world economy grew at the rate of 5.0 percent. In the 1970s the real growth rate dropped to 3.6 percent. By the 1980s the rate had dropped to 2.8 percent and continued this decline in the 1990s when it fell to 2.0 percent. In two decades capitalism lost 60 percent of its macroeconomic momentum (Thurow, 1996: 1-2). Through the 1990s the overall European unemployment rate remained in double digits while the Japanese economy has been stagnating for a decade. The recent capitalist convert, Russia, appears to be demodernizing to Third World levels, while much of the Southern hemisphere has seen its social indicators deteriorating from already disastrous levels.

Theoretical Context

There is a significant body of evidence suggesting that capitalism entered into an economic crisis phase in the late 1960s due to a fall in the rate of profit as a consequence of the costs of production rising faster than productivity and/or price (Brenner, 1998; Cherry, 1987). Crisis in this context does not mean catastrophic economic breakdown or the end to capitalist social relations. Nor does it mean capitalism as usual (since 1945). The difference between capitalism's business cycles and an economic crisis is that with non-crisis cyclical conditions, normal economic activity, within the context of prevailing social relationships, is sufficient to restore prosperity (Gordon, 1980). By contrast, crises undermine the stability of the institutional framework, because as accumulation slackens, less profit is available for the maintenance of those institutions whose relative stability and reproducibility permit the repeated fulfilment of an important socio-economic function.

Capitalism runs on profit. Without adequate profits, firms cannot invest in order to lower their costs of production (e.g. robots), promote research and design in order to invent new products, produce new plant and equipment to meet increases in demand or to generate dividends for their owners. The same firm will not be able to pay debts or advertise, in a word they cannot compete and stay in business. Those firms with higher profits are better able to lower their costs of production, invent new products, and advertise to tell about their "successes" in production. Investments that generate less profits because costs (raw materials, machines and/or labour) are rising faster than productivity and/or price diminish the capacity and incentive to invest again. If this situation becomes the average condition for firms in an economy, stagnation or depression is the expected result.

It is the rate of profit that provides the capitalist class with the product to invest as well as the motive. As the rate of profit falls there is a tendency for investment, productivity, economic growth and tax revenue to follow while unemployment rises.

Evidence

By standard accounting methods between 1965 and 1973 the rate of profit in the U.S. in manufacturing and private business sectors fell by 40.9 percent and 29.3 percent respectively. The profitability decline in the U.S. economy did not bottom out until the early 1980s (Brenner, 1998: 95).

The rate of profit also declined in the other major capitalist economies (Brenner, 1998; Cherry, 1987), albeit not necessarily on the same precise schedule, resulting in global stagnation and the creation of a crisis far more serious and enduring than a normal cyclical downturn. As a result, capitalism has been suffering from a quarter century of economic slowdown. Stagnation has been the manifestation of this crisis in all of the advanced capitalist countries. While the crisis came earlier for some countries than others, the profitability crisis is a global capitalist phenomenon.

The U.S. is the country that appears to be the first to emerge from the crisis. As late as the period 1989-1997 the U.S. economy grew an average of 2.3% a year, less than Germany's (2.6%) and Japan's (2.4%). Even the 1994-1997 period U.S. growth of 3.0% was not significantly higher than Europe's 2.4% (LBO, 1998: 3). It is only in 1997 that the U.S. had emerged with signs of a more vital macroeconomy. The question becomes how has capitalism managed its profitability crisis?

Corporate and State Policy Response
to the Crisis of Profitability

In the face of falling profits corporations are compelled to find means of reducing their costs by lowering their wages and taxes and/or raising their productivity. Some of these methods represent advanced capitalism's "intensive" method of reducing costs through increases in productivity by means of mechanization. However, other methods of responding to the profitability crises have included "a return to extensive methods," including longer hours, lower wages, and deteriorating low cost working and environmental conditions. A generation of high national and international levels of unemployment and "globalization" have made labour more vulnerable. The real and threatened effects of unemployment and globalization (capital flight) tend to lower worker's expectations with respect to wages, benefits and working conditions as well as citizens' expectations with respect to health, education and welfare.

During this period of crisis the conditions of economic stagnation have given rise to a corresponding political response. The real or increased threat of "capital flight" due to competitive pressures, enhanced by the growing technological possibilities to do so, imposed on governments the "need" to introduce attacks on labour in general and state salaried employees in particular. Attacks on the welfare state (in the form of the war on deficits and debts), wages, unions and government in general are, along with the socialization of private debt, arguably attempts by capital to restore profitability by using its increased influence over the state in its own interest.

Why are declining investment (capital strike), unemployment, increasing poverty, falling wages, a shortage of tax revenue, an attack on the welfare state, and qualitative social and institutional change part of this process of restoring profitability? For capital the resolution to the crisis requires means of restoring profitability. A number of strategies have been employed to this end over the past quarter century.

i) Anti-inflation policy

Contemporary economic orthodoxy has failed to establish that inflation rates up to 8% have any negative impact on the economy or that zero inflation maximizes economic growth (Sarel, 1996). And yet the U.S. central bank and many other central banks have made the attack on inflation its prime goal over the past few decades. The war on inflation is accomplished by restricting the availability of money and credit and therefore keeping interest rates high, discouraging investment and making it more difficult for the low profit firms with their relatively inefficient capital to stay in business.

The alternative explanation for this strategy is that the underlying goal is to lower wages and resistance to labour intensity by increasing unemployment and lowering workers' expectations. This helps industry, while preserving the value of the debt and therefore the source of profits of the financial industry.

ii) Tax reform

Tax cuts for the corporate sector and the wealthy help to redistribute income upwards.

iii) Capital flight and free trade

The threat of direct foreign investment in non-unionized countries and areas of developed countries where wages, taxes and environmental regulations tend to favour business, lowers costs and raises profits.

iv) Deregulated industry

Reducing government-imposed regulations tends to lower prices of the affected industry and wages of its workers. The institutional transformation that takes place is such that the firms themselves re-regulate the industries so they may better determine wages and benefits.

v) Downsizing and the merger movement

The weeding out of all but the most productive and profitable means of production results in less capital available as well as layoffs, wage reductions, benefits cuts and speedups at work. The same profitability crisis that led to the downsizing process and the merger movement resulted in a massive number of bankruptcies and a destruction of capital not seen since the Great Depression. The general effect of this is that only the more efficient and profitable capital is left standing.

vi) Deficit/debt mania

A strategic obsession with government deficits and debt, the corresponding attack on the welfare state and the lowering of the taxes of the corporations increases the insecurity and dependency of everybody else. The emphasis on the market, minimalist state and individual/family responsibility are all soldiers in the war against the welfare state reflected in declining state expenditures and the privatization of the public sector.

Is Globalization the Best Explanation for our Changing Political-Economic Environment?

It would be hard to exaggerate the degree to which the concept of globalization has penetrated our culture. It is treated at once as an economic tidal wave and a paralyzer of the state. It has been used to justify deregulation, privatization, environmental degradation, free trade, deficit/ debt mania, high interest rates, zero inflation targets, anti-labour legislation, cuts to social spending and upper income and corporate taxes. These policies are of course executed by individual nation states. The rationale in defence of these policy changes is that the rules established by the now dominant transnational corporations and the uncontrollable high speed market highway they travel on must be obeyed lest you be run over and/or left behind. The trouble with the concept of globalization is that objectively it is largely a myth, while the consequences of its power to organize our thoughts as to how the world works has real effects.

Weiss (1997) identifies a spectrum of hypotheses with respect to globalization ranging from strong to weak. The strong globalization hypothesis views the rapid growth of economic interdependence as a reflection of an emerging supra-national phenomenon which is distinct from the three decades following the Second World War when the expansion of world trade and finance was primarily led by the concerted efforts of nation states through the creation of an international financial system (Bretton Woods) and successive rounds of multilateral tariff reductions under GATT (General Agreement on Tariffs and Trade).

According to this view, the era of internationalism has run it course, and has given way to a new phase of international political economy – a new "globalism" or "borderless" economy, in which the internationalization of production is identified as the driving mechanism of economic integration. In such a "borderless" world it is claimed that footloose transnational corporations (TNCs), rather than nation states, are spearheading "global" economic interdependence eroding the national differences and making domestic strategies of national economic management increasingly irrelevant (Ohmae, 1990; Reich, 1992; Horsman and Marshall, 1994; Hamdani, 1997). In this view, TNCs are claimed to be the dominant economic entities. These truly global TNCs own and control subsidiaries, engage in business alliances and networks in different locations of the "borderless" world, source their inputs of labour, capital, raw materials and intermediate products from whereever it is best to do so, and sell their goods and services in each of the main markets of the world (Dunning, 1997). Globalization is therefore, according to this view, "triggering a process of systematic convergence in which all governments face pressures to pursue more or less similar policies to enhance their national (or regional) competitiveness, vis-à-vis other countries, as locations for international production" (Hamdani, 1997: 3).

The erosion of state power is, however, contested by a second hypothesis of globalization, which holds that states never had the macroeconomic planning power before the emergence of globalization. However, those powers that they had and continue to have are significant (*The Economist*, 7 October, 1995).

In contrast to the strong hypotheses of globalization, the weak hypotheses view the rapid expansion of cross-border trade, investment and technological transfer, and the greater integration of national economies not so much as a reflection of a globalized world, but rather as a more internationalized world where national and regional differences, including national institutions, remain substantial (Chang, 1998; Dymski and Isenberg, 1998; Hirst and Thompson, 1996; Weiss, 1997). From this perspective the external and internal constraints that strong internationalization tendencies impose on the nation states are viewed to be relative rather than absolute, and they represent an evolving history of state adaptation to both external and internal challenges rather than 'the end of state history.' According to this view, many of the recent difficulties national policy makers have experienced with macroeconomic management, such as balancing budgets, have more to do with internal fiscal difficulties caused by the years of slow economic growth, prolonged recessions and demographic changes, than with the 'globalization' tendencies.

Globalization Versus Regionalization of the World Economy

To assess the extent and patterns of globalization and its limits and counter-tendencies, we follow the commonly used quantitative approach with its focus on trade flows of goods and services, and capital flows.

All interpretations of globalization recognize the sheer volume of cross-border flows of capital, goods and services and the growing interdependence and integration among the main world markets. However, the central issues in the debate are three: (i) do these trade and investment flows indicate an historically unprecedented trend; (ii) how substantive are these flows compared to their corresponding flows in earlier periods; and (iii) to what extent are these flows world-wide in scope.

Trade Flows

In their historical comparison of the international economy and its regimes of regulation during the Gold Standard period (1870-1914) with the international economy during the 1980s and early 1990s, Hirst and Thompson (1996) look at a wide range of measures of integration, including the share of merchandise trade (export and imports) in output (gross national product, GNP). Their results indicate that our highly internationalized economy is not unprecedented. In some respects the current international economy is less open than the system that prevailed during the Gold Standard period (1870-1914). Table 1 indicates the extent of internationalization, as measured by the sum of exports plus imports as a percentage of GNP of a number of advanced industrialized countries. In 1973, the share of exports and imports in GNP in most industrialized countries was lower than in 1913.

Table 1. Exports and Imports as a Percentage of GNP

	1913	1950	1973	1994
France	30.0	21.4	29.2	34.2
Germany	36.1	20.1	35.3	39.3
USA	11.2	6.9	10.8	17.8
Japan	30.1	16.4	18.2	14.6

Sources: Madison (1995: 149); OECD (1998).

The degree of integration into the world economy was even more limited for most regions of the developing world, with the exception of East Asia. For the developing countries as whole the share of exports plus imports in GNP rose from an average annual rate 28 percent during the 1960s to 34.4 percent in the 1970s and 38.4 percent in the 1980s (Hirst and Thompson, 1996: 28).

The only region of the developing countries that underwent a great deal of internationalization was East Asia, where the share of exports plus imports in GNP rose from 47 percent in the 1960s to 69.5 percent in the 1970s and 87.2 percent in the 1980s. Africa's share of exports plus imports in GNP actually dropped slightly between the 1970s and 1980, as did the Middle East where the downturn in oil prices reduced the region's share of exports and imports in GNP. The marginalization of most of the low wage regions of the developing countries from the 'globalized' world economy becomes more evident if one focuses on the geographic distribution of trade and investment flows.

Geographic Pattern of Trade Flows

In order to assess the extent to which the recent increases in trade flows have been global in scope, it is necessary to examine trade flows by region of origin and destination. Table 2 indicates that trade flows are highly concentrated among the rich OECD countries in general and within the three large regional trading blocks of the European Union, North American and Japan in particular. In 1996, export and imports by the OECD countries accounted for three quarters of total world exports and imports. The EU as a trading bloc does not appear to be more integrated into the world economy. Intra-EU exports and imports have continued to account for almost 62 percent of the total of EU exports and imports. The growing importance of intra-EU trade indicates a clear trend towards "Europeanization" rather than toward "globalization" as suggested by globalization theorists.

The growing importance of Japan's trade flows with the dynamic Asian economies also indicates a trend towards "Asianization" rather than 'globalization.' As Table 2 indicates Japanese exports to the dynamic Asian economies more than doubled over the period 1972-1996, thus reversing the traditional dominance of trade with the United States.

Table 2. Geographical Structure of OECD Trade

Area/country	Source/Destination	Source of imports			Destination of exports		
		1962	1972	1996	1962	1972	1996
OECD	OECD	72.5	77.7	74.7	72.0	78.5	75.0
European Union	European Union	49.7	59.6	61.5	54.3	61.5	62.2
Japan	United States	32.1	24.9	22.9	28.7	31.3	27.5
	DAEs[1] + China	10.2	12.8	29.3	15.5	16.5	33.2
	European Union	9.6	9.3	14.2	12.1	14.9	15.3
United States	OECD	64.6	77.0	68.0	60.3	73.1	70.1
	DAEs a + China	9.0	6.3	19.1	2.4	4.3	12.9

[1] DAEs are the Dynamic Asian Economies (Taiwan; Hong Kong; Malaysia; Philippines; Singapore; Thailand).
Source: OECD (1998: 288).

Foreign Direct Investment

If trends in trade cannot be used to support globalization theory then it might be suggested that this is to be expected. After all, in a truly globalized economy direct foreign investment might be expected to replace exports, as capital, free to move where it wants, will locate in low wage, low tax countries.

One of the structural changes in the world economy during the post war period has been the change in the relative importance of trade and FDI. The relative importance of trade in the world economy has been declining since the early 1980s. The total accumulated (inward) stock of FDI grew at an average annual rate of 18.2 percent during the period 1986-1990 and 9.7 percent during the period 1991-95 (United Nations, 1998: 2). Over the same period the total nominal value of exports of goods and services grew at average annual rate of 14.6 and 8.9 percent, respectively (United Nations, 1998: 2).

This rapid growth in FDI is often taken by the globalization theorists as proxies for the 'globalization' of production in general and the dominance of TNCs in manufacturing production in particular. Instead of exporting goods, TNCs are serving foreign markets by building factories. However, a careful analysis of the aggregate FDI figures reveals the inappropriateness of these proxies, and thus the misleading conclusions drawn from these aggregate figures (Weiss, 1997: 9).

Not all FDI flows are normally directed towards the establishment of new investment in manufacturing and other productive sectors of the economy of the host country. 'Non productive'/speculative ventures, such as real estate, and the cross-border merger and acquisition activity of TNCs are estimated to account for a major portion of the aggregate FDI flows (Weiss, 1997: 8-9). Cross-border merger and acquisition activity alone accounted for over half of FDI flows in the second half of the 1980s, and as much as 58 percent of FDI flows in 1997 (United Nations, 1998: 19). Merger and acquisition activity expanded dramatically in the United States in the 1980s and 1990s. In 1997, merger and acquisition by foreign TNCs accounted for some 90 percent of FDI flows into the United States (United Nations, 1998: 13). The corresponding ratios for the first and second half of the 1980s were 67 and 80 percent, respectively (Hirst and Thompson, 1996: 71).

The significance of cross-border mergers and acquisitions is that what is taking place is simply a transfer of ownership, as TNCs attempt to consolidate their positions within the three trading blocks.

The available evidence also indicates a redistribution of the stock of outward FDI from primary and secondary towards the tertiary sector (services) over the period 1975-1990 (United Nations, 1992: 18). Because it is not possible to internationally trade many services, TNCs must invest abroad to provide these location specific services. With the growing importance of services in the high-wage economies, investments in services by TNCs are expected to grow in the future.

To judge the significance of the internationalization of production and its recent trend, it may be useful to look at the trend of inward and outward FDI flows relative to the total investment in building, plants, machinery and equipment (fixed capital formation). If the strong globalization hypothesis holds, the data should show a large and increasing share of FDI in total investment. Taking the aggregate FDI figures at their face value, Table 3 indicates that this is clearly not the case. FDI accounted for a small share of investment in both developed and developing countries and there is little indication that these shares are rising.

Table 3. Inward and Outward Foreign Direct Investment Flows (as % of gross fixed investment)

		Annual Averages	
		1986-1991	1992-1996
Total	Inward	3.6	4.7
	Outward	4.1	5.1
European Union	Inward	5.7	6.0
	Outward	8.4	8.6
United States	Inward	6.5	5.0
	Outward	3.4	7.4
Japan	Inward	–	0.2
	Outward	4.0	1.4
Developing countries	Inward	3.4	6.8
	Outward	1.3	2.9

Source: United Nations (1998: 385-386).

Geographic Distribution of Foreign Direct Investment

Like trade flows, investment flows are also almost exclusively concentrated in the advanced industrial states and a small number of rapidly developing industrial economies. In the beginning of the 1990s, 75 percent of the total accumulated stock was located in three trading blocks of North America, the European Union and Japan (Hirst and Thompson, 1996: 63), a proportion which has not changed much since the end of 1970s (Brandt Commission, 1980). The triad, consisting of the European Union, Japan and the United States, also received approximately 70 of the world-wide FDI inflows in 1990, a proportion unchanged from the average of the decade of the 1980s (United Nations, 1992: 20). The dynamic Asian economies accounted for over 60 percent of investment in the developing countries by TNCs. The concentration dropped moderately in the early 1990s as the major economies experienced a recession (United Nations, 1998: 5).

This geographic distribution of investment by the TNCs is clearly in conflict with the strong globalization hypothesis, according to which a growing portion of investment by the TNCs should be world-wide in scope, and the low-wage and low tax developing economies should attract an increasing share of investment by footloose TNCs.

Several explanations are provided in the literature for the concentration of the TNCs activity, especially core technological activity, such as research and development, in the high-wage and high tax home countries.

First, concentration in the same country/region provides a pooled market for knowledge-intensive labour, which tends to be treated increasingly as a fixed cost. With new technologies placing a premium on fixed costs, including machinery, equipment and specialized skills, the importance of raw material, wages and other variable costs is reduced. Second, the concentration allows for a close link between producers and specialized suppliers of inputs, especially in non-assembly operations. Third, home location provides the TNCs with a national institutional support system, including relationships with trade associations, training institutions, and more importantly local and national governments. The latter supporting relationship is of particular importance because "(b)eing generally exclusive rather than open to all, support relationships of this kind constitute a competitive advantage" (Weiss, 1997: 10).

In Hirst and Thompson's (1996: 96) examination of the home bias of the U.S., Japanese, German and the British manufacturing TNCs, the parent operations accounted for between 62 and 97 percent of total assets, and between 65 and 75 percent of total sales in 1992-1993. Similar findings are reported by Tyson (1991). The U.S. manufacturing parent operations accounted for 78 percent of total assets, 70 percent of total sales, and 70 percent of total employment in 1988.

Financial Flows

In the case of money and capital markets, the progressive internationalization of money and capital markets has been even more impressive, especially since the collapse of Bretton Woods in the early 1970s, and subsequent liberalization of exchange and capital controls (see Table 4). The daily turnover on the world's major exchange markets rose by a four fold increase between 1986 and 1993, reaching $1.0 trillion, or about 250 trillion a year (IMF, April 1993: 24), i.e. 33 times the total value of world trade.

The progressive internationalization of money and capital *is* a marked change from the post war period. Whether this progressive internationalization of money and capital markets signifies a radical change indicating a globalized financial market or a tendency toward a globalized market, is, however, unclear, for at least two reasons. First, to assess whether the explosion in the cross-border financial flows represents a new phase in the international economy or simply a greater internationalization of finance, we need to have a relatively clear model of what a truly global financial market would look like. Dymski and Isenberg (1998: 21) provide such a rigorous model:

A financial market is internationalized when assets with idiosyncratic risk/return characteristics – that is, whose risks and returns are unique to the regulatory and banking structure of the country of origin – are sold offshore as well as domestically. A financial market is considered to be truly globalized when it involves the continuous exchange in financial centres around the world of assets whose risk/ return characteristics are independent of national regulatory and banking structures…. Globalization is, in effect, the end point of a process of the separation of financial asset characteristics (including prices) from the idiosyncrasies of their countries of origin.

Despite the explosion in cross-border financial flows during the recent years, the penetration of foreign assets into domestic financial markets is still relatively light and confined within the three trading blocks (Hirst and Thompson, 1996: 40-44). The available evidence also suggests that the "home asset bias" – a tendency to invest in local assets – is strong even in financial markets. The available evidence on "home asset bias" in the equity portfolio of investors from several large industrial economies is quite revealing. The investors in the United States were among the least diversified with the percentage of equity portfolio held in domestic equities equal to 98 percent in 1987, followed by Japan (87%), the United Kingdom (78%), Germany (75%) and France (64%) (Cooper and Kaplanis, 1994). Moreover, whether the internationalizing financial markets will lead to a globalizing financial market remains in dispute (Boyer, 1996; Wade, 1996).

Second, to the extent that the recent phenomenal growth of international financial flows and liquidity was brought about by policy specific and conjunctural factors, such as the international recession and the growth in government debt through the 1990s, the emergence of structural imbalances in payments for a number of large economies, and the liberalization and deregulation of financial markets by national governments and the abandonment of capital controls, these changes may be temporary (Hirst and Thompson, 1996).

The progressive internationalization of money and capital markets acts as a double-edged sword. To the extent that cross-border financial flows spread risk across assets of various nationalities and redistribute savings across nations, such flows may enhance efficiency and capital accumulation.

However, greater internationalization of financial markets also broadens the scope for financial speculation and redistribution of income, wealth, and political power toward a growing worldwide rentier class. As the most recent Asian and Mexican crises indicate, the internationalization of "casino capitalism" makes not only national economies more vulnerable to short-term capital and money movements, but it also contributes to greater interest rate and exchange rate volatility (Felix,

1998). As Keynes (1967: 159) reminded us in 1936: "Speculators may do no harm as bubbles on a steady stream of enterprise. But the position is serious when enterprise becomes the bubble on a whirlpool of speculation. When the capital development of a country becomes a by-product of the activities of a casino, the job is likely to be ill-done".

Table 4. Cross-Border Transactions in Bonds and Equities[1] (as % of Gross Domestic Product)

	1975	1980	1985	1990	1995	1997
United States	4	9	35	89	135	213
Japan	2	8	62	119	65	96
Germany	5	7	33	57	172	253
France	-	5	21	54	187	313
Italy	1	1	4	27	253	672
Canada	3	9	27	65	189	358

[1] Gross purchases and sales of securities between residents and non-residents.
Source: Bank for International Settlements (1998: 100).

What Would Capitalism Like to do to Increase its Profitability? – The World Trade Organization in Context

In the first part of this article we gave an account of the changes that took place within the nation state as a response to capitalism's profitability crisis, which in part were justified by the forces of globalization. In the second section of this paper it was established that the growth in real productive FDI was greatly exaggerated, which suggests that globalization is not by and large the way multinationals have responded to their profitability problem. If globalization is not a fact but rather largely a myth that has been used effectively to reshape society in the interest of increasing capital accumulation, the question becomes: what next?

In 1995 the World Trade Organization (WTO) replaced the GATT. WTO rules have been described as international bill of rights for corporations. Trade negotiations are conducted by trade ministers, where TNCs economic interests are pursued to the exclusion of all else. When the Mulroney government was asked if any environmental assessment had been carried out on the impending free trade agreement it responded that the trade deal was a commercial agreement and that the subject of the environment had not once come up – this in an agreement that dealt with energy, agriculture, environmental standards, forests and fisheries (Shrybman, 1999: 5).

The WTO agreement is an extensive list of policies, laws, and regulations that governments can no longer establish or maintain(Shrybman, 1999: 6). "The WTO has extended the reach of trade rules into every sphere of economic, social and cultural activity. Historically, trade agreements were concerned with the international trade of goods such as manufactured products and commodities. The WTO, however, extended the ambit of international trade agreements to include investment measures, intellectual property rights, domestic regulations of all kinds, and services – areas of government policy and law that have very little, if anything, to do with trade, per se. It is now difficult to identify an issue of social, cultural, economic or environmental significance that would not be covered by these new rules of 'trade'" (Shrybman, 1999: 4).

Trade related investment measures is an example of one of many agreements that are on the agenda that would open all sections of a nation's economy to foreign investment, to prevent governments from favouring domestic corporation, to establish the pre-eminence of corporate rights, and to enable foreign investors to enforce their new rights directly. The WTO agreement on trade in services in the area of health and education would effectively undermine the mechanisms with which Canada has maintained its commitment to public health care and education. Such an agreement would require governments to provide the same subsidies and funding support to private hospitals and schools as they make available to non-profit institutions in the public sector (Shrybman, 1999: 16).

Of course, these rules do not apply only to Canada but any government or community that attempts to infringe on TNCs "rights".

Here are some examples of typical U.S. state laws or legal principles that conflict with the WTO: laws that promote investment in recycled material markets; that allocate public deposits or banking business based on community reinvestment performance or local presence; that impose "buy local" requirements of preferences for state procurement; and that make state procurement contingent on certain social or human rights considerations, like the Macbride principles and Burma-selective purchase laws. Ninety-five laws have been identified as potentially "WTO-illegal" in California alone, according to the Georgetown University Law Center. How do we know this? Japan, the European Union and Canada publish documents every year that list American laws they consider WTO illegal (Borosage, 1999: 21).

WTO authority and influence stem from its powerful enforcement tools that ensure that all governments respect the new limits it places on their authority-trade sanctions that can cost hundreds of millions. While previous trade agreements allowed for similar sanctions, they could only be imposed with the consent of all GATT members, including the offending country. Now WTO rulings are automatically implemented unless blocked by a consensus of WTO members (Shrybman, 1999).

The World Trade Organization has a great deal of potential to improve the profitability of the TNCs by lowering their taxes, their costs of production through its effects on labour and environmental legislation, and by its ability to commodify much of what was out of the reach of the for-profit sector.

"Footloose capital is free riding on less mobile taxpayers, getting the benefit of services provided by governments in high-taxing countries while paying taxes in low-tax jurisdictions, if at all.... Some EU governments also argue that tax competition makes it ever harder to tax mobile factors of production such as capital. Instead, they complain, they have to increase taxes on less mobile factors, notably labour, which may drive jobs away." (*The Economist*, 2000: 9). Footloose capital of course need not move to the third world, but in the EU case simply from France to Ireland, even after Ireland's growth has been subsidized by the EU.

While the World Trade Organization did not invent these "opportunities" it would make them more possible. So-called globalization cannot explain the ability of MNCs to extort low taxes from the state or to privatise the health or education sectors. These are political acts reflecting the relative power of capital at this juncture in our history.

Conclusion

Capitalism runs on profit. There is a significant body of evidence suggesting that capitalism entered into an economic crisis phase in the late 1960s due to a fall in the rate of profit as a consequence of the costs of production rising faster than productivity and/or price. In the face of falling profits corporations are compelled to find means of reducing their costs by lowering their wages and taxes and/or raising their productivity.

In the face of falling profits corporations are compelled to find means of reducing their costs by lowering their wages and taxes and/or raising their productivity. Some of these means include mechanization, longer hours, lower wages, and deteriorating working and environmental conditions. The real and threatened effects of unemployment and globalization (capital flight) tend to lower worker's expectations with respect to wages, benefits and working conditions as well as citizens' expectations with respect to health, education and welfare.

The trouble with the concept of globalization is that objectively it is largely a myth, while the consequences of its power to organize our thoughts as to how the world works has real effects.

A careful examination of trade flows suggests that our highly internationalized economy is not unprecedented. In some respects the current international economy is less open than the system that prevailed during the Gold Standard period (1870-1914). Moreover, trade flows have been highly concentrated among the rich OECD countries in general and within the three large regional trading blocks of the European Union, North American and Japan in particular.

One of the structural changes in the world economy during the post war period has been the rapid growth of FDI. However, not all FDI flows are directed towards the establishment of new investment in manufacturing and other productive sectors of the economy of the host country. 'Non productive'/speculative ventures, such as real estate, and the cross-border merger and acquisition activity of TNCs are estimated to account for a major portion of the aggregate FDI flows. FDI accounts for a small share of investment in both developed and developing countries and there is little indication that these shares are rising.

The progressive internationalization of money and capital markets has acted as a double edged sword. It may enhance efficiency and capital accumulation by spreading risk across assets of various nationalities and redistributing savings across nations. Greater internationalization of financial markets and the internationalization of casino capitalism have also broadened the scope for financial speculation and redistribution of income, wealth, and political power toward a growing worldwide rentier class while making national economies more vulnerable to short-term capital and money movements.

Finally, the World Trade Organization can be seen as a having the purpose and potential to improve the profitability of the TNCs by lowering their taxes, their costs of production through its effects on labour and environmental legislation, and by its ability to commodify much of what was out of the reach of the for-profit sector.

References

Bank for International Settlements (1998). *68th Annual Report*. Basle, Switzerland: Bank of International Settlements.

Borosage, R. (1999). The Battle in Seattle, *The Nation*, Dec. 6.

Boyer, R. (1996). "The convergence hypothesis revisited: globalization but still the century of nations?" In *National Diversity and Global Capitalism*, edited by S. Berger and R. Dore, pp. 29-59. Ithaca, N.Y.: Cornell University Press.

Brandt Commission. (1980). *North-South: A Programme for Survival*. London: Pan Book.

Brenner, R. (1998). "Uneven Development and the Long Downturn: The Advanced Capitalist Economies from Boom to Stagnation, 1951-1998." *New Left Review* 229: 1-265.

Chang, Ha-joon. (1998). "Globalization, transnational corporations, and economic development: can the developing countries pursue strategic industrial policy in a globalizing world economy?" In *Globalization and Progressive Economic Policy*, edited by D. Baker, G. Epstein, and R. Pollin, pp. 97-113. Cambridge: Cambridge University Press.

Cherry, R., et al. (eds.). (1987). *The Imperiled Economy, Book 1*. The Union for Radical Political Economics, New York.

Cooper, I. and Kaplanis, E. (1994). "Home bias in equity portfolio, inflation hedging, and international capital market equilibrium." *Review of Financial Studies*, 7(1), pp. 45-60.

Dunning, J. (1997). "The advent of alliance capitalism," In *The New Globalism and Developing Countries*, edited by J. Dunning and K. Hamdani, pp. 12-50. New York: United Nations University Press.

Dymski, G. and Isenberg, D. (1998). "Housing finance in the age of globalization: from social housing to life-cycle risk." In *Globalization and Progressive Economic Policy*, edited by D. Baker, G. Epstein, and R. Pollin, pp. 163-194. Cambridge: Cambridge University Press.

The Economist. (2000). "Globalisation and Tax Survey," January 29th, p. 9.

The Economist. (1995). "The myth of the powerless state," October 7, pp. 15-16.

Felix, D. (1998). "Asia and the crisis of financial globalization." In *Globalization and Progressive Economic Policy*, edited by D. Baker, G. Epstein, and R. Pollin, pp. 163-194. Cambridge: Cambridge University Press.

Gordon, D.M. (1980). "Stages of accumulation and long economic cycles." In *Process of the world System*, edited by T Hopkins and I. Wallerstein, pp. 9-45. Beverly Hills, Calif: Sage Publications.

Hamdani, K. (1997). "Introduction." In *The New Globalism and Developing Countries*, edited by J. Dunning and K. Hamdani. New York: United Nations University Press.

Hirst, P. and Thompson, G. (1996). *Globalization in Question: The International Economy and the Possibilities of Governance*. Cambridge, UK: Polity Press.

Horsman, M. and Marshall, A. (1994). *After the Nation State*. London: Harper Collins.

International Monetary Fund. (1993). *International Capital Markets, Part I, Exchange Rate Management and International Capital Flows*. Washington, DC: IMF, April.

Keynes, J. M. (1967). *The General Theory of Employment, Interest and Money*. London: Macmillan

Left Business Observer. (1998). The U.S. boom. 81: 3.

Maddison, A. (1995). *Monitoring the World Economy, 1820-1992*. Paris: Development Centre of the Organization for Economic Co-operation and Development (OECD).

Ohmae, K. (1990). *The Borderless World*. New York: Collins.

Organisation for Economic Co-operation and Development (OECD). (1998). *OECD Economic Outlook*. Paris: OECD, June.

Reich, R. (1992). *The Work of Nations*. New York: Vintage.

Sarel, M. (1996). Nonlinear Effects of Inflation on Economic Growth, *IMF Staff Papers*, 43 (1), March, pp. 199-215.

Shrybman, S. (1999). *The World Trade Organization: A Citizen's Guide*. James Lorimer & Company Ltd., Toronto.

Thurow, L. (1996). *The Future of Capitalism*. Penguin Books, New York.

Tyson, L. (1991). "They are not us: Why American ownership still matters," *The American Prospect*, Winter, pp. 37-49.

United Nations. (1988). *Transnational Corporation in World Development: Trends and Prospects*. New York: United Nation, Centre on Transnational Corporations.

United Nations. (1992). *World Investment Report 1992: Transnational Corporations as Engines of Growth*. New York: United Nations.

United Nations. (1998). *World Investment Report 1998: Trends and Determinants*. New York: United Nations.

Weiss, L. (1999). Globalization and the Myth of the Powerless State. *New Left Review*, Vol. 225, pp. 3-27.

Wade, R. (1996). "Globalization and its limits: reports of the death of the national economy are greatly exaggerated." In *National Diversity and Global Capitalism*, edited by S. Berger and R. Dore, pp. 60-88. Ithaca, N.Y.: Cornell University Press.

Chapter Three

Undoing the End of History: Canada-Centred Reflections on the Challenge of Globalization

by William K. Carroll

"There is a wide consensus that prosperity can best be achieved by harnessing the enormous capacity of private markets to create a better standard of living for all." – *Canadian Finance Minister Paul Martin, May 2000*

"There is a global democratic deficit which now manifests itself in various forms through environmental, economic and social protest and we have to face that fact." – *London Stock Exchange Chair Donald Cruickshank, May 2000*

Introduction

In April, 2000, CEOs of leading Canadian corporations held their Summit 2000 meeting in Toronto. They are members of the Business Council on National Issues, a group which since the mid-1970s has led the way in articulating a political consensus for Canada's corporate elite. The key conference document opens with a tribute to "Canadian values" – sharing, caring, environmentalism and the like – and sets about to ensure that these values will "triumph in a competitive world." It insists that "global economic

---

Note: An earlier version of this chapter was published in the *Socialist Studies Bulletin* (No. 63/64, January-June 2001: 5-31). It was revised for publication while the author was a fellow in residence at the Netherlands Institute for Advanced Study in the Humanities and Social Sciences.

integration and the rapid advance of technology are changing the rules of competition for companies and countries alike." The report envisages a future in which Canadians and their enterprises maintain an enviable status as "world leaders" rather than "regional followers" – attracting the big corporations and head offices, cutting-edge technology, and rich people whose ideas and money produce prosperity, and in the process pay most of the government's bills. Through a lowering of corporate and personal income tax rates, "we must make Canada a compelling place for Canadians and foreigners alike to invest their money in our people and ideas, and to build growing global enterprises." As the summit report made its intended media splash, other voices quickly entered the fray – the voice of labour in a response by Canadian Labour Congress President Ken Georgetti, which satirically compared Canada's corporate elite to crocodiles in need of another grotesque feeding; the voice of government, as federal Finance Minister Paul Martin chastised the business leaders for their criticisms of a beleaguered administration trying its best to facilitate the Business Council's objectives, but not getting sufficient buy-in from corporations disloyal to the national interest; even the voice of Canada's own self-declared "national newspaper," whose editorial affirmed the Council's analysis that taxes and regulations are destroying Canada's competitive edge, adding that political leaders now have a "duty to see Canada in a global context, and *to generate public support for whatever changes are required to ensure that this country remains in the first rank*" (emphasis added).[1]

This example is an exhibit of the authority and finality with which corporate capital speaks today, of how state officials and news media add nuance to that voice, and of how organized labour and other movements try to pry open fissures in the discourse – whether by satirizing elite opinion or by more direct action. Recent protest in Seattle, Quebec City and elsewhere against some of globalization's most prominent agencies may prove to be no more than a hiccough in the orderly construction of a new world order, confidently proclaimed more than a decade ago by U.S. President George Bush. The future, of course, is perennially up for grabs; and as social scientists and social activists we have no crystal ball. What is worth asking at this point is how neoliberal globalization – the combination of globalized economics and market-driven politics that the Business Council statement instantiates – has gained its sense of inexorability and how, alternatively, movements committed to social justice and ecological sustainability are challenging that fatalism with bids for a renewal of democratic politics. This article focuses primarily on the first question, and secondarily on the second one.

The obduracy of neoliberal globalization is rooted in recent transformations of high modernity's landscapes and signposts. For more than two decades the legacy of the modernist left, of movements for distributive justice, whether ossified in state-socialist formations or in welfare states, has been under attack by a virulent new right. In place of the vision of a progressive movement "forward" toward collective emancipation – toward freedom in the sense of self-actualization and equality in the sense of universal satisfaction of basic needs – neoliberal intellectuals champion "the end of history." The phrase appears in the title of an influential book by former Reaganite policy analyst Francis Fukuyama (1992), who posits that the ideal of liberal democracy marks the final end of history – a world "free of contradictions" (p. 211) toward which all human societies are evolving (p. 48), a system ideally suited to meet the human needs of self-esteem, reason and desire. In this scenario, all the worthwhile socio-political transformations have occurred; what lies ahead is the insistence that the liberal freedom to choose takes precedence over claims to distributive justice. The minimal state is the face of humanity's future: government's proper role is simply to enact and enforce the laws that sustain "the free market system."

How inevitable is all this? I argue that the obduracy of neoliberal globalization is an integral yet contestable element of social control in contemporary capitalism, contributing to the reproduction of a deeply problematic way of life. This sense that, as Margaret Thatcher put it, "There is no alternative," needs to be probed carefully if democratic alternatives *are* to be effectively advanced. The obduracy of the present globalized capitalist order depends for its persuasive power upon two kinds of practices that de-historicize our world. One represents certain human relations as unalterable facts of nature – this is the phenomenon of *reification*. The other secures popular consent to a specific way of life by representing it as normative and universal, with the effect that dissent appears at odds with the common sense of our world – this is the phenomenon of *hegemony*. As devices for legitimating capitalism, reification and hegemony have a long history, and critical analysis of them goes back eight decades to the original formulations of Lukacs and Gramsci. The formidable achievement of neoliberal globalization is to have deepened the naturalization of human practices and to have created a new common sense commensurate with conditions of global capitalism. The result is a wide-spread sense that history has indeed come to an end in the renewed vigour of the American way. Yet people make their own history. The practices that legitimate the new regime must be continually accomplished if they are to retain their persuasive force, and popular protests against Asian Pacific Economic Cooperation (APEC) (Vancouver, 1997), the Multinational Agreement on Investment (MAI) (Paris, 1998), the World Trade Organization (WTO) (Seattle, 1999), the International Monetary Fund/World

Bank (Washington, 2000) and the Free Trade Area of the Americas (Quebec, 2001) suggest that "globalization from above" may well have met its antithesis in a globalization of progressive politics, from below.

Neoliberal Globalization and the New Imperialism

Admittedly, globalization – whether from above or below – is a problematic term. It invites us to exaggerate the differences between our present era and the past, when a strong case can be made that the same dynamics of uneven capitalist development have continued into the present (Tabb, 1997). Moreover, as an orienting concept "globalization" is amorphous and in many usages apologetic: it lacks the critical edge that terms like imperialism have had.[2] Indeed, what globalization mainly intimates is that since the 1970s imperialism has entered *a new phase*. The basics of imperialism continue to be discernible in the ensemble of practices and relations within which monopoly capital accumulates in an international field. But when we compare it to the classic imperialism that analysts like Bukharin (1973) knew,[3] the new imperialism has several distinct features.

First, this is an imperialism without much in the way of borders, colonial empires and rivalries – an ultra-imperialism, in Kautsky's prescient phrase.[4] Part of this can be seen in the elaboration of supranational governance structures such as the WTO, themselves both responses to and custodians of the increasing cross-penetration of capitals, which has become so extensive that sharp nationally-organized rivalry is increasingly without foundation.

Secondly, this is an imperialism that entails a transformed relation between core and periphery. Not only has state socialism collapsed, but in an era of post-colonialism, national oppression at the hands of the major powers is no longer a highly salient factor. In the circumstances, the imperial project becomes "the reconstruction of command and underdeveloped economies" – through structural adjustment programs and the like – within the framework of "a global liberal hegemony" (Bush and Szeftel, 1999: 167). Instead of an articulation of capitalist and pre-capitalist modes of production, the new imperialism involves (a) a selective industrialization of the periphery which (b) globalizes mass consumerism yet (c) continues imperialism's super-exploitation of low-wage labour on the periphery while (d) collaterally dragging working-class subsistence in the core downward. With the establishment of advanced capitalist production on the periphery, and even of periphery-based TNCs, the very concepts of core and periphery have been transformed (Burbach and Robinson, 1999: 28). Mexico now has more billionaires than Canada; and hinterland areas of Canada have become favoured locations for TNCs interested in closing down high-wage, unionized plants and relocating under high-tech, non-union conditions.[5] Indeed, we have witnessed a selective "peripheralization of the core" (Cox, 1987), as in the "wild zones" of American inner cities, where living standards now resemble those of many "Third World" sites (Lash and Urry, 1994).

Thirdly, this is an imperialism which embodies qualitative advances in both the productive forces and the economic circuitry of capital. If finance capital refers to a coalescence of big industrial and financial capital under conditions of capitalist internationalization, ultra-imperialism has brought transformation to both sides of this nexus. On the industrial side, the generalization of information technology throughout the capitalist economy has cheapened costs, eliminated jobs, and shifted the balance of power away from nationally-organized labour movements (Menzies, 1996). On the financial side, the revolution has been no less significant, and has been driven in part by the generalization of the same technologies, which have enabled the formation of a global financial market featuring stateless money-capital that circulates in a proliferation of speculative instruments, often with only glancing relationships to concrete production of use-values (Stanford, 1999). Ultra-imperialism brings with it a more flexible and transnational circuit of finance capital, in which the very distinction between industrial and financial capital tends to blur, as corporations enter directly into the world of finance, for instance through the securitization of their debt, and as financial institutions become major consumers of the new post-industrial information technologies.

What is perhaps most significant in the new imperialism is the cumulative impact of the rapid growth in cross-national trade, credit and investment since the early 1970s, which has subverted the distinction between cross-border and domestic flows – all of which become subject to the same calculation. "The global integration of accumulation means that economic calculations of all kinds – from purchases in the supermarket to the determination of the prime interest rate – are subject, quite explicitly, to international calculation" (Bryan, 1995: 13). For businesses and state bodies, *the fact that competitors function in a globalized field is enough to lead to the embrace of a standpoint of global capital* (Ross and Tracte, 1990: 7-9). It is this shift in the general horizons of economic calculation – for various agents at various sites of the world system – that marks our present era. Globalization's obduracy is grounded in the enhanced *structural power* that capital has attained, as internationalized economic circuitry poses the constant threat of capital withdrawal for any jurisdiction whose policies stray very far from the new paradigm.

What the paradigm prescribes is a "globalization of the state," not only through supra-national bodies such as the IMF but through a "redefinition of the role and purpose of government in the emerging world order" (Gill,

1995: 85-6). The state's role in international competition now takes the form not of promoting "*its*" *capitalists* – the logic of classic imperialism – but of promoting its *territory* as an attractive site for investment (Burbach and Robinson, 1999). This aspect of the new imperialism is effectively conveyed in Amoore and Dodgson's (1997) conceptualization of neoliberal globalization as a political project that entails 1) the protection of the interests of capital and expansion of accumulation; 2) the tendency towards homogenization and harmonization of state policies and even state forms in the direction of protecting capital and expanding accumulation; 3) the elaboration of a layer of transnationalised institutional authority above the states, with the aim of penetrating states and re-articulating them to global capital accumulation; and 4) the exclusion of dissident social forces from the arena of policy formation, thereby insulating the neoliberal state forms against the societies over which they preside.

In this market-driven approach to governance the state becomes a somewhat of an accessory to capital accumulation and its structure of class domination. The constituent elements of neoliberalism – the emphasis on "sound money" and low inflation, the attacks on the power of unions, the policies of fiscal retrenchment and the downsizing of social services, of privatization, of 'flexible labour markets', of deregulation and free trade – all magnify the impact of global market forces on working people and communities, thereby shifting the balance of class power toward capital (Teeple, 2000). I want to focus on the reasons why a strong sense of inexorability has accompanied the consolidation of this new regime, beginning with an analysis of reification.

Reification: Naturalizing Global Market Society

In his seminal essay on reification and the consciousness of the proletariat, Lukacs (1971) notes that capitalism is a way of life in which social relations appear as relations between things, most immediately in the form of commodities – including labour power – interrelated through the market. With reification, human practices and relations take on a thing-like, natural character which denies their own historicity – as in the notion of "the economy" as a mechanism whose movement can be measured. A compelling example in our everyday lives is the regular business reports broadcast on radio and television, which represent capitalism not as an ensemble of social relations but as a collection of objects whose prices oscillate – with pork-belly futures up today and gold down tomorrow. Lukacs makes three claims of relevance to an analysis of globalization's inexorability:

1. Reification is grounded in the commodity form. It gains its force as the commodity form becomes universalized, subjecting "the whole of

society ... to unified economic laws" (1971: 81-2) which *appear to be* *natural*, not historical, in character.

2. Reification entails both *"objective form" and "subjective stance"*: it structures both the objective field of subject-object relations and the subjective field of psycho-cultural life, as material life takes the form of an "economy" whose laws can be comprehended and respected and as subjects come to view their own agency as a thing separate from self – a commodity to be sold in exchange for income enabling one to make consumer-choices in the economy.

3. As the notion of objects having natural prices becomes commonplace, reification brings a mode of *quantitative, calculative rationality* to an increasing array of human endeavours – the bureaucratic, the legal, the political, the cultural. The quantified norms of the market, transposed into other fields, comprise an objective structure of social relations whose subjects tend display a characteristic mentality. Rather than question and attempt to transcend a problematic way of life, the reified mind accepts the *immediacy* of existing arrangements, the forms of capital, as authentic representatives of societal existence. Hence, Lukacs's pessimistic prognosis, which is not to be mistaken for his last world on reification: "Just as the capitalist system continuously produces and reproduces itself economically on higher and higher levels, the structure of reification progressively sinks more deeply, more fatefully and more definitively into the consciousness of man" (1971: 93).

Globalization, of course, involves precisely the subjection of humanity to capital's unified economic laws. Accumulation on a global scale means the integration of commodity, consumer and financial markets into a single totality, the deepening of capitalist colonization of culture, and the marginalization of collectivist alternatives which previously presented instances, however problematic, of a different way of life. The commodity form has come to shape if not dominate the everyday lives of most of the world's population, attaining an historically unprecedented aura of univer-salization. As more aspects of human relations become ensnared in a world market which seems to have no outside and no end, the pessimistic scenario of a cumulative deepening of reified consciousness becomes ever more compelling. We can discern this aspect of reification at three moments in the globalized circuit of capital.

In production, the increasingly globalized character of competition subordinates workforces to the exigencies of naturalized, quantified norms – productivity indices and profit rates, often micro-managed down to specific plants and offices. Complementing this representation of alienated human relations as competitive laws of nature is a reified view of the productive forces through which labour processes are being dramatically restructured. Technological determinism has long been an aspect of the ideology of progress, underwritten by the objectifying purposes to which technologies are put in the service of accumulation.[6] The proliferation of information technologies takes this further in reifying not only hardware but codes, and in presenting technological change as "the driving force of globalisation." Within this naturalized discourse, the social and political interests that are *designed into* new technologies disappear (Noble, 1996), as changes in science, technology and production methods are held directly to determine the future for workers, managers, states and communities (Amoore and Dodgson, 1997). In the fetishized world of global cyberspace "digital flows are used by 'virtual corporations' to link automated machines to just-in-time inventory systems, connect dispersed production sites, accumulate and mine data about consumer tastes and habits, and forge new marketing opportunities, coordinating these activities on a global scale and as swiftly dispersing them" (Dyer-Witheford, 1999: 122).

In consumption, what Baran and Sweezy (1966) called "the sales effort" has been broadened and deepened, its strategies for mobilizing and channelling desire honed to maximal efficiency. As recreation, schooling and other fields become infused with commercial practices, it appears only natural that everyday life be organized around money, markets, and ubiquitous corporate logos (Klein, 2000). With the globalization of consumer capitalism identities can be built around the promotional culture of transnational capital, as consumers identify with objects and logos rather than with other subjects such as the workers behind the products. The allure of this aspect of reification is especially strong in the affluent North: capital's global circuitry veils the fact that the lives of the purchaser of athletic shoes here, and the makers of those shoes there, are entwined, while the culture of consumer capitalism instrumentalizes the economy as a faceless mechanism for matching earnings with desires. But the reification that founds consumerism is increasingly a world-wide phenomenon:

> The faithful gather to worship the new icons in malls – temples raised to the glory of all forms of consumption. All over the world these centres of shopping fever promote the same way of life, in a whirl of logos, stars, songs, idols, brands, gadgets, posters and celebrations.... All this is accompanied by the seductive rhetoric of freedom of choice and consumer liberty, hammered home by obsessive, omnipresent advertising (annual advertising expenditure in the US exceeds $200 billion) that has as much to do with symbols as with the goods themselves. Marketing has become so sophisticated that it aims to sell not just a brand name or social sign, but an identity. All based on the principle that having is being (Ramonet, 2000).

In investment, globalization releases enormous international flows of fictitious capital at the speed of light.[7] With the globalization of financial capital since the 1970s, the volume and forms of stateless fictitious capital have proliferated, enhancing capital's structural power,[8] driving the neoliberal agenda and fuelling the Thatcherite myth that "there is no alternative" to the race to the bottom. In reflecting on the implications of casino capitalism, Mellos points out that the shift in capital's centre of gravity away from productive investment and toward speculation has brought a new form of reification. The objective reality of volatile, unpredictable capital movements supports a reified consciousness of spontaneous risk-taking and possessive individualism:

> The world appears uncertain and reified consciousness associates this uncertainty with natural forces. The return of individualist values of independence and negative liberty can be explained, at least in part, by this reified understanding which reasons that 'in an uncertain world, my needs come first' (1999:132).

These reifying practices in production, consumption and investment find their counterpart in the neoliberal state. What neoliberalism has achieved is a reinscription of the commodity form within politics itself. As policy is disciplined to a set of market-mimetic, quantitative calculations of debt/deficit levels, currency exchange rates, interest rates, etc., all of which take precedence over qualitative issues of human need or environmental sustainability, the space for a proactive state shrinks.

The organization of state practices around such calculations excludes the citizenry from much of the politics of the state, which is framed and pursued within technocratic discourses and expert systems. As with so much of globalization, this eventuality is not in itself new. Indeed, neoliberalism has refined technologies of power first associated with the welfare state.[9] However, developments such as the "new public management" have deepened the reification of state politics by introducing capitalist managerial techniques directly into the public sector (Rose, 1999: 150). Increasingly, quantified accounting schemes discipline professionals to a machinery of governance that maximizes predictability, performance and control. As government agencies and departments become "calculable spaces" (Miller 1994: 253) the state becomes little more than a naturalized conduit for spending "taxpayers' money", and compelling arguments can be advanced for augmenting both value-for-money and national competitiveness by decentralizing public administration and by introducing competition into intrastate relations, whether the competing units be ministries, municipalities, school boards, or individual schools.

Hegemony: Globalization as Common Sense

This discussion of the neoliberal state brings us to a second device through which globalization has been made to appear inevitable. Hegemony is not about the naturalization of humanly constructed social relations. Hegemony is rule by consent. It is "the orchestration of the wills of the subordinates into harmony with the established order of power" (Gitlin, 1987:242). Within such an order, the particular interests of the dominant appear as the general interests of all, as in the taken-for-granted notion in liberal politics that a healthy investment climate is in the public interest. It is "by weaving its own cultural outlook deeply into the social fabric" (Adamson, 1980: 149) that a dominant class wins the consent of subaltern groups. Woven into a way of life, such world views acquire "a validity that is 'psychological'; they 'organise' human masses, and create the terrain on which men move, acquire consciousness of their position, struggle, etc." (Gramsci, 1971: 377). To take up the issue of hegemony is to explore the production of the common sense of an age, for in achieving the status of common sense a political project gains its persuasiveness and obduracy.

The first question to pose, then, is *how neoliberal globalization became common sense*. An adequate historical answer to this question would obviously require much more space than is available here, and would oblige us to consider the relationship between the triumph of neoliberalism and the historical failures of state socialism, social democracy and national liberation movements to construct democratic alternatives to capitalism. Suffice it to say, in the broadest terms, that from the first experiment in full-blooded neoliberal policy in Pinochet's Chile, where Milton Friedman and his colleagues helped design a free market regime under the protective cover of the police state, through the Thatcher and Reagan governments in the 1980s, neoliberalism became the normative outlook for governments around the world, roughly in step with the increased internationalization of capital that it both facilitated and responded to. This hegemony is a major ideological accomplishment, but like all hegemonies "has continually to be renewed, recreated, defended, and modified" (Williams, 1977: 112); our opening exhibit from the BCNI gives an example of one of the latest initiatives in the ongoing construction of neoliberal hegemony.

Broadly, we may distinguish two sociological bases for this hegemony, both of which have contributed to the sense of inevitability surrounding neoliberal globalization. In the first place, and here the BCNI statement is particularly instructive, *the very success of neoliberal regimes* in the 1980s and 1990s in securing the conditions for more globalized accumulation now enables neoliberalism to be presented as a paradigm in step with the times and continually validated by the very practices it informs. In Canada, neoliberal transformation proceeded in great part "by stealth"

(Battle, 1998; Bradford, 1999), in a process I have characterized elsewhere as a passive revolution (Carroll, 1990; cf. McBride and Shields, 1993: 119, 139ff). The key initiatives in establishing the conditions for neoliberalism to be woven into the fabric of life in Canada were the continental free trade agreements. The political rider to economic integration was policy harmonization over time, and given the size of the American economy and the well-established hegemony of neoliberalism there, the trade deals made it possible in the 1990s to promote neoliberal harmonization and deregulation in Canada as a new common sense, well suited to the new reality of continentalism.

A second sociological basis for neoliberal hegemony has been the formation of an *historic bloc* of leading cultural, economic, political forces, mobilized behind the project of globalization. Through their active support for the hegemonic project, these forces have made it a compelling reality. The last decades of the twentieth century was an era in which the crisis of fordist-Keynesian regulation, dating from the 1970s, provoked various neoliberal initiatives aimed both at dissolving the historic bloc that had organized consent in the post-war boom era and at constructing a new historic bloc around the economic nucleus furnished by capitalist globalization and post-industrial accumulation. In this period, what Gill (1995b: 86) has called a *transnational historic bloc*, composed of globalizing capitalists, incipient institutions of global governance such as the Trilateral Commission and the World Economic Forum, and various organic intellectuals active internationally in political, cultural and economic fields, began to take shape (cf. Robinson and Harrison, 2000; Carroll and Carson, 2003). It orchestrated a project of "globalization from above" that sought to discipline local populations to new accumulation norms, while offering the allure of cosmopolitan consumer choice and increased affluence for abstract individuals possessed of a morally worthy attitude of entrepreneurship. The emergence of this bloc in the 1970s and its subsequent consolidation and extension beyond elite groups to the popular classes have provided a social base for the common sense of neoliberal globalization.

If these developments help account for the consolidation of neoliberal globalization as common sense, they do not consider how this hegemonic project has achieved a specific psycho-cultural effectivity, how it persuades subordinate groups to acquiesce to "the inevitable." Much could be said on this matter, but let me briefly make three observations.

The first has to do with how the project negotiates the national question. Nationalism has long been a fundamental element in organizing consent within a world system of divided sovereignties. By appealing to shared values and culture it establishes "a supra-class identity" which when aligned with the state appears to transcend class struggle, as the state seems to act "in the interest of the national body" (Atkins, 1986: 30). The key move in neoliberalism has been to mobilize a "national interest" around the ideology of *international competitiveness*, thus presenting "international class dominance as national economic necessity" (Bryan, 1995: 190). Canada is an interesting case on this score. Because the main vehicle for neoliberal transformation has been the continental trade deals, construction of a compelling national interest around "international competitiveness" has been problematic. Although continentalism has been trumpeted as a means of enhancing international competitiveness, the prospect of Canada's absorption into the American behemoth seems to renounce the national interest altogether (Carroll 1990: 408; McBride and Shields, 1993: 38-9). Left-nationalist critics argued in the late 1980s that the creation of North American economic space would lead to a "race to the bottom" in which the welfare of Canadians would be sacrificed on the altar of competitiveness. A decade after implementation, it is clear that Canadian policies in areas such as income taxation and unemployment insurance have been harmonized downward so that they now more or less correspond to post-Reagan American standards.[10] But if in Canada a sense of "selling out the national interest" weakened neoliberal hegemony in its formative phase, the North-South pull of continentalism may be creating conditions for a North American historic bloc, as internalization of American corporate structures and values cumulatively changes the notion of "what constitutes the Canadian national interest" (Clarkson, 1988: 28).

A second feature of neoliberal hegemony has been its program of moral and intellectual reform, producing new political discourses and subject positions for a globalized world. Neoliberal common sense has required that the social-democratic culture of entitlement, the sedimented product of decades of reform, be supplanted by a reassertion of bourgeois morality according to which freedom can be measured as the inverse of income given over to taxes. A marker of this new common sense is the Fraser Institute's calculation of "Tax Freedom Day." Introduced unobtrusively in 1976 when the Institute was barely two years old and still on the margins of Canadian political life, by 1999 Tax Freedom Day had become a regularly observed "event" in the mass media, if not a household phrase (Fraser Institute, 1999; cf. Lee, 2002). What initiatives like Tax Freedom Day signify is a shift in the notion of citizenship from the "social citizen" of the welfare state "articulated in the language of social responsibility and collective solidarities" (Miller and Rose, 1990: 23) to citizenship as a combination of enterprise and consumer choice. Neoliberal citizenship means that "individuals are now constituted as active purchasers and enterprises in pursuit of their own choices: vouchers in education, housing and other services replace 'paternal' forms of distribution" (Isin, 1998:

175). One instance of this turn, as public pension schemes atrophy for lack of funding, is the conversion of upper-stratum workers from a labour aristocracy, incorporated into the dominant historic bloc through high wages, into an *investor aristocracy*, incorporated through their RSPs and other investments (Harmes, 1998: 114).[11] In neoliberalism, the citizen-as-consumer and the affluent worker-as-investor become elements in a discursive chain linking capital, state and nation with the subject positions of citizen, consumer and investor, and validating the leadership of private business in national and international life.

As a third distinctive element in neoliberal hegemony, we can consider the material and symbolic concessions that neoliberalism extends to subordinate groups to secure their allegiance. Here, the project runs into possible difficulties. At the World Economic Forum in 1996, organisers Klaus Schwab and Claude Smadja observed that the social forces leading globalisation face "the challenge of demonstrating how the new global capitalism can function to the benefit of the majority and not only for corporate managers and investors" (quoted in Rupert, 2000: 135). The ever-widening economic disparities of unregulated global capitalism mean that the investor aristocracy is likely to be permanently outnumbered by the working poor and relative surplus population. Neoliberalism in its Thatcherite casting was a two-nations project (Jessop et al, 1988): its pattern of material concessions rewarded the entrepreneurial individual while excluding organized labour and the structurally disadvantaged, in a betrayal of the Keynesian class compromise. Yet we are well past the destructivist phase of neoliberal transition led by Thatcher. Perry Anderson points out that,

> ideologically, the neo-liberal consensus has found a new point of stabilization in the 'Third Way' of the Clinton-Blair regimes. The winning formula to seal the victory of the market is not to attack, but to preserve, the placebo of a compassionate public authority, extolling the compatibility of competition with solidarity. ... The effect of this combination ... is to ... kill off opposition to neo-liberal hegemony more completely. ... we could say that the Third Way is the best ideological shell of neo-liberalism today (2000: 11).

In the new structure of concessions the labour left is marginalized – its voice does not carry and its traditional concerns seem parochial, old-fashioned and unrealistic. What neoliberalism offers as material concessions to the atomized worker-consumer are jobs and lower taxes, but only on the condition that obstacles to investment and unsupportable state programs are removed. Such promises offer cold comfort to globalization's many victims, and for this reason the neoliberal historic bloc is comparatively "thin," as many subaltern groups are excluded (Cox, 1987).

Neoliberalism may secure consent more effectively in the area of symbolic concessions. In the Third Way, we find a cooptation of the new 'politics of recognition' that Nancy Fraser (1995) sees as paradigmatic to our post-socialist times. The validation by governments of "civil society," viewed as a diverse collection of private associations and identity groups which stand in for the formerly intrusive state – together with hip niche-marketing corporate strategies – activates non-class identities in symbolically integrating subordinate groups into the new order.[12] Indeed, the retreat from a commonality politics into a pluralistic politics of identity has dovetailed nicely with neoliberalism, not only in deflecting attention from class issues but in fragmenting the opposition into many contending identities whose claims seem incommensurable. As each identity group speaks for itself, it becomes difficult for groups to speak to one another, across the boundaries of identity (Epstein 1991: 25; Gitlin, 1995). It is, as David Tetzlaff reminds us, to capital's advantage if the challenges it faces remain isolated and local – "held beneath the global, multinational scale at which capital operates. Thus it is to capital's interest to keep its subject population as fragmented as possible" (1991: 29). Pluralism – the celebration of human diversity – is a core value of democratic socialism, but when inscribed within a discourse of essentialized identities and market rationality it complements neoliberalism's attacks on working-class solidarities, in a scenario of "divide and conquer." This, too, belongs to the common sense of neoliberal globalization.

Conclusion

I have focused here on some ways in which reifying and hegemonizing practices have created a sense that neoliberal globalization is inescapable. This is bad news for those concerned with democracy and social justice. Yet it remains the case that people make their own history. The future is open to alternatives. What is remarkable about the past few years, since, say, the outpouring of resistance in Chiapas that rained on NAFTA's opening-day parade on 1 January 1994 (Holloway, 2002), is how protests have begun to challenge much of neoliberal globalization's finality and authority.

Paradoxically, neoliberalism's victory – the rational tyranny of the global market – has reinvigorated opposition from below, which, like neoliberalism itself, has begun to throw off the national castings of Keynesian class compromises and to pose its politics in a global field. One of the remarkable implications of neoliberalism has been to vindicate a class dialectic that post-modern fashion consigned to the dustbin of history. As the neoliberal historic bloc takes shape, particularly in the form of its peak governance bodies such as OECD, APEC, the IMF and the WTO, a growing collection of counter-hegemonic movements have begun to shadow its activities, making effective use of both a global mass media and a rapidly developing internet alternative media.[13]

We may distinguish several types of initiatives, adding up to a globalization-from-below:

- mass political revolts against globalisation, including the three weeks of strikes and protests in France in 1995 (Krishnan, 1995) and popular protests that brought down the Argentine government in December 2001 (Cibils, 2002);
- people's summits organized to coincide with major international meetings, such as the NGO Forum on Women '95 at Beijing, the World Social Forum, and the G6B;[14]
- movements that organize locally around global issues, as in protests on North American campuses against NIKE and other TNCs;[15]
- organizations whose expressed purpose is to coordinate resistance on a wider scale than national movements, such as the Third World Network, Common Frontiers, and the International Forum on Globalization (Amoore and Dodgson 1997; Wilson and Whitmore 1998: 18); and
- use of the internet as a tool for democratic politics, as in the posting of the MAI draft text on the Multinational Monitor's website in 1998 (Coburn, this book).[16]

It is in these initiatives that we can discern challenges to the reifying and hegemonizing practices reviewed above and, perhaps, prospects for undoing the end of history.

These movements *shatter reification* by disrupting what otherwise appears as a natural unfolding of global rationalization, exposing it as a project posited from a particular standpoint. Reification, as Lukacs knew, expresses the standpoint of capital, which has no interest in going beyond its immediate needs to accumulate. Others, however, have different needs which require them to consider the interconnected, humanly-produced character of our world, the implication of each person in the lives of others. By putting people *visibly into motion*, as Mellos (1999: 137) emphasizes, popular movements against neoliberal globalization fracture the naturalized images of competition in the global casino, of new technologies and displaced workers as teleological necessities, of possessive individualism as humanity's natural state, of quantified accounting schemes as appropriate forms of governance. The effect of such activism is not only to shatter the imagery. People in motion are people in transition. Ultimately, the struggle against reification is a struggle to produce "new people" – "people with a new conception of themselves – as subjects capable of altering their world" (Lebowitz, 1992, p. 143) and keen to participate in democratic governance.

By the same token, these movements *contest the common-sense of neoliberal globalization* and its claims to represent the general interests of humanity. They question the authority of unaccountable elites, the equation of freedom with the abstract individual, the reduction of citizenship to a form of consumerism, the rationality of a race to the bottom under the sign of competing nationalisms, the morality of an economic formation that guarantees permanent material disparities, and the ecological viability of that same formation. They also offer hope of moving beyond the fragments of identity politics, of building bridges across movements and borders, of harnessing the new information technologies into networks of communicative action and empowerment, of constructing a transnational counter-hegemonic bloc around a project of democracy, sustainable development, human welfare and social justice.

Activists in Canada have played major roles in these democratic movements, and there are socio-political reasons why Canada has been and may continue to be a propitious site for pursuing the politics of globalization from below.

In the first place, location next door to the American behemoth and the permeability of Canadian capitalism – its heavy reliance on trade, the high levels of foreign investment dating from the 1950s – meant that political currents critical of globalization had already stirred by the 1970s, when the current wave of globalization was just forming, and before 'globalization' even entered public discourse. The left-nationalism of the 1960s and 1970s entailed a critique of American imperialism, and provided a basis for organizing against the Free Trade Agreement in the 1980s – giving rise to a vibrant popular sector that did not dissipate after the signing of NAFTA but has continued to develop.[17] Activists in Canada got a head start in the politics of globalization compared to those in other capitalist democracies and in this regard may be further along on the learning curve.

More significantly, because Canada has been "internally divided by competing nationalist claims" (Albo and Jenson, 1997: 226), the basis for a solid national hegemony has always been weak, with regional, provincial, and ethnic identities continually contesting the universalizing moves to construct a singular national identity. Canada, as Gordon Laxer argues, is a state-nation in which the "Tory touch" of classical conservatism legitimated a large public sphere "and laid the groundwork for social liberal and social democratic governments to implement programs whereby all citizens had the right to high-quality health care, education and welfare" (Laxer, 2000: 63). By the 1980s the main pillars of "Canadian identity" were liberal multiculturalism and a social-democratic program of universal state services such as Medicare and the Canadian Broadcasting Corporation. Broad popular support for such services meant that critics of the trade agreements could play the nationalist card in the 1980s; but just as importantly the multicultural strain may have helped activists to begin transcending nationalist political limits by the 1990s. The trajectory of the Council of Canadians illustrates this movement. From its origins in 1985 as a liberal-nationalist group focused on the American threat to Canadian sovereignty, the Council reinvented itself in the 1990s. On the basis of lessons learned in the national context, it played a key role in 1998 in opposing MAI and in advocating a Citizens' MAI based on the identity of citizens' movements worldwide.[18]

These features of Canada contrast sharply with its southern neighbour. It is in the United States that the reifying and hegemonizing practices that lend to globalization such a lustre of fatefulness have been most ubiquitous. Given the vast size of the American market and the legacy of post-war American power worldwide, the new imperialism finds its virtual centre at a point somewhere between Wall Street, Washington and Hollywood. There, as they say, money talks, and the commodification of culture and politics is common sense. The free market is officially celebrated, and the strong state, notably the criminal-justice system and the military, presents a well-oiled machine for dealing with threats to the unfettered disposition of property, whether domestic or international. Many Americans identify closely with the American imperial state and are deeply invested in a competitive individualism that interpellates them as consumer-citizens in the freest society on earth. A minority of Americans – many of them affluent and conservative – participate in political life to the extent of voting, and most media discourse is framed in remarkably insular terms, making for a highly parochial, image-driven political culture. The trajectory of American labour – one of cooptation into the Democratic Party, McCarthyite repression of the left, the embrace of business unionism and the predictable collapse of membership in the second half of the twentieth century – has rendered the United States a political wasteland in which class struggle is mostly waged from above and hardly recognized as a reality (Davis, 1986, Boggs, 2000). In the wake of the September 11, 2001 attacks on the World Trade Center and Pentagon, the Bush Administration's "war without end" against "terror" now provides an ideological cover for stepped-up surveillance and repression of political activism of all stripes, whether "at home" or abroad.[19]

If projects of revolutionary transformation have been mainly launched at the "weak links" of imperialism, it is the strong link that poses the greatest obstacle to global democracy. The disorganized state of the American left is an unspoken premise for the hegemony of neoliberal globalization, and for the American imperial state. Yet the mass protests in Seattle in November, 1999, in Washington in April, 2000 and in Quebec a year later suggest that this premise is no more inevitable than other aspects of globalization examined here. On this issue, Canada's location and the permeability of its border may be propitious for globalization-from-below. At Seattle, "the important role of Canadians, and particularly the Council of Canadians, was widely recognized and appreciated."[20] A strong activist sector in Canada, advancing an agenda of social justice *vis-à-vis* the Canadian state but – crucially – working with a renewed left in the USA and, indeed, with critics of globalization in Mexico, could make signal contributions not only to resisting neoliberal globalization on this continent but to a proactive democratic movement worldwide.

Against this hopeful scenario, it is not difficult to imagine a different future. The current conjuncture in Canada is marked by a collapse of the social-democratic left and by vigorous attempts to "unite the right" around full-fledged harmonization and continentalism, a project largely endorsed by neoliberal governments in Ontario, Alberta, and British Columbia. In the coming years, the right may win decisively; the Business Council may get its coveted tax reductions, and a good deal more – in which case globalization-from-above and all that it drags in its train will become more entrenched in this corner of the world. But not without a struggle. Perhaps all that is certain in these uncertain times is that history has not reached an end. The struggle, for better or worse, continues.

Notes

1. See Toronto *Globe and Mail*, 4 April 2000, p. A13, 5 April 2000, p. A15, 10 April 2000, p. A1; 7 April 2000, p. A16.

2. Indeed, in our time, imperialism "has become a non-word, an unfashionable word" (Sivanandan, 1991), a term partially eclipsed by globalization. Before 1984, for instance, none of the social-science articles abstracted in *Sociological Abstracts* included "globalization" in the title; between 1984 and 1993, slightly fewer titles contained "globalization" than contained "imperialism"; between 1994 and 1999, titles that contained "globalization" outnumbered those containing "imperialism" by more than five to one (search executed on June 9, 1999).

3. In its classic form, as analysed by Bukharin, imperialism was a system of Hobbesian states in rivalry, of national monopoly capital overreaching its borders in pursuit of higher profits on the periphery which in part furnished a fund with which a labour aristocracy could be bribed into quiescence (Blaut, 1997: 385). In such a system, international competition bred political conflict and war, as national fractions jostled for control of space and markets. This indeed was the dynamic of imperialism until 1945: a Hobbesian world order of pitched inter-state rivalry in the core and of intense national oppression of colonized peoples, within an articulation of capitalist and precapitalist modes of production. In this

periodization the *Pax Americana* that followed World War II comprised a two-and-a-half-decade-long transition from nationally-organized imperialism to the new imperialism. Hardt and Negri (2000) offer a similar periodization, although they describe a post-1960s paradigm shift from (classical) imperialism to a USA-centred and highly networked empire built not upon the closed spaces of competing national sovereignties but upon an "imperial sovereignty" whose space is "always open" (2000: 167).

4. Writing during World War I Kautsky speculated that "...imperialism, the striving of every great capitalist State to extend its own colonial empire in opposition to all the other empires of the same kind, represents only one among various modes of expansion of capitalism" and that "...the result of the World War between the great imperialist powers may be a federation of the strongest", "a holy alliance of the imperialists", a new phase of capitalist expansion which represents "the translation of cartellization into foreign policy: a phase of *ultra-imperialism*, which of course we must struggle against as energetically as we do against imperialism, but whose perils lie in another direction, not in that of the arms race and the threat to world peace" (Kautsky, 1970: 45-6). My approach to ultra-imperialism is indebted to the work of Steven (1994) and Patnaik (1999).

5. As Bryan Palmer points out, "...we need to appreciate a new imperialism, concentrated not on the Third World...but on the underdeveloped peripheries and marginal enclaves of unevenly developed but economically advantaged nation-states" (Palmer, 1994:122).

6. Val Burris gives an account of the typical process: as social relations become mediated by mechanical and electronic technical apparatuses, relations of supervision are depersonalized and labour processes atomized – with the result that "social arrangements that were once visibly the product of human agency now appear as technological imperatives" (1987: 37).

7. On the concept of fictitious capital see Marx (1978). Jim Stanford's (1999) distinction between the "paper economy" and the "real economy" provides a useful analysis of the case of contemporary Canada.

8. Bernard Lietaer has observed that "currency traders are effectively 'policing' governments by selling off a nation's currency when they are dissatisfied with that government's policies, thus creating a currency crisis". CCPA *Monitor*, March 1998:17.

9. As Bradford argues, technocratic Keynesianism and neo-liberalism have constituted Canada's governing paradigms since the 1940s, and the embedding of the former in the 1940s "made it highly likely that neo-liberalism would triumph in the 1990s" (1999: 50). "At both critical junctures in twentieth-century Canada, policy innovation occurred through political stealth guided by paradigms celebrating either the technocratic efficiency of neutral expertise, as in the 1940s, or the neo-classical efficiency of unfettered markets, as in the 1990s" (ibid: 42).

10. Chernomas and Black (1996), for instance, observe that the massive 1995 cuts to unemployment insurance were not only intended to save money, but also to intensify competition in the labour market by impoverishing a significant portion of the unemployed workforce. As a result of these changes, only a minority of unemployed workers were deemed eligible to receive benefits, a situation matching the prevailing patterns of coverage in the USA.

11. A recent study shows that 49% of Canadian adults now own corporate shares directly or through mutual funds, up from 13% in 1983 (Blackwell, 2000).

12. As Swift notes, in the context of neoliberal globalization "it might seem that civil society has simply been captured by the dominant ideology, which stresses the need for private NGOs and ill-defined 'communities' to look after public welfare and public provision" (1999: 136). The Free Trade Area of the Americas (FTAA), an initiative to extend NAFTA hemispherically, has recently issued an "open invitation to civil society" to submit briefs on trade matters relevant to the FTAA (see www.ftaa-alca.org/spcomm/soc2_e.asp). However, the neoliberal rendition of civil society is only one version; movements for "globalization from below" present a sharp alternative that would democratize both states and markets (ibid, 147; see also Drainville, 2001).

13. For a fuller discussion of these issues as they pertain to a research program I have pursued with Bob Ratner, see Carroll and Ratner (2000).

14. For documentation of the first-mentioned see www.igc.org/beijing/beijing.html. The World Social Forum, first organized in June 2000, has taken this practice into a new phase by establishing a venue for democratic movement politics, whose annual meeting in the Brazilian city of Porto Alegre coincides with the meeting of the neoliberal World Economic Forum in Davos, Switzerland. See Klein (2001). Along similar lines, the G6B (Group of Six Billion) "people's summit" was held in Calgary in June 2002 as a parallel to the G8 meeting staged in the remote resort community of Kananaskis. The people's summit was organized by a coalition of movements and NGOs led by the Edmonton-based International Society for Peace and Human Rights (http://www.peaceandhumanrights.org/).

15. See for instance, the website of the United Students Against Sweatshops, at www.umich.edu/~sole/usas/.

16. An example of use of the internet for political organizing can be found at the website of Global Exchange, and associated links: www.globalexchange.org/. See also the sites of alternative news organizations such as Rabble (http://www.rabble.ca/), Straight Goods (http://www.straightgoods.com/), ZNET (http://www.zmag.org/weluser.htm), Common Dreams (http://www.commondreams.org/), the Independent Media Center (http://www.indymedia.org/) and the Guerilla News Network (http://www.guerrillanews.com/).

17. As markers of this progression see the collections edited by Lumsden (1970), Drache (1985) and Jackson and Sanger (1998).

18. As the most recent document in this initiative, see Confronting Globalization and Reclaiming Democracy: Report of the Citizen's Inquiry into MAI. Issued in 1999, it is available at the Council of Canadians website: http://www.canadians.org/campaigns/campaigns-mai-confronting.pdf. See also the Council's guide for activists, which rejects "the old ideas of 'nationalism' and 'national sovereignty' and proposes as a common basis of action a *"popular sovereignty"* that "reflects the dreams and aspirations of people who live in a political community (like a neighbourhood, city, province or country) and who remain connected with peoples around the world in the struggle for social and economic justice" (www.canadians.org/documents/citizen_agenda.pdf).

19. In October 2001 the USA Patriot Act revoked guidelines from the 1970s that prevented the FBI from spying at will on domestic organizations and introduced the new category of "domestic terrorism," threatening to transform protestors into terrorists if they engage in conduct that "involves acts dangerous to human life." The proposal by Bush of a new Department of Homeland Security in June 2002, to have a staff of 169,000 and a $37 billion budget, was another ominous sign of a quantum leap in political repression within the USA. On the former, see the American Civil Liberty Union's analysis, available at http://www.aclu.org/congress/l110101a.html. On the latter see Fiske (2002).

20. "New round, turn around. The battle in Seattle." Editorial, Canadian Dimension, February 2000 (34:1), p. 4.

References

Adamson, Walter L. (1980). *Hegemony and Revolution*. Berkeley: University of California Press

Albo, Greg, and Jane Jenson. (1997). "Remapping Canada: The state in the era of globalization." Pp. 215-39 in *Understanding Canada: Building on the New Canadian Political Economy*, edited by Wallace Clement. Montreal: McGill-Queens University Press.

Amoore, Louise, and Richard Dodgson. (1997) "Overturning 'globalisation': resisting the teleological, reclaiming the 'political'." *New Political Economy*, 2 (1), pp. 179-195.

Anderson, Perry. (2000). "Renewals." *New Left Review* (II) 1: 5-24.

Atkins, Fiona. (1986). "Thatcherism, populist authoritarianism and the search for a new left political strategy." *Capital & Class* 28: 25-48.

Baran, Paul A. and Paul M. Sweezy. (1966). Monopoly Capital. New York: *Monthly Review Press.*

Battle, Ken. (1998). "Transformation: Canadian social policy since 1985." *Social Policy and Administration* 32 (4), pp. 321-340.

Blackwell, Richard. (2000). "Share ownership on the rise." *Toronto Globe and Mail*, 27 May: B1.

Blaut, J. (1997). "Evaluating Imperialism." *Science & Society* 61(3): 382-93.

Boggs, Carl. (2000). *Corporate Power and the Decline of the Public Sphere*. New York: Guilford.

Bradford, Neil. (1999). "The policy influence of economic ideas: Interests, institutions and innovation in Canada." *Studies in Political Economy,* 59 (summer): 17-60.

Bryan, Dick. (1995). *The Chase Across the Globe*. San Francisco: Westview Press.

Bukharin, Nikolai. (1973) *Imperialism and World Economy*. New York: Monthly Review Press.

Burbach, Roger and William I. Robinson. (1999). "The Fin de Siecle Debate: Globalization as Epochal Shift." *Science & Society* 63(1):10-39.

Burris, Val. (1987). "Reification: A Marxist perspective." *California Sociologist,* 10 (1): 22-43.

Bush, Ray, and Morris Szeftel. (1999). "Commentary: Bringing imperialism back in." *Review of African Political Economy,* 26 (80): 165-169.

Carroll, William K. (1990). "Restructuring capital, reorganizing consent: Gramsci, political economy, and Canada." *Canadian Review of Sociology and Anthropology,* 27 (3): 390-416.

Carroll, William K., and Colin Carson. (2003). "The network of global corporations and elite policy planning groups: A structure for transnational class formation?" *Global Networks*, 3 (1).

Carroll, William K., and R.S. Ratner. (2000). "Social movements and counter-hegemony: Lessons from the field." Presented at *Marxism Today: A Renewed Left View. Instituto Superior de Arte*, Havana, February 17.

Chernomas, Robert and Errol Black. (1996). "What kind of capitalism? The revival of class struggle in Canada." *Monthly Review,* 48(1):23-34.

Cibils, Alan. (2002). "Argentina: The demise of neoliberal economics?" ZNET. Available at http://www.zmag.org/content/Economy/cibils0120.cfm, 20 January.

Clarkson, Stephen. (1988). "Continentalism: The conceptual challenge for Canadian social science." Pp. 23-43 in *The John Porter Memorial Lectures 1984-1987*. Montreal: Canadian Sociology and Anthropology Association

Coburn, Elaine. (2002). "Capitalism, class and collective action: Emerging conflicts and contradictions." This volume.

Cox, Robert W. (1987). *Production, Power and World Order.* New York: Columbia University Press.

Drache, Daniel and Duncan Cameron (eds.). (1985). *The Other MacDonald Report.* Toronto: Lorimer.

Drainville, André. (2001). "Quebec City 2001 and the making of transnational subjects." Pp. 15-42 in Leo Panitch and Colin Leys (eds.), *Socialist Register 2002.* London: The Merlin Press.

Dyer-Witheford, Nick. (1999). *Cyber-Marx: Cycles and Circuits of Struggles in High-Technology Capitalism.* Chicago: University of Illinois Press.

Epstein, Barbara, 1991 "'Political correctness' and collective powerlessness." *Socialist Review* 21 (3/4): 13-35.

Fiske, Robert. (2002). "Bush's Titanic War On Terror." ZNET, 13 June. Available at http://www.zmag.org/content/Mideast/fisk_june%2013.cfm.

Fraser, Nancy. (1995). "From redistribution to recognition? Dilemmas of justice in a 'post-socialist' age." *New Left Review 212*: 68-93.

Fraser Institute. (1999). "Challenging Perceptions: Twenty-Five Years of Influential Ideas." Vancouver: Fraser Institute, http://www.fraserinstitute.ca/publications/books/challenging_perceptions/.

Fukuyama, Francis. (1992) *The End of History and the Last Man.* New York: Free Press.

Gill, Stephen. (1995) "Theorizing the interregnum: The double movement of global politics in the 1990s." Pp. 65-99 in Bjorn Hettne (ed.), *International Political Economy: Understanding Global Disorder.* Halifax: Fernwood Books.

Gitlin, Tod. (1987). "Television's screens: Hegemony in transition." In D. Lazere (ed.), *American Media and Mass Culture: Left Perspectives.* Berkeley: University of California Press

_____ (1995). *The Twilight of Common Dreams.* New York: Metropolitan Books.

Gramsci, Antonio. (1971) *Selections from the Prison Notebooks.* Edited and translated by Quintin Hoare and Geoffrey Nowell Smith. New York: International Publishers.

Harmes, Adam. (1998) "Institutional investors and the reproduction of neoliberalism." *Review of International Political Economy,* 5 (1): 92-121.

Holloway, John. (2002). *Change the World Without Taking Power.* London: Pluto Press.

Isin, Engin F. (1998). "Governing Toronto without government: Liberalism and neoliberalism." *Studies in Political Economy,* 56: 169-1.

Jackson, Andrew, and Matthew Sanger (eds.), 1998 *Dismantling Democracy: The Multilateral Agreement on Investment (MAI) and its Impact.* Toronto: Lorimer.

Jessop, Bob, Kevin Bonnett, Simon Bromley, and Tom Ling. (1988). *Thatcherism: A Tale of Two Nations.* Cambridge: Polity Press.

Kautsky, Karl. (1970). "Ultra-Imperialism." *New Left Review,* 59:41-6.

Klein, Naomi. (2000). *No Logo.* Toronto: Knopf Press Canada.

_____ (2001). "Farewell to 'The End of History': Organization and vision in anti-corporate movements." Pp. 1-14 in Leo Panitch and Colin Leys (eds.), *Socialist Register 2002.* London: The Merlin Press.

Krishnan, Raghu. (1995). "The first revolt against globalization." *Monthly Review,* 48(1) December, pp. 1-22.

Lash, Scott and John Urry. (1994). *Economies of Signs and Space.* London: Sage.

Laxer, Gordon. (2000). "Surviving the Americanizing new right." *Canadian Review of Sociology and Anthropology,* 37 (1): 55-75.

Lebowitz, Michael A. (1992). *Beyond Capital.* London, Macmillan.

Lee, Marc. (2002). "The Tax Freedom daze. Opinion piece." Canadian Centre for Policy Alternatives. Available at www.policyalternatives.ca, June 27.

Lietaer, Bernard. (1998). "From the Real Economy to the Speculative." *CCPA Monitor* 4(19 March):16-18.

Lumsden, Ian (ed.). (1970). *Close the 49th Parallel etc. The Americanization of Canada.* Toronto: University of Toronto Press.

Lukacs, Georg. (1971). "Reification and the consciousness of the proletariat." Pp. 83-222 in Georg Lukacs, *History and Class Consciousness.* Cambridge, Mass.: MIT Press.

McBride, Stephen, and John Shields, 1993 *Dismantling a Nation: Canada and the New World Order.* Halifax: Fernwood Books.

Marx, Karl. (1978). *Capital, volume III.* Moscow: Progress Publishers.

Mellos, Koula. (1999). "Reification and speculation." *Studies in Political Economy,* 58 (Spring): 121-40.

Menzies, Heather. (1996). *Whose Brave New World?* Toronto: Between the Lines.

Miller, Peter, and Nikolas Rose. (1990). "Governing economic life." *Economy and Society,* 19 (1), pp. 1-31.

Miller, Peter. (1994). *Accounting and objectivity: The invention of calculating selves and calculable spaces.*

Palmer, Bryan. (1994). *Capitalism Comes to the Backcountry.* Toronto: Between the Lines.

Patnaik, Prabhat. (1999). "Capitalism in Asia at the end of the millennium." *Monthly Review,* 51(3):53-70.

Petras, James. (2000). "The Third Way: Myth and Reality." *Monthly Review,* 51 (10): 19-35.

Ramonet, Ignacio. (2000). *"United States goes global: The control of pleasure.* Le Monde Diplomatique, May.

Robinson, William I., and Jerry Harris. (2000). "Toward a global ruling class? Globalization and the transnational capitalist class." *Science & Society,* 64 (1): 11-54.

Rose, Nikolas. (1999). *Powers of Freedom.* Cambridge: Cambridge University Press.

Ross, Robert J.S., and Kent C. Tracte. (1990). *Global Capitalism: The New Leviathan.* Albany: State University of New York Press.

Rupert, Mark. (2000). *Ideologies of Globalization.* London: Routledge.

Sivanandan, A. (1991). "Whatever Happened to Imperialism?" *New Statesman and Society South Supplement,* 4 (172 11 October):13-14.

Stanford, Jim. (1999). *Paper Boom.* Toronto: Lorimer/CCPA.

Steven, Rob. (1994). "New World Order: A New Imperialism." *Journal of Contemporary Asia,* 24(3):271-296.

Swift, Jamie. (1999). *Civil Society in Question.* Toronto: Between the Lines.

Tabb, William. (1997). "Globalization is *an* issue, the power of capital is *the* issue." *Monthly Review* 49 (2), pp. 20-30.

Teeple, Gary. (2000). *Globalization and the Decline of Social Reform: Into the Twenty-First Century.* Toronto: Garamond Press.

Tetzlaff, David. (1991). "Divide and conquer: Popular culture and social control in late capitalism." *Media, Culture and Society,* 13: 9-33.

van der Pijl, Kees. (1995). "The Second Glorious Revolution: Globalizing Elites and Historical Change." In, *International Political Economy: Understanding Global Disorder.* Bjorn Hettne, ed. Pp. 100-128. London: Zed Books Ltd.

Williams, Raymond. (1977). *Marxism and Literature.* Oxford: Oxford University Press.

Wilson, Maureen G., and Elizabeth Whitmore. (1998). "The transnationalization of popular movements: Social policy making from below." *Canadian Journal of Development Studies,* 19 (1):7-36.

Chapter Four

Explaining Local-Global Nexus: Muslim Politics in Turkey

by Yıldız Atasoy

Introduction

Islamist capitalists build on the shifting features of the world economy and economic development while promoting the idea of diverting development away from its "Western" moorings. In Turkey, a growing number of engineers, business groups and industrialists are part of the pro-Islamic political movement. These Islamists constitute the country's fastest growing capital groups. They do not represent an "anti-West" brand of radical Islam but are in fact perfectly aligned with the global capitalist system. The growing importance of these Muslim capitalists in politics reflects the transformation which has occurred in development patterns in Turkey since the 1980s.[1]

If we are to fully comprehend the global economy, it is important to analyse the influence of local cultures on economic development projects. We can think of this influence in terms of an active incorporation of non-Western cultures into the shaping of the global economy. This calls into question the theoretical premises of economic activity which have dominated development literature since the end of World War II.

The development literature reflects a broad range of competing theoretical positions. Nevertheless, virtually all the studies of the post war era have tied the idea of development to the historically specific experience of Europe (Evans and Stephens, 1988), as revealed in limitless economic growth, and linear and evolutionary social change (Shanin, 1997). The nation-state was also conceptualized as a uniquely European historical model of political organization (Tilly, 1990), providing a coordinating framework for capitalism (Mann, 1986). In the post war development literature the two facets of European experience, (economic development and the nation-state), were integrated into a universal model of social change to be imitated and applied elsewhere. Many scholars presently argue for the necessity of incorporating local cultures into an analysis of economic development, against the universal assumption behind Western notions of development.

Political Islam in Turkey has played an increasingly active part in the shaping of economic development projects in the last twenty years. It is widely recognized that an Islamist movement in Turkey has its roots in the former Ottoman Empire. Despite certain historical continuities between the Ottoman Empire (1299-1923) and the Republic of Turkey, founded in 1923, each period in Turkish history has produced its own unique version of political Islam, but my goal is to uncover how Turkish Islamists responded to the development ideas of the 1980s and 1990s, and whether this response has allowed them to frame a distinctly Islamist approach to the global economy.

There is no evidence to suggest that Islamic groups propose a culturally distinct theory of capitalism with uniquely Islamic patterns of development. There is a group of Islamist capitalists in Turkey who participate competitively in the global capitalist economy. Although they highlight Islam to constitute a culturally different category in world politics, these Islamists do not appear to envision Islam as a form of oppositional politics forged against globalization. What we are seeing is the emergence of a critique of a development ideology which regards European experience as a universally replicable transcultural pattern. This critique is based on their understanding of the relationship between a development ideology and the historical relations of poverty and wealth creation.

My analysis proceeds in two steps: 1) I situate the Islamism of the 1980s and 1990s as a historically specific movement which emerged in the context of the neo-liberal reorganization of the global economy; 2) I assess the shaping of an Islamic ideology in Turkey during this period by distinguishing between the ideas of the pro-Islamic political parties, Islamist thinkers, and Islamist capitalists. Islamists in Turkey are not a unified category. There are many Islamist groups with a variety of ideological orientations. For example, a group known as the "Islamist intellectuals" developed a critical agenda against global capitalism and against the idea of development. Gulalp (1997) evaluates their ideas as an Islamist manifestation of post-development theory. But, a group known as the "Islamist capitalists" are perfectly comfortable with participating in the global economy and supporting those political changes which facilitate it (Atasoy, forthcoming). These various groups have their own differential approaches to the connections between local cultural elements and the global economy.

Reorganization of the Global Political Economy and Islam

During the formative years of the post-1945 world economy the primary political objective of the U.S. was to organize a multilateral open world economy (Block, 1977). The post-war American strategy was designed to prevent the competitive growth of European national economies. This project involved bringing an end to European protectionism, which was historically established around the bilateral trading relations of Western European states with their colonies. American policy makers had seen the national independence of the colonies as a crucial step in breaking the political basis of protectionism. Breaking colonial ties involved the U.S. provision of "aid" to the former colonies of Europe (Wood, 1986). An ideology of "development" was also invented within this context (Esteva, 1992). These colonial areas were to be "developed" under a program of industrialization to be financed by the provision of American aid. The term "Third World" was also among the concepts invented by U.S. policy makers. It was used to refer to the former colonies of Europe and the newly independent states of Asia, Africa, and the Americas which were collectively defined as "underdeveloped", and, therefore, in need of industrialization (Hoogvelt, 1982).

Between the 1960s and early 1970s, development was still understood as a project of industrialization for the development of Third World states. But it added a new dimension: it required planning for its successful implementation (Ferguson, 1990). This symbolized an attempt to establish strong bureaucratic supervision over its course. The new emphasis on planning took place within the general conditions of the difficulties encountered by the U.S. in constituting an open world economy in the face of growing European protectionism (van der Pijl, 1984). In order to remedy the situation, the U.S. further promoted the idea of national industrialization which was to be implemented through strict bureaucratic control over the economy by a professional technocratic class whom Ferguson calls "development managers." This era was also known as the era for the consolidation of the national principle in postwar developmentalism (Kitching, 1989). Nevertheless, the states were never autonomous in formulating their policies from the general policies shaped within Cold War world economic conditions (Friedmann, 1991).

During the 1960s Cold War era, Turkey adopted planning to oversee its national industrialization programs. The military coup of 1960 brought "planning" into the economy and reinstated the political power of bureaucrats in the coalition politics of capitalist industrialization (Keyder, 1987). The goal was to develop a heavy industrialization program within the State Planning Organization, to be carried out by state economic enterprises (SEEs) and large private industrial capitalists. Given the fact that large industrialists had little weight in the Turkish economy and the fact that organized labour was yet to become a reality, the ultimate goal of development managers was to prepare the economic and political-social ground for them to become dominant players. The elevation of development managers and large industrialists into a politically powerful category was not in the interests of the rural and urban small producers. Thus, the entire period of the 1970s was rampant with constant political tensions between and within political parties over the allocation of scarce resources and income distribution among various fractions of capital.

These tensions were intensified by the way governments planned to create an urban working class for industry. In the historical absence of such a class, governments of the period adopted a policy of encouraging migration from rural areas to the cities. Since Turkish agriculture did not experience a class polarization which would have led to large scale rural migration for the formation of an urban working class (Keyder, 1987), governments were active in creating the conditions for a migration from rural to urban areas with a high urban wage policy. The 1960s witnessed a massive rural to urban migration in Turkey. The population of the four largest cities increased by 75 per cent. One out of every ten villagers migrated to urban areas. However, as urban job creation was not successful (Paine, 1974: 33), rural migrants entered into urban class politics as marginal "workers" within the informal economy.

The development managers sought to remedy the potential political problem of increasing urban unemployment by exporting excess urban labour to Western Europe. In the early 1970s Germany alone absorbed nearly 100,000 of these workers annually (Paine, 1974: 33), 13.3 percent of an economically active population of 15 million in 1972. Governments were willing to send workers abroad because migration would reduce unemployment and increase foreign exchange earnings. By the early 1970s, remittances from Turkish workers in Europe added 1 per cent to the annual growth of the GNP (Paine, 1974). This enabled the governments to import capital goods and raw materials without accumulating much foreign debt. Labour migration was also beneficial for easing domestic political tension resulting from increasing unemployment rates (Abadan-Unat, 1993). Due largely to labour exports, unemployment figures remained more modest than they would have otherwise. Those who could not be "exported" joined the ever expanding marginal economy, building on unused public or private lands on city outskirts. These new settlements were basically shanty towns or, as is commonly referred to in Turkish, *gecekondus* (built over night). Although improved over time, these *gecekondus* lacked an infrastructure: they had no water, electricity, roads or sewers in the formative years of the 1960s.

Government encouragement of labour migration to Western Europe linked Turkish industrialization to the European economic reconstruction movement. Since the Berlin Wall shut off the continuing supply of labour from East Germany in 1961, the labour shortage problem was especially acute for Germany. In 1970, vacancy figures in labour markets reached close to 800,000 in Germany (OECD. *Main Economic Indicators*). Europe solved its labour shortage problem by recruiting migrant labour on a temporary basis, largely from its former colonies. While France recruited from North Africa, Germany received labour from Turkey and other Southern European countries. In Germany in 1974 the proportion of migrant workers to the total labour force was 10.3 per cent, most of whom were Turkish. In France the figure was 10.8 per cent (EUROSTAT, 1984: 168-169). With the participation of migrant labour, European economies in general, and Germany in particular, achieved strong economic growth rates, increased their exporting capacity and accumulated capital. In so doing they were able to establish themselves as strong competitors to the U.S. economy (Armstrong, et al. 1991).

The mutually beneficial effects of labour migration lasted until the 1973 energy crisis. Because of the rise in oil prices and the economic recession that followed, EEC countries terminated further recruitment of foreign workers and encouraged return migration back to labour exporting countries. Between 1974 and 1975 the number of foreign workers employed in European industry fell by more than 20 percent (Leithauser, 1988: 179). In the same period Turkish labour migration to Europe came to an end. This also resulted in a drop in workers' remittances in the Turkish economy from $1.4 billion in 1974 to $982 million in 1977. This had the effect of seriously constraining the financing of national industrialization plans. As a result, Turkey experienced a dramatic slowdown in job creation. The number of unemployed increased threefold between 1974 and 1978. By the end of the 1970s the unemployment rate was close to 16 percent of the economically active population (Kepenek, 1984: 374). The issue of job creation became a crucial political problem as an increasing number of "unexportable" workers joined the informal sector of the urban economy, living in *gecekondus*, and increasing pressure on the political system.

In the context of the unfolding history of the world economic crisis and the political and military conjuncture of detente, as well as Turkey's conflicts within NATO with Greece over Cyprus, Turkey became a marginal state in its relations with the U.S. (U.S. Senate, 1980). This reduced Turkey's capacity to receive long-term loans from the U.S. and other external official sources. Coupled with a decline in workers' remittances from Western Europe, this underscored a crisis in the postwar development regime in Turkey.

As was the case with Turkey, development projects for other Third World countries were also premised on the availability of official foreign aid. The world economic recession had undercut this premise. A general reorientation of "petrodollar" surpluses into a new regime of capital flows to the Third World was a policy option designed to bring the crisis to an end (Frobel et al., 1980). High oil prices had generated dollar surpluses for oil exporting countries which were deposited in transnational private bank accounts. The reorientation of the post war aid regime thus consisted of a shift in post-war policy from long-term official lending to short-term private loans by transnational banks. These loans became the basis for the reorganization of the postwar world economy during the 1980s, with the establishment of a global manufacturing system (Gereffi, 1994). Within this process of "globalization," the states of the Third World increased their import of financial and investment capital from private sources, and industrial production was relocated from Western Europe and North America to Southern Europe, parts of Latin America and South East Asia. But, the flow of petrodollar surpluses to the Third World also reversed a developmentalist policy orientation of full employment and social welfare provision (van der Pijl, 1984). Third World states have adopted policies designed to increase their international competitiveness for attracting investment and financial capital, pushing them into deeper short-term debt relations with the private banks while helping transnational companies increase their profit rates.

Turkish governments also received short-term loans from transnational private banks in order to increase investment capacity and create jobs. The high levels of financial and investment imports, sustained by short-term loans[2], exacerbated by increasing oil prices and decreased workers' remittances and exports, created the conditions for a debt crisis in the late 1970s. Since then, Turkey has become a debtor state, unable to pay its debts accumulated over the years. As a result, the total foreign debt which was US$13.5 billion in 1980 rose to US$ 104.5 billion in 1999. Within this total, the overwhelming majority of short term total debt is private, while private debts also make up about 30 percent of the total long terms debt (Kazgan, 1999: 270). Starting in 1978, the IMF imposed a debt repayment program, transferring short-term private loans (negotiated between large private industrialists and banks) into long-term public loans. Considering the fact that more than three-quarters of the short term loans were private loans (Kazgan, 1999: 130), the state's ability to repay its debt was further diminished.

The broad political-economy perspective elaborated here helped to frame the context for the growth of a political Islam after the 1980s. Political Islam emerged as an oppositional movement to a particular strategy designed earlier by the development managers of the state. Even though it is multifaceted and cannot be reduced to a single overarching ideological project (Ozis, 1997), political Islam in Turkey has been successful in designing concrete anti-poverty projects in its appeal to the poorest and most marginalized segments of the urban and rural populations.

Following the oil crisis of the 1970s oil exporting states in the Middle East increased their wealth and import capacity. Turkey, struggling under an ever-increasing debt burden, adopted a new foreign policy of cultivating close relations with Muslim states in the region. The idea was to create the conditions for large private industrialists and exporters to get into the lucrative Middle Eastern markets. With that goal in mind, Turkey became a founding member of the Organization of the Islamic Conference (OIC), which emerged in 1972 as an international organization of solidarity of Muslim states.

The OIC emphasizes the comprehensiveness and self-sufficiency of Islam in providing a moral basis for Muslim states' economic and political autonomy. The OIC charter was based on the notion of Islamic solidarity on the issues of sovereignty, independence and territorial integrity for each member state (al-Ahsan, 1988). Nevertheless, the OIC was created to constitute "a bloc of Muslim countries" committed to the greater unity of all Muslims. Its founding principle was the Islamic idea of *ummah*. The basis of Muslim *ummah* was the spiritual-moral unity among individuals who accept Islam as a way of life. This definition of *ummah* transcends national principles and rejects the Western idea of the nation-state. Although the OIC has recognized the nation-state as the organizing principle in the state system, it promotes a larger loyalty to Islam beyond national ideologies.

There have been steps taken in this direction of a unified *ummah*. The International Shariat Congress which convened in Pakistan in 1976 has adopted the principle of restructuring the constitutional frameworks of OIC member states according to Islamic principles. In order to recreate Islamic unity, the Congress required all Muslim states to first recognize and accept their Islamic attributes and then establish a confederation under the guidance of a commonly elected leader. This conference, organized and financed by the Saudi transnational financial organization *Rabitat al-Alam al-Islami*, has designed a program for Islamist political movements in Muslim countries. These movements build on the platform of rejecting Western ideas and culture, including the idea of the nation-state, to return to the notion that Muslims constitute one community. Since the OIC accommodates the nation-state, these nationally conceived Islamic movements would be the first step in building the *ummah* around the OIC. For their part, Turkish Islamists continually work towards greater Muslim cooperation within the OIC.

The Islamic movement framed by the international Sharia conference was reinforced by the Islamic Revolution in Iran and the Soviet invasion of Afghanistan. The political rise of Islam in regional politics, and the changing balance of military power, helped the U.S. revitalize its Cold War mentality in relation to Islam and socialist movements in the Middle East. Halliday (1984) refers to this as the "second Cold War." The second cold war re-established Turkey's military-strategic importance for Western oil interests in the region (Bromley, 1991). Moreover, in order to counter the international spread of radical Shia Islam, the U.S. encouraged a more moderate Sunni Islam. This plan, designed under the Carter regime, granted Saudi Arabia a leadership role in the emerging "moderate Sunni Islamic bloc" around the OIC, and was played out by the growing circulation of Saudi petrodollars.

The Saudi-based *Rabitat al-Alam al-Islami*, the *Dar al-Maal al-Islami,* and the *al Baraka Group* became the major institutions circulating Saudi capital transnationally among Muslim member states of the OIC. The World Bank Structural Adjustment Loans (SALs) were also linked to Saudi capital. The World Bank recycled petrodollar surpluses deposited in the private banks of the Euromarkets to debtor states under the SAL program. From 1974 to the end of 1981 total current account petrodollar surpluses were approximately $450.5 billion for OPEC members. Saudi Arabia alone accounted for 42 per cent of the surplus (Oweiss 1983). Between 1980 and 1987 Turkey received US$13 billion. The offer of loans was an expression of American support for Turkey as a frontline state strategically positioned to thwart the possible spread of Islamic revolutionary movements in the region.

With the end of the Cold War in 1991, the integration of the global economy under American leadership has become more problematic. Economic globalization has intensified intercapitalist competition and paved the way for the emergence of new political and economic regional arrangements (Gereffi, 1994), among them the EU and NAFTA. As Gereffi observes, these new regional arrangements are also fragmenting the old Third World along several fault lines in terms of their ability to find niches in the global economy. Turkey finds its niche in terms of its strategic relevance to U.S. interests, standing at the crossroads of almost every issue of importance to the U.S. on the Eurasian continent. In addition to linking newly founded Muslim states of the Caucasus and Central Asia to the West, the 1991 Gulf War and the U.S. war in Afghanistan have also deepened Turkey's involvement in the protection of U.S. oil interests in the region –

an involvement which is utilized by Turkey as a bargaining tool for more economic aid. In contrast, however, Islamist groups argue for the establishment of an Islamic economic and political bloc, along the lines of the OIC, to mediate the uneven links of Muslim countries to the global political economy.

The Rise of Political Islam in Turkey

Class competition among private capitalists for state funds was intense during the economic crisis of the 1970s. Struggles were played out over the government allocation of foreign exchange among the various segments of private capital (Eralp, 1990). Small and medium sized industrial firms were on the losing end of this process, while large industrialists were supported, in order to earn much needed foreign exchange. The East Asian export-oriented industrialization model was emulated in Turkey. In the process, not only smaller firms but also their regions were discriminated against. While the large exporting companies, located in the metropolitan region of Istanbul, were supported, smaller cities of the Anatolian region, containing small to medium sized industrial and commercial interests, lost out (Barkey, 1990).

The diversification of interests between large corporations and small to medium sized industrial firms translated into a political conflict. Large industrialists advocated a move away from protection in favour of export promotion, while Anatolian commercial-industrial groups were the strongest supporters of state protection (Ilkin, 1993). The economic demands of smaller fractions of private capital articulated into a political opposition movement based on Islam and economic protection.

The state was increasingly unable to protect smaller capital groups and labour, and as a result, the developmentalist social coalition politics formed between development managers and private capital groups broke up. This break-up also fragmented the populist political framework of the Justice Party, the centre-right political party, which was dominant in the 1960s and 1970s. It was out of this context that political Islam saw significant growth during the 1980s and 1990s.

The National Order Party (NOP), founded in 1970, was the first pro-Islamic party. Banned during the military coup of 1971, it remerged under a different name in 1972 as the National Salvation Party (NSP). Again banned by the military coup of 1980, it was re-established in 1981 as the Welfare Party (WP). The political leader of all three parties was the same man, Necmettin Erbakan. Although it became a power broker in the 1970s, the NSP's votes fluctuated around 10 per cent. The Welfare Party, on the other hand, turned into a major political movement during the 1990s by increasing its votes from 7.2 percent in 1987 to 21.4 percent in 1995. As the leading political party in Turkey, it formed a coalition government with the centre-right True Path in 1996. Subsequently, the government was forced to resign by the military in 1998, which claimed that it was behind the growth of reactionary religious forces against the secular regime, The Welfare party was closed down and its leader Erbakan was banned from politics for life. The military's manoeuvre in this case is generally regarded as a "soft military coup" because the military did not actually take over the government, although it firmly established its tutelage over civilian governments. In the same year the pro-Islamic party was re-established under a new name, the Virtue Party. In 2001 the Virtue was fragmented into two competing pro-Islamic factions. The Justice and Development Party (Ak Parti) and the Happiness Party (Saadet Partisi) were thereby founded.[3]

Several scholars have analysed the rise of political Islam in Turkey within the conceptual framework of modernization theory (Toprak, 1981; Tapper, 1991). Modernization theory speculates that the social bases of political Islam, understood as the reactionary mobilization of traditional cultural values, will eventually be weakened under the influence of further industrialization and urbanization. Keyder (1997), writing within an international political economy framework, develops a similar argument and advocates a full realization of the promises of modernization. According to him, the choices made by the modernizing elites delimited the scope of modernization in Turkey as they did not attempt to accommodate the popular resentment of the rural and urban lower classes with the modernization projects. Similar to Barrington Moore's (1966) suggestion that authoritarian modernization projects from above produce a popular reaction to them, Keyder also suggests that the popular resentment of the masses gave way in Turkey to a resistance culture around Islam. For Mardin (1997), however, unless wider daily-personal social relations are analysed and the power of Islam is recognized as a discourse of day-to-day social activity, it does not appear to be an easy task to answer the question of why and how these masses will crystallize their resentment around Islam.

I argue that political Islam in Turkey grew within the developmentalist context of industrialization as an opposition movement of the urban poor, as well as the emerging Anatolian-based fractions of private capital and well-educated professionals. These groups struggle to re-position themselves within an economy which has been under a neoliberal restructuring since the 1980 military coup. However, in a fashion reminiscent of C. Wright Mills' (1959) "Sociological Imagination," they construct their political struggles in the nexus of the interaction between their own personal narratives of the self and family, and the material conditions of their existence as marginalized groups in society. The pro-Islamic parties are instrumental in politically articulating these struggles.

By invoking the principle of social justice, the pro-Islamic parties blamed the development managers of the state, whom they defined as corrupt for appropriating the nation's wealth and wasting it on a small number of large private industrialists from the Istanbul region. Within this line of thinking, the emphasis of the NSP was nationalist, advocating a "heavy industrialization" program as the route to be taken for Turkey's national independence from the West (Saribay, 1985). In addition to the issues of Western imperialism, the "just economic order" rhetoric of the WP gave greater attention to the cultural-moral issues for improvements in income distribution and the material position of the poor (Ozis, 1997: 753). This was WP's response to the negative aspects of neoliberal economic restructuring in Turkey for the masses.

According to the State Planning Organization (1996), the 20 percent richest segment of the population increased their share in income distribution from 49.9 percent in 1987 to 54.9 percent in 1994. The incomes of the poorest 20 percent of the population decreased from a very low 5.2 percent in 1987 to 4.9 percent in 1994. While 80 percent of the population comprised of all segments of society (excepting the richest) enjoyed an income share of 45 percent in 1994, a decrease from a 50.1 percent share in 1987, the richest 20 percent experienced an increase in income. The same statistics also reveal a decline in the income of the middle classes from a share of 35 percent in 1987 to 31 percent in 1991. The regional distribution of incomes was worse for cities in Central and Eastern Turkey compared to Istanbul and surrounding area. The WP's "just economic order" rhetoric thus built on such consequences of the neoliberal structuring in the Turkish economy. Nevertheless, the WP did not see any contradiction between a social justice-oriented distributional program and private wealth accumulation, as such wealth accumulation is seen as being perfectly consistent with the basic Islamic principles.

In addition to a commonly held principle of social-justice in their redistributive policies, the NSP and WP diverge in their approach to the role of the state in the economy. NSP's emphasis during the 1970s was on the state's active involvement in "heavy" industrialization projects (Erbakan, 1975). The WP's economic program for the 1980s and 1990s is consistent with neoliberal economic structuring as it reveals an uncompromising stand in private capital accumulation and economic growth. The WP has advocated the adoption of an export-oriented economic model as revealed in the experiences of South East NICs. This is related to the fact that the WP tries to accommodate the interests of the newly emerging Islamist capitalists in its party program. Yet, both parties saw economic growth as facilitated by education in modern sciences and advanced technology. They also share a "Third Worldist" perspective with regard to economic "imperialism" and the global spread of Western cultural values, arguing against the imitation of Western ways (Erbakan, 1975; 1990). They propagate an Islamic world view against the appropriation of Euro-American values, ideas, customs, and fashions. Both parties also argue that national principles should be enhanced by reference to Islamic spirituality and morality perspectives in daily life practices.

These perspectives reflect Islamist desires to be moored to the Islamic moral-spiritual universe in their definition of society, and the elaboration of the self linked to society. I examine the significance of this in connection to the ideas of a prominent Turkish poet and a well-known Kurdish thinker. Both lived before the present era of globalization, but their ideas continue to be influential.

Necip Fazil Kisakurek: Islamist Moorings and the Self

N. F. Kisakurek (1905-1983) has been an icon for Turkish Islamists especially during the late 1970s. He did not receive a religious education but attended a series of modern-secular schools, one in Paris where he studied modern French literature. In the process, Kisakurek developed a firm grasp of Western theories of modernization. There was no organized Islamic movement in Turkey when he began to disseminate his ideas. He published his writings in the periodical *Buyuk Dogu* (Great East) which, after 1943, was closed down several times but continued to appear until the 1960s. The *Buyuk Dogu* became a vehicle for the transmission of an Islamic message to a wide audience. Although jailed many times, Kisakurek continued to deliver his message against the backdrop of increased anxiety about secular nationhood in Turkey. He was deeply disappointed with the spiritual emptiness of the newly created Turkish society.

N. F. Kisakurek wrote about the meaninglessness and emptiness of the secularization discourse in Turkey, a discourse which, according to him, lacked sympathy or affection for the values of everyday life practices. His works drew on the cultural contrast of the East and West as opposite poles of emotional and symbolic value. He wrote:

> My brain has become the shelter of deep anxiety about the 'absolute truth' …. My soul is like an aching tooth …. Even if the Oceans were made of ink, if all the trees constitute only one pen, they would still not suffice to express my distress in depth (N. F. Kisakurek, *Buyuk Dogu*, N. 1, 1943).

The source of his "distress" was the diffusion of Western cultural values in society. These values symbolized the great "evils" of life as they impoverished the human soul. They included: materialism, conspicuous consumption, egoism, instrumental reason, moral decadence and so on

(*Buyuk Dogu*, N. 2, 1943 and N. 19-26, 1944). Kisakurek's remedy for these "evil" influences involved a revitalization of values based on affection, caring, and sympathy. He hoped to give back to people that lost feeling of connection and communion. He believed that Turkish modernization projects had actually produced greater inequality and had done nothing to improve human happiness. These projects were unable to construct a meaningful personal story linking the self to family, community and the history of the larger society. For him, the goal of development must be sought within the development of the self, living virtuously within the locally experienced culture of one's community. Instead, under the imposition of Western life styles, people found themselves alienated from their cultural surroundings which increasingly created the conditions for what Hannah Arendt (1961) has named a "mechanistic atomism" of mass societies. This condition was created by all the forerunners of the westernization project whom Kisakurek called "Spurious Heroes."

In his approach Kisakurek totally demystifies the abstract notion of modernization and development which the secular state managers conceived of as the replication of Western ways of life. Instead, Kisakurek sees development in terms of the growth and enrichment of the self arising out of a world view which is meaningfully rooted in everyday practices and as free as possible from the Westernizing forces of disenchantment.

Said Nursi and Development
The writings of Said Nursi (-1960), similar in a way to those of Kisakurek, were based on the cultural-symbolic opposites of Western and Eastern-Islamic civilizations. The primary theme in his writings is the need to mobilize Muslims in their daily life as individuals, and as members of a community, in order to combat the expansion of "materialist Western ideologies" into their inner world (Mardin, 1989: 67-69). The awakening of the Islamic community would be a result of the mobilization of the individual "through his or her heart." Individuals would cultivate their faith through readings of the Koran and its interpretation.

Said Nursi understood the Western concept of development as a cause of moral decay. According to him, Western civilization was based on the following principles:

> its point of support is force and aggression; its aim is benefit and self interest; its principle of life is conflict; its tie between communities is racism and negative nationalism; its fruits are stimulation of the appetites of the soul and increasing the needs of human kind ... It is because of its founding principles as such that Western civilization has negated the happiness of human kind. Because, Western civilization is based on these negative principles, it has brought bad

consequences for human kind like: wastefulness, poverty, idleness, egoism and cast the great majority, like 80 per cent, into wretchedness. (Quoted in Canan, 1991: 197, 201).

Said Nursi wrote:

Because Western civilization as it stands today has acted contrary to the divine fundamental laws, its evils have been greater than its benefits. The real goals of civilization which are general well-being and happiness in this world have been subverted. Since wastefulness and vice have predominated over frugality and contentment, and laziness and the desire for comfort over endeavour and service, it has made wretched humankind both extremely poor and extremely lazy … (Said Nursi, *Emirdag Lahikasi*, 1959: 98).

The moral corruption was evidenced by a change in human needs under the influence of a mass consumption economy. He wrote:

While in the primitive state of nomadism (for example), people only needed three or four things. And those who could not obtain these three or four products were two out of ten. The present tyrannical Western civilization has encouraged consumption, abuses and wastefulness and the appetites, and, in consequence, has made nonessentials into essentials, and has made this so-called civilized person in need of twenty things instead of four. And yet he can only obtain two of these twenty. He still needs eighteen. Therefore, contemporary civilization impoverishes humankind … (Said Nursi. *Emirdag Lahikasi*. 1959: 98).

According to him, Western civilization was established on foundations contrary to the achievement of human happiness. A strengthening of faith at the individual level was the first requirement in overcoming corruption; religion would regulate consumption patterns. The establishment of an Islamic society around Koranic principles was the second task. However, unless the first task of strengthening the faith of individuals was completed, the second task could not begin. The third task for Said Nursi was the unification of Islamic countries to form a bloc against "evil" influences from the West. For Said Nursi, any attempt to bring Muslim countries into a framework of cooperation, rather than competition and conflict, was to be welcomed as a positive step in the articulation of a Muslim resistance movement against Western domination.

Said Nursi linked an "internal jihad" with the external one. The internal jihad was about the morality of the individual – self-purification of individual life – to be achieved by living under the guidance of Koranic principles. The external jihad was a collective struggle of all Muslims against the expansion and domination of "corrupt" Western values. His understanding of "development" represented an ethical journey away from a secular principle of individual citizenship toward instituting the primacy of a moral community.

Said Nursi linked virtuous community living to economic growth projects. Economic growth demanded advancements in science and technology. Besides providing a sense of dignity and self-worth, he saw Muslim advances in science and technology as the precondition for the self-sufficiency of the Muslim community. According to him, the scientific knowledge necessary for technological innovation and industrial development was present in the Koran. The task of a Muslim was to discover that knowledge and use it for the progress of an Islamic society at large. Since he saw a constancy in Koranic principles, he argued against the temporal and fragmented nature of the developmentalist ideology and presented Islam as a comprehensive system of human emancipation.

The Naqshbandi Order

In addition to the political influence of the ideas of Kisakurek and Said Nursi on the shaping of an Islamist ideology, a parallel influence was exerted by the Naqshbandi Sheikh Mehmet Zaid Kotku. Kotku was a Preacher and Prayer Leader employed by the state. The mosque where he had officially worked until his death in 1980 became the Naqshbandi centre for his teachings (Mardin, 1991).

In contrast to Kisakurek and Said Nursi's emphasis on disseminating their ideas through print media, Kotku's emphasis was on *sohbet* (gathering, conversation) with a small group of people. Those who were in his inner circle obtained highly strategic positions in the government bureaucracy and in politics later during the 1980s and 1990s. These included Prof. Necmettin Erbakan (the founding leader of the pro-Islamic NSP and WP and former Prime Minister of the 1995-1998 coalition government); Korkut Ozal (Minister of various coalition governments during the 1970s); and Turgut Ozal (former Prime Minister and President of Turkey during the 1980s and 1990s).

Sheikh Kotku showed remarkable success in capturing the discourse of secular intellectuals and understanding the problems of modernity and economic development. Under his leadership, the focus of the Naqshbandi tariqa was on an Islamic definition of the needs structure and consumption norms to be joined with the indigenous potential of industrial production. Kotku's primary emphasis was on the development of a "truly" national industry (Mardin, 1991: 134). He advised his followers to refrain from using imported customer goods, particularly food and clothing, and to establish a national industrial development plan in order to avoid falling into what he called a "colonial status" (Kotku, 1984a; 1984b). This led his followers working in the State Planning Organization in 1970s to formulate strategies for heavy industrialization in Turkey.

The other dimension of Kotku's ideas pertains to the problems of the moral-spiritual enrichment of the self in society. This became the cornerstone of Naqshbandi teachings during the 1980s and 1990s under Kotku's successor Prof. Cosan, Professor in the Faculty of Theology at Ankara University. Cosan gave great emphasis to the spread of Naqshbandi teachings on faith and national economic growth. The dynamism for a society mobilized towards economic growth was to be found in morally-disciplined individuals who were highly educated in the subjects of modern science and technology. In addition to the traditional Naqshbandi method of *sohbet*, Cosan disseminated his ideas to a large audience through the use of print media, fax, and electronic mail.

Common to all these examples of Turkish Islamist thinking is their uncompromising stand with regard to the emotional growth and moral-spiritual strength of the self, education in modern sciences and advanced technology, and a program based on social justice in distributional policies. Pro-Islamic political parties have been active players in articulating these elements into an Islamist movement of opposition.[4] While the NSP integrated them into a nationalist program of heavy industrialization during the 1970s, during the 1990s the WP consolidated them within a neoliberal economic strategy to constitute the very foundations for expressing and organizing individual and group identity. I will further examine the political expression of these elements in relation to the competitive growth of Islamist capitalists and professionals in the 1990s.

Islam and the Global Economy

Although political Islam has emerged as a movement expressing the grievances of the poor and marginalized segments in society, it also expresses the interests of the newly emerging "Islamist bourgeoisie" (Ozis, 1997). The Islamist bourgeoisie consists of well educated, upwardly mobile young professionals, industrialists and business groups from smaller cities in the Anatolian region. They emerged as the fastest growing new group of capitalists in the specific context of the neo-liberal restructuring of the economy. They now constitute the power base of political Islam (Sakallioglu, 1996: 243) in a cross-class alliance with the poor and disadvantaged. Not feeling part of the established economic and political elite, their struggle is directed towards repositioning themselves in the economy.

Most of these professionals have an engineering background and were educated in the secular school system (Gole, 1993). They come from modest lower-middle class family origins in small Anatolian cities and rural areas. Much of their upward social mobility was due to their education in highly secular fields of science and technology. They received their Islamist education at home from their families, from their informal education in private Koran schools, and within the Sufi *sohbet* circles. Their informal education in Islam plays an important role in the linking of an Islamic worldview and the practical economic activity of wealth accumulation.

Islamist business groups ventured into the competitive market economy in the 1980s. Among them are a number of large holding companies and medium-sized firms with extensive export-oriented production activities. These companies received a significant boost during their growth years in the 1980s from the inflow of Saudi-based petrodollars and migrant workers' remittances from Germany. Moreover, the large holding companies have also mobilized hidden wealth in Turkey. Islamic financial institutions offer an interest-free market share for the investment of the unused wealth of devout Muslims, similar to the operation of mutual funds in North America. Well-educated professionals undertake the management of these firms and funds. In linking an Islamic morality with the capital accumulation process, the Islamic professionals take the example set by the Prophet Mohammed, who himself was a merchant in Madina. They believe their economic success to be based on continued capital accumulation due to their education in modern science and advanced technology.

Among these large Islamist firms are those which are established in the labour-intensive export field of textiles and clothing and those which are active in the more complex and sophisticated export of consumer durables, such as cars and refrigerators. They also invest in the international markets of North Africa, the Balkans, the former Soviet Union and the Middle East. These holding companies are either founded by the followers of Said Nursi or directly affiliated with the Naqshbandi order (Bulut, 1999: 75-76).

For example, with approximately 500 affiliate-firms, finance and insurance companies, the Fethullah Gulen group, which follows Said Nursi, is among the richest of Islamist groups and the fastest growing of all capital fractions in Turkey. Enver Oren's Ihlas Holding is also affiliated with a particular branch of the Nur movement. Its economic activities cover many areas including the media, marketing, insurance/finance, electrical appliances, machinery, food, construction and foreign trade (Ihlas Holding Annual Report, 1997).

Gulen (1997) sees Islam as a moral-spiritual value forming a cultural matrix within which economic activity can take place. According to him, the worldly affairs of the economy should not be conflated with the spiritual rules of religion; they are separate. But, economic activity must be embedded within the cultural sphere of religion in order to guide the practical pursuit of wealth creation. Gulen differentiates between religion and the economy. He sees them as separate spheres of human activity, but he also believes the two are deeply intertwined. This may be attributed to his attempt to impose a moral constraint on an unregulated market economy. Nonetheless, he still identifies wealth creation as the most important goal for Islamists in order to strengthen their position in society.

The growth of Anatolian-based medium and small sized firms since the 1980s also warrants further mention, given their role in increasing exports. These firms organized the Independent Association of Industrialists and Businessmen (MUSIAD). MUSIAD is not an exclusively Islamist business organization. It represents companies founded by both Islamist and secularly oriented individuals. Nevertheless, it refers to Islam in its class strategy of representing smaller capital interests against the traditional domination of Istanbul-based large capital groups (Bugra, 1998: 528-530). Although there are large holding companies within MUSIAD, such as Kombassan Holding (which represents the capital of more than 30,000 shareholders), the majority of MUSIAD members are medium-sized firms from Anatolian cities and smaller towns. Also referred to as "Anatolian tigers," these firms produce manufactured goods for export, as well as domestic markets.

Similar to the patterns of economic globalization experienced by companies in other Third World nations (Gereffi, 1994), manufacturing in textiles and clothing, food, and consumer electronics represents the leading edge of their participation in global markets. In an attempt to establish export niches in textiles and clothing within the world economy, MUSIAD advocates closer economic ties and political relations with Muslim countries while discouraging ties to the Customs Union with the EC, (which Turkey entered in 1996). For example, MUSIAD proposed a "Cotton Union" to be established among Turkey, Pakistan, Uzbekistan and Turkmenistan (MUSIAD 1996). MUSIAD sees such a union as a strategy for increasing the international competitiveness of these countries in cotton-textiles and related fields.

These industries tend to be labour-intensive at the manufacturing stage, which contributes to their competitiveness in markets. Although there is no statistical information available to show the employment patterns in Islamist firms, it is well known that a majority of the workers employed in the export-oriented textile and clothing industry are married women with children (Eraydin, 1998). Many of these women work in their homes for lower wages with no social security benefits, as their jobs are situated within the very complicated social networks of the informal economy. They see paid work as an extension of their housework, while defining paid work as a matter of helping out a fellow male subcontractor who may be a relative or the husband of a neighbour. According to research conducted by White (1991) on women workers in the informal sector of Istanbul, some of these women are religiously-oriented and refrain from participating in the male dominated public sphere of paid work. They do not consider themselves as wage earners and believe their primary responsibility is to their children and home. Although they work for more than 45 hours a week producing clothes, they still do not think of themselves as "working" women because they continue socializing with their neighbours and minding children while they do their paid work. They believe they are housewives who are only helping out a neighbour or a relative. When the economy entered into crisis in 1998, it was inevitably women employed in the lower subcontracting chains of the informal cotton economy that suffered most. Turkish newspapers have documented that "fainting seizures, psychotic fevers, frenzy, and hysteria" were among the symptoms experienced by these women who lost their paid work in the export-oriented cotton towel production.

Conclusion

I have explored some of the issues concerning the relationship between political Islam and economic development in Turkey. It is clear that Islam cannot be understood by viewing it as representing a single meaning derived from an inward-looking history. Such a position gives primary attention to ideological tensions between the so-called Islamic world and the West, and reduces Islam and the West to certain essences of civilization. In contrast, I have situated the rise of Islam in the historical context of the neo-liberal reorganization of the global political economy. This makes it rather difficult to ask such questions as: What does Islam do (or not do) to Western ways of "modernity"? Rather, we are required to pose the question: Who constructs and mobilizes Islamic cultural values and for what purposes? This leads us to recognize that there is uncertainty in the political meaning of Islam as various actors refer to "it" differently, according to context.

What is essential, then, is to explain the conditions under which various groups within the pro-Islamic movement are involved in the elaboration of a role for Islam in the economy. Each Islamist group has its own reasoning. The capitalists are perfectly in tune with participating in the global economy, while behaving consistent with Western notions of instrumental rationality towards the goal of capital accumulation. They want to reposition themselves within the economy. By elaborating on an emotional content for political Islam, Islamist thinkers create enabling frameworks for the poor and the marginalized, as well as for the newly rising Islamist capitalists. These frameworks provide the means for these groups to use Islam as a moral-cultural resource in their definition of the self, their families, and their position in society. In the process, the pro-Islamic party, building on a cross-class alliance, actively articulates these interests into a political program of economic and social justice.

The foregoing discussion of the relationship between Islam and the economy, as seen from the historical context of Turkey, compels us to reorient our perspective beyond simple essentialist generalizations about "Islamic" and "Western" so that we may better investigate the role of local cultures in economic practice. Islam appears to be contextualized by various groups in their responses to conjunctural political-economic pressures. Rather than morally prescribing social behaviour, Islam is viewed as a critical resource re-configuring specific social relations and recreating frames of reference. In Turkey, where there exists a widespread distrust of the ability of the state to deliver the economic benefits of development, Islam becomes a political project of opposition framing behaviour on moral grounds for the pursuit of material-instrumental ends and social goals.

The concept of "social capital" (DiMaggio, 1994; Smart, 1993) is useful here in demonstrating how Islam is constituted as a frame which generates cultural signals and norms that engender trustworthy social relations and cultural bonds among a variety of actors. What is implicit here is the mobilization of cultural values to realize immediate material goals. This presents the danger of reducing Islam to manipulative tactics for the purpose of gaining instrumental ends. However, this falsely assumes that there is a universal mode of expressing Islam, a point which I hope has been definitively refuted in this article. My research suggests that Islam has been constituted as forming a frame of action in harmonizing economic activity with culturally globalized Western ways, characterized by instrumental rationality and capitalism (Ritzer, 2000). But, such an action is not a static-manipulative act because pro-Islamic parties, Sufi groups and Islamist thinkers are involved in an active political process of articulating multiple claims raised by various segments in society into a political project. This process has increased their bargaining power in society – a process which was initially rooted in a shift of state policy for the neo-liberal restructuring of the economy.

The foregoing analysis reveals the complicated way in which globalized Western ways enter into Islamic framing in repositioning these morally entitled groups in the economy. As this pattern highlights complex cultural flows, it is very difficult to view Islamic politics as informing an active resistance against Western cultural patterns. It seems that Islam becomes part of a hybrid form emerging from the meshing of local, national, and global discourses. This suggests that, similar to East Asian capitalism (Hamilton, 1994), Islam has become part of a complicated plurality in the organization of the global economy – one that does not give rise to its own version of capitalism, nor challenges the globalization of Western capitalism.

Notes

1. This is consistent with recent scholarship on the "Third World" which calls into question the "Eurocentric" bias in notions of economic development (Escobar, 1995; Rist, 1998). These studies highlight local/national differences in politico-cultural experience and "decentre" our understanding of development from its European origins. For example, Pigg's (1992) emphasis is on "hybrid" patterns in social change which emerge from a fusion between the local and the global in the development history of Third World societies. These fusions reposition Western patterns in a way that can no longer be defined as "Western." Escobar (1995), on the other hand, argues that Western ways constitute globalized structures in such fusions. He sees the mobilization of indigenous local cultures and experiences as essential to developing alternative patterns to the globalization of capitalism. The "post-development" literature is built on this idea of the mobilization of local knowledge against the globalizing structures of Western ways.

2. Short-term debts were almost non-existent during the early 1970s, amounted to 60 percent of the total debt in 1977.

3. The unfolding history of the development of the pro-Islamic parties is a fascinating story which deserves serious investigation of its own. In this section of the paper I examine an Islamist articulation of an opposition movement from those whose interests were adversely affected by the economic crisis of developmentalism. Since the Justice and Development, and Happiness parties have just been founded from within a short-lived Virtue party, I will not focus on them but on the pro-Islamic ideology of the former National Salvation Party of the 1970s, as well as the Welfare party of the 1980s and 1990s.

4. It must be noted that the pro-Islamic parties are not the only ones in the political articulation of these elements. Since the establishment of the multi-party regime in Turkey in 1945, Islam has been an important player in party politics and incorporated into the secular structure of the state. Starting from the Democrat Party of the 1950s, the centre-right Justice Party of the 1960s and 1970s, the Motherland Party of the 1980s and 1990s and the True Path of the 1980s and 1990s were actively involved in articulating these elements politically. I should add that in addition to these centre-right parties, the Democratic Leftist Party of the 1990s has also recognized Islam as fundamental to the national culture in its party program.

References

Abadan-Unat, N. (1993). "Impact of External Migration on Rural Turkey" in *Culture and Economy: Changes in Turkish Villages* (P. Stirling, ed.). London: The Eothen.

Al-Ahsan, A. (1988). *The Organization of the Islamic Conference*. Herndon, Va: The International Institute of Islamic Thought, Islamization of Knowledge Series N. 7.

Arendt, H. (1961). *The Origins of Totalitarianism*. New York: Meridian Books.

Armstrong, P., A. Glyn, J. Harrison. (1991). *Capitalism Since 1945*. Oxford: Basil Blackwell.

Atasoy, Y. (forthcoming). "Cosmopolitan Islamists in Turkey: Rethinking the Local in a Global Era", *Studies in Political Economy*.

Barkey, J. H. (1990). *The State and Industrialization Crisis in Turkey*. Boulder: Westview Press.

Block, F. (1977). *The Origins of International Economic Disorder*. California: University of California Press.

Bromley, S. (1991). *American Hegemony and World Oil.* Pennsylvania: Pennsylvania State University.

Bugra, A. (1998). "Class, Culture, and State: An Analysis of Interest Representation by Two Turkish Business Associations." In *International Journal of Middle East Studies* Vol. 30: 521-539.

Bulut, F. (1999). *Yesil Sermaye Nereye? (The Green Capital).* Istanbul: Su Yayinlari.

Buyuk Dogu (Great East). (1943). Vol. 1-2 and 19-26.

Canan, I. (1991) "Said Nursi's View of Civilization", *Panel: Bediuzzaman Said Nursi.* Istanbul: Yeni Asya Yayinlari.

DiMaggio, P. (1994). "Culture and Economy", *The Handbook of Economic Sociology* (N. Smelser and R. Swedberg, eds.). Princeton and New York: Princeton University Press and Russell Sage Foundation.

Eralp, A. (1990). "The Politics of Turkish Development Strategies", *Turkish State, Turkish Society* (A. Finkel and N. Sirman, eds.). London: Routledge.

Eraydin, A. (1998). "Turkiye'de Uretim Yapisinin Donusumu ve Esnek Uretim Orgutlenmesi ile Yeni Istihdam Bicimlerinin Ortaya Cikisi (The Emergence of New Employment Patterns in Turkey), Paper Presented at the International Conference on Bilanco 1923-1998: Turkiye Cumhuriyeti'nin 75 Yilina Toplu Bakis.

Erbakan, N. (1975). *Milli Gorus (National Outlook).* Istanbul: Dergah Yayinlari.

(1990). "Welfare Party 3rd. General Congress: The Opening Speech". Ankara: Pamphlet Published by the Welfare Party.

Escobar, A. (1995). *Encountering Development.* Princeton: Princeton University Press.

Esteva, G. (1992). "Development", *The Development Dictionary* (W. Sachs, ed.). London: Zed.

EUROSTAT. (1984). *Employment and Unemployment.*

Evans, P. S. and J. D. Stephens. (1988). "Development and the World Economy", *Handbook of Sociology*, (N. Smelser, ed.). Newbury Park, CA: Sage.

Ferguson, J. (1990). *The Anti-Politics Machine.* Cambridge: Cambridge University Press.

Friedmann, H. (1991). "New Wines, New Bottles: Regulation of Capital on a World Scale", *Studies in Political Economy*, N. 36, Fall.

Froebel, F., J. Heinrichs, and O. Kreye. (1980). *The New International Division of Labour.* Cambridge: Cambridge University Press.

Gole, N. (1993). "Engineers: Technocratic Democracy", *Turkey and the West* (M. Heper, A. Oncu and H. Kramer, eds.). London: I.B. Tauris & Co Ltd.

Gereffi, G. (1994). "The International Economy and Economic Development", *The Handbook of Economic Sociology* (N. Smelser and R. Swedberg, eds.). Princeton and New York: Princeton University Press and Russell Sage Foundation.

Gulalp, H. (1997). "Globalizing Postmodernism: Islamist and Western Social Theory", *Economy and Society* Vol 26, N. 3: 419-433.

Gulen, F. (1997). *Prizma: 2 (Prism: 2).* Izmir: Nil

Halliday, F. (1984). *The New Cold War.* London: Verso.

Hamilton, G. G. (1994). "Civilizations and the Organization of Economies", *The Handbook of Economic Sociology* (N. Smelser and R. Swedberg, eds.). Princeton and New York: Princeton University Press and Russell Sage Foundation.

Hoogvelt, A. (1982). *The Third World in Global Development.* London: MacMillan.

Ilkin, S. (1993). "Businessmen: Democratic Stability" in *Turkey and the West* (M. Heper, A. Oncu and H. Kramer, eds.). London: I.B. Tauris & Co Ltd.

Kazgan, G. (1999). *Tanzimat'tan XXI. Yuzyila Turkiye Ekonomisi (Turkish Economy from Tanzimat to the XXI Century).* Ankara: Altin Kitaplar Yayinevi.

Kepenek, Y. (1984). *Turkiye Ekonomisi (Turkish Economy).* Ankara: Savas Yayinlari.

Keyder, C. (1987). *State and Class in Turkey.* London: Verso.

(1997). "Whither the Project of Modernity?: Turkey in the 1990s", *Rethinking Modernity and National Identity in Turkey* (S. Bozdogan and R. Kasaba, eds.). Seattle and London: University of Washington Press.

Kitching, G. N. (1989). *Development and Underdevelopment in Historical Perspective.* London: Methuen.

Kotku, M. Z. (1984a). *Cihad (Jihad).* Ankara: Seha.

(1984b). *Mu'minin Vasiflari (The Qualities of the Believer).* Ankara: Seha.

Leithauser, G. (1988). "Crisis Despite Flexibility: The Case of West Germany", *The Search for Labour Market Flexibility* (R. Boyer, ed.). Oxford: Clarendon Press.

Mardin, S. (1997). "Projects as Methodology: Some Thoughts on Modern Turkish Social Science", *Rethinking Modernity and National Identity in Turkey* (S. Bozdogan and R. Kasaba, eds.). Seattle and London: University of Washington Press.

(1991). "The Naqshbandi Order in Turkish History" *Islam in Modern Turkey* (R. Tapper ed.). London: I.B. & Co Ltd Publishers.

(1989). *Religion and Social Change in Modern Turkey: The Case of Bediuzzaman Said Nursi.* Albany: State University of New York Press.

Mann, M. (1986). *The Sources of Social Power Vol. I.* Cambridge: Cambridge University Press.

Mills, C. W. (1959). *Sociological Imagination.* Oxford, London, New York: Oxford University Press.

Moore, B. (1966). *Social Origins of Dictatorship and Democracy.* Boston: Beacon Press.

MUSIAD. (1996). *Pamuk Birligi (Cotton Union).* Istanbul.

OECD. *Main Economic Indicators.*

Oweiss, I.M. (1983). "Petrodollar Surpluses: Trends and Economic Impact" in *L'Egypte Contemporaine* LXXIVeme ANNEE, Juillet-Octobre, No. 393-394, Le Caire.

Ozis, Z. (1997). "The Political Economy of Islamic Resurgence in Turkey: The Rise of the Welfare Party in Perspective." *Third World Quarterly,* 18/4.

Paine, S. (1974). *Exporting Workers.* London: University of Cambridge, Department of Applied Economics, Occasional Papers 41.

Pigg, S. L. (1992). "Inventing Social Categories Through Place: Social Representations and Development in Nepal", *Comparative Study of Society and History*, 34: 491-513.

Rist, G. (1997). *The History of Development.* London: Zed.

Ritzer, G. (2000). *The McDonaldization of Society.* Thousand Oaks, CA: Pine Forge Press.

Said Nursi. (1959). *Emirdag Lahikasi.*

Sakallioglu, U. C. (1996). "Parameters and Strategies of Islam-State Interaction in Republican Turkey", *International Journal of Middle East Studies.* Vol. 28. Pp. 231-251.

Saribay, A.Y. (1985). *Turkiye'de Modernlesme: MSP Ornek Olayi (Modernization in Turkey: the Case of the NSP).* Istanbul: Alan Yayincilik.

Shanin, T. (1997). "The Idea of Progress", *The Post-Development Reader* (M. Rahnema and V. Bawtree, eds.). London, Dhaka, Halifax, Cape Town: Zed Books, University Press Ltd., Fernwood Publishing, David Philip.

Smart, A. (1993). "Gifts, Bribes, and Guanxi: A Reconsideration of Bourdieu's Social Capital", *Cultural Anthropology* Vol. 8, N. 3: 388-408.

State Planning Organization. (1996). *A Comparison of the 1994 Temporary Results of the Income Distribution Survey with the Results of the 1987 Income Distribution Survey.* Ankara.

Tapper, R. (Ed.). (1991). *Islam in Modern Turkey.* London: I.B. & Co Ltd Publishers.

Tilly, C. (1990). *Coercion, Capital, and European States, AD 990-1990.* Cambridge: Basil Blackwell.

Toprak, B. (1981). *Islam and Political Development in Turkey.* Leiden: E.J. Brill.

U.S. Senate. (1980). *Turkey, Greece and NATO: The Strained Alliance.* A Staff Report to the Committee on Foreign Relations, 96th Congress 2nd Session.

van der Pijl, K. (1984). *The Making of an Atlantic Ruling Class.* London: Verso.

White, J. (1991). "Linking the Urban Poor to the World Market: Women and Work in Istanbul", *Middle East Report* N. 173.

Wood, R. (1986). *From Marshall Plan to Debt Crisis.* Berkeley: University of California Press.

Part III Global Politics:
The Role of Non-Governmental and
Governmental International Oranizations

Chapter Five

Globalization,
Competitiveness and
Human Security: Revisited

by Helen O'Neill

There is a widespread perception among people in all walks of life and in all parts of the world, that the pace of change today is very fast, and in many ways unexpected and beyond their control. Much of the blame for the sense of unease and insecurity is being put on processes and changes occurring at the "global" level. The ability to influence, let alone control, such changes is perceived to be beyond the capability of the individual person or community – and even, in many cases, the individual nation state. What kinds of processes and changes are causing such feelings of insecurity – within rich countries as well as poor ones?

Was not the ending of the Cold War supposed to have been an example of positive change and to have reduced people's fears by ridding the world of the ultimate threat to peace and security – that of global military conflict? It is true that the repercussions for Europe and the rest of the world from the events of 1989 and the ending of the Cold War have been largely positive. Much needed reforms, both political and economic, have been launched inside developing countries and transitional economies and they are perceived to have brought widespread benefits to many people. At the global level, a greater sense of security from the threat of nuclear war has

Note: This is a thoroughly revised and updated version of a paper with the same title published in 1997 as 'Globalization, Competitiveness and Human Security' in Cristobal Kay (ed), *Globalization, Competitiveness and Human Security – Papers from the Vienna Conference of EADI* 1996, London, Frank Cass.

taken root. Yet, and also to a large extent perceived to originate at the global level, new types of uncertainties and insecurities are gaining ground. Which specific threats to human security are now causing so many people to fear for their lives and livelihoods? Many of them have international or global dimensions in the sense that their root causes can be traced to events and processes occurring outside their own territories. Two such processes are globalization and competitiveness. The key question is: what are the implications for human beings in their everyday lives of what is described as "globalization" in the world today, and the relentless competition among globalizing actors? To put it more colloquially: how are things "out there" affecting people "in here"? This gives rise to other questions: does globalization imply that national governments are powerless to act in the global arena, or even in the national arena on global issues? What kind of role is being played by non-governmental organizations (NGOs) in filling any policy vacuums? Do the main international economic organizations need further reform to enable them to fulfil their mandates? Finally, what are the main research challenges facing academics today in the field of globalization?

Human Security and Human Insecurity

Our understanding of development has evolved over the past few decades in terms of both approach and substance. The process is universally seen as a multidimensional one and the most useful approach to understanding it is acknowledged to be multidisciplinary. However, while there is still a necessary concern with the determinants of economic growth and of social and political change at the national level, the implications for people, as beneficiaries more than as labour "inputs," is increasingly becoming the main concern. There has been a shift in focus from places to people: from growth as an outcome to growth as an input; and from people and their capabilities as development inputs, to the enhancement of human choices and capabilities as the outcome.

Galtung included in his dimensions of human development, not just satisfaction of basic needs such as food, shelter, health and education, but also work, freedom of impression and expression, freedom of movement, political participation, greater equality and social justice, self-reliance (the capability of self-sufficiency in a crisis), and sustainability (Galtung, 1976: 261-265).

The UNDP defines human development as the process of expanding the range of people's choices – and more recently of their capabilities as well. In its 1994 Human Development Report, it introduced the new – distinct but related – concept of human security. It has two aspects, first, safety from such chronic threats as hunger, disease and repression and, second, protection from sudden and hurtful disruptions in the patterns of daily life. It is, of course, related to human development in the sense that human security means that people can exercise their expanded choices (and develop their capabilities) safely and freely and can be relatively confident that the opportunities they have today are not totally lost tomorrow (UNDP, 1994, 23).

The components of human security fall under two main headings, freedom from fear and freedom from want (two key principles underlying the United Nations Charter). The UNDP produced a multidimensional list of aspects of human security and the various threats that can be identified under each heading as follows: economic security (the threats to which include unemployment, insecure jobs, income inequalities, poverty, homelessness); food security (inadequacies in terms of food availabilities and food entitlements); health security (infectious and parasitic diseases, new viruses including HIV/AIDS, respiratory infections from polluted air); environmental security (degradation of air, water, soil and forests); personal security (conflicts, crime, violence against women and children, terrorism); community security (ethnic clashes); and political security (violation of human rights) (*ibid*: 24-25).

The World Bank introduced the concept of security into its *World Development Report* 2000 which, like its previous start-of-decade reports in 1980 and 1990, was focused on the theme of poverty. In defining poverty, the World Bank included fear for the future within it. For the poor, this fear relates to uncertainty regarding their capability to cope with crises. It defines insecurity as exposure to risk and lists the main sources of insecurity as: natural risks (droughts, floods, landslides, earthquakes); health risks (illness, injury, disability, epidemic); social risks (crime, domestic violence, terrorism, civil strife, war); economic risks (unemployment, harvest failure, growth collapse, technology- or trade-induced terms of trade shocks); political risks (riots, political default on social programmes, *coups d'état*); and environmental risks (pollution, deforestation, nuclear disaster) (World Bank, 2000: Ch. 5).

In its 1999 *Human Development Report*, the UNDP links, for the first time, its concept of human security with that of "advancing globalization." When human security is under threat anywhere it can affect people everywhere when it states: "Famines, ethnic conflicts, social disintegration, terrorism, pollution and drug trafficking can no longer be confined within national borders". It points out that, while some global challenges to human security arise because threats within countries rapidly spill beyond national frontiers, such as greenhouse gases and trade in drugs, other threats take on a global character because of the disparities between countries – disparities that encourage millions of people to leave their homes in search of a better life, whether the receiving country wants them or not. It adds that frustrations over inequality – in incomes and in political power – often build up into serious civil conflicts between groups, whether ethnic, religious or social.

Human security is a universal concern. There are many threats that are common to all people, rich and poor alike, but their intensity may differ from one part of the world to another [UNDP, 1994:22]. The UNDP claims that, in seeking security, people in rich countries tend to focus on the threat of crime and drug wars in their streets, the spread of deadly diseases like HIV/AIDS, soil degradation, rising levels of pollution, and the fear of losing their jobs. People in poor countries have similar concerns but they tend to focus more on liberation from the continuing threats of hunger, disease, and poverty.

In fact, if we differentiate between rich and poor *people*, rather than rich and poor *countries*, we find that the human insecurities world-wide may look more alike. Food security, for example, has become an intense issue in Europe as manifested in fears, not about the availability of food, but rather its safety from the effects of animal diseases, pesticides on fruit and vegetables, and milk and water contamination, to mention but some of the perceived threats. There is universal agreement that the spread of the BSE virus can be explained by the unrestrained deregulation of the animal-feed industry in the mid-1980s by the government of one European Union (EU) member state intent on promoting the global competitiveness of its food industry. Thus a measure of food security could include not just quantitative indicators (food availability and entitlements) but also a qualitative one (food safety).

As regards economic security, the concerns of rich and poor people, although differing in intensity, include many similar elements. The insecurity associated with the threat of unemployment is concentrated most among the unskilled in poor and rich countries alike. Within labour markets in both rich and poor countries, it is not just unemployment (no job) that is seen as a threat to economic security, but also job insecurity, manifested by an increasing tendency toward contract and casual jobs (what competitive global actors tend to praise as "labour flexibility").

Widening income inequalities constitute another threat to economic security. While life expectancy and some other social indicators have shown general improvements over the years, income inequalities between rich and poor countries, as well as among developing countries, tended to widen during the 1980s compared with the period 1965-80 (Griffin and Khan, 1992: 2). Current data suggest that these inequalities are also rising within many developing countries – and some industrialised countries (UNDP, 1996: 13-17, UNDP, 1999: 38-39). The 1996 OECD *Employment*

Outlook provided evidence of widening earnings inequalities in OECD countries which, it claimed will lead to "more marginalization of people (social exclusion) – and increased pressure on welfare budgets" (*Financial Times*, 16 July 1996, 4). The OECD blamed substantial labour and product market reforms for the increase in social exclusion in the U.S. and the UK during the first half of the 1990s. It also suggested that countries with generous welfare benefits and widespread unionisation of workers have a less unequal distribution of earnings than those that do not. Yet, according to the UNDP's *Human Development Report* 2000, globalization and the pressure for a flexible labour market are compromising workers' rights and protections. It states that trade union membership in the non-agricultural labour force has declined in many countries – both developing and OECD. Moreover, it claims that, of the 27 million workers in the world's 845 export processing zones, many are not allowed to join unions, "a clear violation of workers' rights and human rights" (UNDP, 2000:41).

Although widely criticised by the more aggressive globalizing corporations and their advisors, workers' rights and welfare benefits, important contributors to economic security, probably enhance labour productivity – considered to be one of the key factors in the competitiveness of nations.

Competitiveness: Do Nation States Compete?

Everyone would agree that individuals compete with each other and also that enterprises compete. But, do nation states compete? While Porter (1990) doubts that they do, nonetheless his influential book the *Competitive Advantage of Nations* explores the determinants of "national competitiveness" and the "competitive advantage of nations" – which he defines as "the decisive characteristic of a nation that allows its companies to create and sustain competitive advantage in particular fields" (Porter, 1990: 84-85). He equates national competitiveness with productivity – the productivity with which a nation's labour and capital are employed – stating that it must be continually improved. While Porter claims that no nation can be competitive in everything, it could also be added that the same applies in the case of large enterprises. No enterprise, no matter how profitable, can be competitive in the production of all products – even though their penchant for mergers and take-overs might suggest that they believe that they might be. The recent trend toward "downsizing" in many large corporations, especially those that are competing in global markets, suggests that once they come to this conclusion, they can be totally ruthless in shedding those parts of their operations that are not considered profitable enough to justify maintaining them – or the workers whose livelihoods depend on them.

The United Nations Conference on Trade and Development (UNCTAD) argues that the term national competitiveness includes a broad set of factors such as "productivity, technological innovation, investments, export and import prices, trade and capital balances, working conditions, taxes, political stability etc." (UNCTAD, 1995: 4). This list begins to sound rather like the list of factors used by the World Economic Forum (WEF) and the International Institute for Management Development (IMD) when they attempt to measure and compare the levels of competitiveness of various countries around the world.

Up until 1996, WEF and IMD together produced an annual *World Competitiveness Report* in which they ranked 40-50 (mainly industrialised) countries according to a wide range of factors. In 1996, they split up and each produced its own report (*Global Competitiveness Report* and *The World Competitiveness Yearbook* respectively). Inevitably, their approaches have much in common. However, there are some interesting differences between them.

WEF and IMD both use a number of "factors" to compile their indices of competitiveness but these factors in turn are divided into a very long list of sub-factors or "criteria," bringing the total number of variables used by them to over 200 in the case of IMD and to over 300 in the case of WEF. Each uses a combination of "hard" data (published statistics) and "soft" data (survey data compiled from executive opinion surveys) in compiling their sub-factors.

The eight factors used by IMD to measure competitiveness are: Internationalisation and openness of the economy; the Domestic economy (including savings, investment and cost of living); the Government sector (including public expenditure and fiscal policies, state efficiency, justice and security, and the legal and regulatory environment); Financial institutions, including their size and transparency; Infrastructure (both physical and technological), environment and energy; Management (including productivity, labour costs, and corporate culture); Science and technology (including R&D expenditure, technology management and scientific environment); and People (including skills and access to education, unemployment levels, working hours, welfare and social services, equality of opportunity, quality of life, and attitudes and values). WEF's list of "factors" are fairly similar to that of IMD. Aspects of a number (although by no means the majority) of the elements that go to make up the concept of human security are to be found among the vast array of sub-factors in these two competitiveness reports.

Had the territorial coverage of the reports been universal, instead of being confined to fewer than sixty countries, it would have been interesting to have attempted to compare the conclusions of WEF and IMD in relation to the contribution of their common sub-factors to national competitiveness and the conclusions of the UNDP regarding their importance for human security. It goes without saying that, in a number of instances, what the UNDP might consider as a positive contribution to human security might be considered as a threat to national competitiveness by WEF and IMD. To take a few examples: job security, guaranteed old age pensions, and a comprehensive welfare programme would all contribute positively to human security. In contrast, WEF and IMD associates them with "inflexibility" of labour markets and "social costs" – both of which constitute threats to national competitiveness.

Evidence to suggest that nations do compete with each other is to be found in the competing incentives packages (grants, tax breaks, "a pool of young computer-literate workers" and so on) offered by (especially contiguous) nations and regions that compete with each other to attract foreign direct investment (FDI). IMD would describe such packages as part of the attempt of countries to become "attractive" to foreign investors. It states that "nations approach the process of internationalisation by being "attractive and/or aggressive'" (*ibid*: 6). Some nations focus on attractiveness by creating a domestic environment that is conducive to FDI being made *inside* their country (it points to the example of Ireland) while others aggressively strive to enter international markets by making direct investments *outside* their countries and through exports (for example Japan). IMD claims that only the U.S. seems to manage both approaches equally.

According to IMD, nations manage two types of economies: one (proximity) that is close at hand and one (globality) that is far-reaching. The first adds value close to the end user while globality assumes that the factors related to production need not necessarily be actually near the end user. There are risks in pursuing the latter option – and many of them have consequences for human security. As IMD puts it: "It affects decisions regarding the degree of exposure, regulation and, eventually, social volatility of the economy" (*ibid*: 7). We could repeat the question posed at the beginning of this article: how are things "out there" affecting people "in here"?

The 1990 *World Competitiveness Report* described three types of society: (1) what it called the South European Model, characterised by weak infrastructure, business regulation and social protection, a parallel economy, and low labour costs; (2) the North European Model, characterised by a strong emphasis on stability, social consensus and regulations; and (3) the Anglo-Saxon Model, characterised by deregulation, privatisation, labour flexibility, and a higher acceptance of risk. It claimed a shift had occurred from the North European model to the Anglo-Saxon one during the 1980s "triggered perhaps by the Reagan and Thatcher years" (*ibid*). In its 2000 report, it claimed that the Anglo-Saxon model was still "prevailing" and that EU legislation "has moved towards more deregulation and privatization" (IMD, 2000: 11).

Prowse (2000) draws attention to the newly-named concept of "presenteeism" in the UK or the tendency for employees to work longer and longer hours. He claims that this "presenteeism culture" hurts nearly everyone especially families and most especially children. People are not working more hours because they choose to do so; rather, they are victims of the "stadium effect". When one person in a crowded stadium stands up, he can see better. But soon everyone is standing up and nobody can see any better and everyone is more uncomfortable than before. Prowse claims that the same thing has happened with working hours. The first companies to demand more hours gained a competitive advantage. But this soon disappeared since all employers are now doing it – and, as in the stadium, everyone is worse off. The movement of more women into paid employment is desirable but, unless more men undertake more parental and home-making activities, children suffer as a result of parental absenteeism. The "long hours culture …contributes to the death of the family", particularly when both parents are working long hours, "since a family exists as a living entity only if its members interact". Presenteeism has not come about from personal choice or even a change in values. As Prowse puts it: "Rather our seemingly free choices are conditioned by institutional changes – such as the global intensification of competition – which nobody planned or intended" (Prowse, 2000: XXIV).

Threats to human security arise, not just within countries (from tensions between the economy of globality to the economy of proximity), but also between countries and regions. The so-called "giants" of *Fortune* magazine's "Global 500" were being praised during 1995 for having "pushed across borders to seize fresh markets and swallow up local competitors" (*Fortune*, 1996) while the CEOs of many global enterprises listed in *Business Week's* "Global 1000" were describing their sector of industry as having become "brutally competitive" causing them to "come to work every day on the razor's edge of a competitive battle" (*Business Week*, 1996: 49). Both magazines concluded that the only way for these enterprises to remain competitive is "to go global" and begin investing overseas.

Globalization

Globalization is one of the most widely used – and misused – words in the field of international relations today. It appears to have many meanings. Because of the many interpretations attaching to the term, there are wide differences of opinion regarding its perceived implications for the world economy, its constituent parts, and for human security. Some would argue that globalization is spreading so fast that it spells the end of the national economy and the role of national governments in policy-making. Others question whether it is appropriate to use the term "globalized" to describe the present state of the world economy claiming that it differs only quantitatively, and not qualitatively, from the one that operated during the *pax Britannica* period prior to the First World War. However, some of these economists also argue that history suggests that the current internationalization (or globalization) of the world economy may be a fragile process that could be reversed if the distribution of benefits arising from it is considered to be unjust by a majority of governments or civil society groups.

In any debate, it is important to have clarity regarding concepts. The key issues to be explored are: is globalization happening? Is the world becoming internationalised in an entirely new way? If it is, has it positive or negative consequences – and for whom? Which are the key actors involved in the process? Does globalization threaten the human security of the weak? Does it significantly reduce the capability of national governments – and, through them, inter-governmental and international organisations – to intervene in ways that can ensure positive outcomes for human security? The world still has borders: are nation states, rather than transnational corporations (TNCs) still the most influential actors in international relations; can they (or perhaps the more powerful among them, or partnerships of them?) still exercise a decisive influence on the global political economy and its consequences for human security? As in all such debates, it is appropriate to begin by exploring the various definitions.

When it first emerged, the term globalization referred almost exclusively to economic events and trends. More recently, it is being interpreted in a multidimensional way. It is seen, not only as an economic process but also one that has socio-political and cultural dimensions. Nevertheless, it is notable that the main debates still centre around its economic aspects and implications. On the whole, economists who question whether "globalization" is a reality and whether there is anything fundamentally "new" about today's more integrated world, interpret the concept in economic terms exclusively and tend to equate this concept of economic globalization with increased internationalization of trade and investment flows. On the other hand, those who claim that today's world is a globalized one are often taking a more multidimensional (socio-economic, political, and cultural) approach. Among economists, those who claim that the world economy is indeed now globalized in a "new" way tend to include micro as well as macro aspects of international "interconnectedness" in their definitions of globalization. In particular, they point to greater linkages at the level of production within and between transnational corporations and other global networks such as those among researchers and among non-governmental organisations.

There is general agreement at this stage that the process, however defined, has both positive and negative implications for most countries and communities but that the benefits tend to favour the relatively rich and powerful and the costs tend to be borne disproportionately by the relatively poor and marginalized – in rich as well as in poor countries. Most of the papers and reports produced by government departments and international organisations tend to define globalization in very general terms and, as a result, tend to conclude that the process can be potentially positive for all countries and groups within them while acknowledging that, to date, its impacts have been uneven and have tended to benefit the better off and more powerful countries and people. What is needed, most of them claim, is better "governance" and better policy choices by governments, international institutions, the private sector, and civil society.

Economists describe globalization as a process driven by technological change and having production, investment, and trade dimensions. On the production and investment sides, globalization is defined as the process by which enterprises (related or unrelated) become interdependent and interlinked globally through strategic alliances and international networks. Alliances may be for individual projects or may be more long-term. On the trade side, globalization is associated with increasing liberalization which, in turn, promotes increasing trade links. The growth of trade can also result from the splitting up of production processes and their location in often widely-dispersed plants or "production chains" (car engines produced in one country, bodies in a second, the marketing function in another, and so on), a process that induces more trade during the course of production. By 2000, it is estimated that TNCs account for about a third of world output and two-thirds of world trade.

Cook and Kirkpatrick (1996) distinguish between "shallow" integration of the global economy (through trade in goods and services and capital, increasingly related to flows of FDI) and "deep" integration (which they call globalization) which occurs at the level of production. "Cross-border activities within multinational corporations and within networks established by them have reinforced linkages between national economies to the extent that intra-firm trade is estimated to account for around 40 per cent of global trade" (Cook and Kirkpatrick 1996, 6). They acknowledge that government policy can foster "deep" integration but imply that the multinationals are the main actors. They state: "It is the multinationals that have more often been the major impetus for globalization, which in many instances has led, rather than followed, government policy actions" (*ibid*, 10, with an accompanying reference to the 1993 *UN World Investment Report* p. 113).

Regionalization, although a concept distinct from globalization, is nonetheless related to it. It can be either "market-led" or "policy-led" or both.

Market-led integration is characterised by increasing economic linkages among a group of contiguous countries but without any accompanying institutional or policy framework while "policy-led" integration is a process that is initiated through an international agreement designed to promote trade among a group of contiguous countries. Regional integration schemes lead to increased intra-regional trade (described as shallow integration) but, in order to get a foothold in the expanded markets of other regional groupings, enterprises in one region will tend to begin investing in other regions. Often these foreign branches of TNCs compete with domestic enterprises for local resources and markets but, more recently, there is an increasing tendency for foreign direct investment (FDI) to become involved in strategic alliances with domestic firms. The result is "deep" integration, or integration at the level of production, facilitated through "investment creation" across regions (O'Neill, 1993). In this way, the processes of regionalization and economic globalization become interlinked.

Increasingly, as tariffs have become less important as impediments to international trade flows, the focus of liberalizing efforts has shifted to non-tariff barriers and especially to reducing differences between countries (or regions) in trade and investment policies, as well as differences in standards, regulatory environments, and government involvement in the economy. Thus, deregulation and privatization are seen as promoting international trade and investment, or internationalization – or, in the language of some, "globalization".

Technological progress, not only in production, but more especially in communications (transportation and information technology) is widely perceived as a major driver of globalization, facilitating wider and faster linkages between people and places. The integration of financial markets is perhaps the most remarkable manifestation of the role of the new information technology (IT) in the so-called globalization process. In 1977, about US$18 billion of foreign exchange was traded daily; by 2001 the figure was US$1,500 billion – and less than five percent of that amount was connected with trade flows. In the mid-1980s, there were a few thousand host computers for the internet; by the end of the 1990s, the number had increased to nearly 50 million. Between 1960 and 2000, during which time the population of the world doubled, the total number of kilometres travelled by people in cars, buses, trains and airplanes increased more than fivefold (Homer-Dixon, 2001).

Some analysts link competitiveness and globalization in their definitions of globalization. Thomas Friedman, a columnist with the *New York Times,* defined it as "that loose combination of free-trade agreements, the Internet and the integration of financial markets that is erasing borders and uniting the world into a single, lucrative, but brutally competitive marketplace"

(*New York Times*, 7 February 1996). Day and Reibstein define it rather similarly but also perceive globalization as the driving force of new forms of competitiveness. According to them: "Globalization and technological change are spawning new sources of competition, deregulation is changing the rules of competition in many industries, markets are becoming more complex and unpredictable and information flows in a tightly wired world permit companies to sense and react to competitors at a faster rate" (Day and Reibstein, 1996: 2).

Although most definitions and analyses of globalization to date have tended to focus on its economic aspects – and especially its trade, investment, and economic governance aspects – the process is increasingly being described as a multidimensional one. Scholars other then economists are now increasingly analysing globalization. The RAWOO (2000) report lists the main themes that engage individual disciplines. Political scientists are concerned with the "globalization of politics" which they consider as an extension of multilateralism (Rosenau, 1990); the key themes of geographers are the relativization of distance and the dialectical relationship between globalization and localization; in philosophy, the focus is on planetary ethics, universal morality, and global reflexivity; in ecology, major themes include global warming and "spaceship earth"; and in cultural studies, the focus is on the global village and the implications of "McDonaldization" (RAWOO, 2000: 15). According to Robertson (1992), some distinguish between globalization as an objective or empirical process of economic and political integration, while others interpret it as a subjective process unfolding in consciousness, or "the collective awareness of growing global interconnectedness" (*ibid*). According to RAWOO, what is important is the general awareness of globalization as a "multifaceted, layered process".

The fact that globalization is now being presented as a process that is broader than economic and that it is being analysed by scholars across a broad range of disciplines does not mean that a truly *interdisciplinary* approach has yet become embedded. Clearly, however, *definitions* of globalization are now increasingly multidimensional.

Despite the growing interest among researchers from a wide range of disciplinary backgrounds – and the tentative emergence of multidisciplinary and interdisciplinary studies – some analysts remain cautious about using the term "globalization" to describe the processes that are occurring at world level today. In particular, some mainstream economists are reluctant to describe the current wave of increasing internationalization of the world economy as "globalization." This sceptical school includes Hirst and Thompson (1996), Bairoch and Kozul-Wright (1996), and O'Rourke and Williamson (1999). They all take an historical perspective. Hirst and

Thompson argue that the present stage of global development is merely one of a number of distinct conjunctures of the international economy that have existed since an economy based on modern industrial technology began to be generalised from the 1860s. They even go so far as to state that in some respects (for example, in relation to labour mobility), the current international economy is *less* open than the regime that prevailed from 1870 to the outbreak of the First World War. In relation to capital mobility, the sceptics claim that it is not leading to a massive shift of investment and employment to developing countries. In common with many other economists and most NGOs, they are concerned about the distributional aspects of the current stage of global integration, even if they are cautious about describing it as globalized. They claim that, with the exception of a small number of newly industrialized economies, developing countries remain marginalized in both investment and trade. Trade, investment and financial flows are concentrated in the Triad (or G3) of Europe, Japan and North America and this dominance seems set to continue (Hirst and Thompson 1996, 3, Bairoch and Kozul-Wright, 1996: 5). O'Rourke and Williamson warn us that, while many pundits, both at the end of the 19th century and equally at the end of the 20th century, have tended to extrapolate the immediate past into the indefinite future and have predicted the ever-increasing integration of the international economy, history shows that globalization can be reversed. All economic change produces losers as well as winners and if the losers are not adequately compensated, and if they are sufficiently powerful politically, then they may use the political process to undo those changes which they dislike most.

Clearly, although there may not be agreement among economists about the use of the term "globalized," all are agreed that, according to their own definitions, the process currently extends to a minority of peoples, most of whom live in the Triad composed of Europe, North America and Japan. But, not all who live in the Triad benefit from globalization and the global competitiveness which drives it – and is in turn driven by it.

International organizations are particularly concerned about the distributional aspects of globalization and are anxious to show that it can be beneficial for human security and for all people. It is notable that almost every United Nations organisation and international financial institution that has held a major conference or published a major report in recent years has included the word "globalization" in its title (UNDP, 1999, World Bank, 1999, UNCTAD, 1999 and 2000a, DFID, 2000, RAWOO, 2000). Their definitions tend to be broad. The current era displays growing worldwide "interconnectedness" (DFID, 2000: 15 and RAWOO, 2000: 5) that results from "shrinking space, shrinking time and disappearing borders" and integrates "not just the economy but culture, technology and governance"

(UNDP, 1999: 1). Development goals are now being pursued in a landscape "that has been transformed economically, politically, and socially" (World Bank, 1999: 31). DFID adds that globalization is reflected in "the diffusion of global norms and values, the spread of democracy and the proliferation of global agreements and treaties, including international environmental and human rights agreements" (*ibid*, 15). All of these international organizations claim that better global governance is needed in order to ensure that the benefits of globalization can be spread equitably. Oman (1994) would go further. He sees the need for "deep" international policy integration if globalization is to benefit all people.

Globalization, Competitiveness and Human Security: Can it be a Positive-Sum Game?

There are conflicting views among analysts as to the implications of globalization for human development and for reduction of human insecurities. On the one hand, the "optimistic" school of thought argues that globalization will lead to a greater integration of developing countries into the global economy and there will be net benefits. As a result, there will be convergence at the global level. The "pessimistic" view, on the other hand, is that globalization is largely confined to the North, has already widened existing inequalities and marginalized the vast majority of developing countries, and this process of divergence continues. At the beginning of the 21st century, the sources of pessimism have become more broad-based and – in some cases – more shrill.

Thurow and Kapstein belong to the extreme pessimistic school. Thurow claims that, since the fall of communism, the capitalist system has had no competitor to curb its excesses, especially the tendency of the new technologies to lead to job losses and cause downward pressure on the wages of the unskilled. Many companies are "ripping up the implicit social contracts". He sees growing inequalities between rich and poor both inside and between countries, large-scale unemployment, increased homelessness and (like Prowse in 2000) the breakdown of the family, leading to a "vicious circle of individual disaffection, social disorganisation and a consequent slow downward spiral" (Thurow, 1996: 7). He warns that the very poor will become socially excluded and will retreat into religious fundamentalism or extremism. As a result, capitalism itself is doomed. Kapstein is equally gloomy. He claims that the "postwar bargain has been broken." The global economy "is leaving millions of disaffected workers in its train. Inequality, unemployment, and endemic poverty have become its handmaidens" (Kapstein, 1996: 16). The forces acting on today's workers "inhere in the structure of today's global economy, with its open and increasingly fierce competition on the one hand and fiscally conservative units – states – on the other" [*ibid*, 17]. Governments are supposed to act as protectors of the weak. Easing pressures on the "losers" of the new open economy must now be the focus of economic policy if the process of globalization is to be sustained but, he claims, "systemic pressures are curtailing every government's ability to respond with new spending. Just when working people most need the nation-state as a buffer from the world economy, it is abandoning them" (*ibid*, 16). This poses a challenge not just to policy makers, he states, but to modern economics as well.

Of course, this is not the first time that the end of capitalism has been predicted. But perhaps the "announcement effect" of Marx's *Das Kapital* induced it to reform only when a communist system in the USSR became a reality. Do the effects of human insecurity have to cause socio-economic disintegration before their "announcement effect" causes public and private actors to intervene decisively?

Schwab and Smadja, president and managing director respectively of the WEF, do not believe that globalization is a positive-sum game. They identify the "megacompetition" associated with the process as the main threat to human security. In their words,

> The lightening speed at which capital moves across borders, the acceleration of technological changes, the rapid evolution of management and marketing requirements increase the pressure for structural and conceptual readjustments to a breaking point. This is multiplying the human and social costs of the globalization process to a level that tests the social fabric of the democracies in an unprecedented way (International Herald Tribune, 1 February 1996).

It is certainly interesting to read the following extracts from the two people at the top of the organisation that produces the annual *Global Competitiveness Report*:

> The megacompetition that is part and parcel of globalization leads to winner-take-all situations; those who come out on top win big, and the losers lose even bigger...[and]... The way transnational corporations have to operate to compete in the global economy means that it is now routine to have corporations announce new profit increases along with a new wave of layoffs...[and]...For those who keep their jobs, the new sense of insecurity means the demise of corporate loyalty bonds. It is not yet clear that corporations have fully realized the consequences that this will have on their future performance [*ibid*].

Schwab and Smadja, no less than the leaders of the G7 or the EU, are concerned to ensure the survival of the "new global capitalism" and that it not become synonymous with "free market on the rampage, a brakeless train wreaking havoc". They call for action from both governments and corporations in order to save capitalism. Their policy advice to governments sounds like "business as usual": they are exhorted to improve training and education, communications infrastructures, "entrepreneur-incentive fiscal policies", and to "recalibrate social policies". Nevertheless, they advise corporations "to look to their social responsibilities."

This notion that corporations have formal social responsibilities, in addition to their contractual ones to employees and shareholders, has been spreading in recent years. According to Suzman, it is largely spurred by the spectre of growing social exclusion (quoted in *Financial Times*, 17 June 1996). He reports on an organisation, the European Business Network for Social Cohesion, which has been formed to encourage companies throughout the EU to take seriously the issue of corporate involvement in the community and, in particular, job creation through investment in training and economic regeneration projects. Two 1996 U.S. reports, commissioned by the White House's National Economic Council, one by a business group and the other by labour, concluded that the social contract between business and its workers had been "falling apart under the strains of competition." They both reported that "companies have less room for manoeuvre in the competitive global environment" [*ibid*]. It is appropriate to note that these views come from the country that was ranked number one in IMD's world competitiveness report and number five in WEF's report of that year. It was also number one in the rankings of the Fortune 500 global corporations and of *Business Week's* global 1000 corporations, and number two in the HDI rankings of the UNDP that same year. In 2000, the U.S. was number one in the rankings of both WEF and IMD and number three in the HDI rankings.

UN organizations, with their universal memberships, are probably under some pressure to present the positive as well as the negative sides in the globalization debate. While, they sometimes appear to be more concerned about the risks arising for countries left out of the process than the risks affecting countries incorporated into it, nevertheless, they are concerned about the distributional aspects of globalization and tend to highlight its negative implications for weak actors, both nationally and internationally.

UNDP sees globalization, not necessarily as a positive-sum game, but as "a two-edged sword…. with winners and losers" and a process that caused divergence, rather than convergence, in many cases. In its 1999 *Human Development Report*, it identifies the benefits of globalization as: "global markets, global technology, global ideas and global solidarity" which can "enrich the lives of people everywhere, greatly expanding their choices. The growing interdependence of people's lives calls for shared values and a shared commitment to the human development of all people" (UNDP, 1999: 1). Although it presents both sides, it claims that income inequality is increasing in many countries that have opened their economies. When it focuses on trade and investment flows, it states that, while some developing regions owe their current prosperity and human development to international trade, "others have been vulnerable to its vagaries" ...[and].... "The risk is not just that the benefits of globalization will bypass these nations. The risk is that these countries will become increasingly marginal as their shares of world trade and international capital flows continue to decline" (UNDP, 1996: 59). It warns that today's globalization is being driven by market expansion – opening national borders to trade, capital, information – which is outpacing governance of these markets and their repercussions for people and that more progress has been made in norms, standards, policies and institutions for open global markets than for people and their rights. Linking globalization to competitiveness, UNDP states that, while competitive markets may be the best guarantee of efficiency, they are not necessarily the best guarantee of equity. It echoes many of the concerns voiced by analysts of the current national pursuit of global competitiveness when it states:

> Liberalization and privatization can be a step to competitive markets – but are not a guarantee of them. And markets are neither the first nor the last word in human development. Many activities and goods that are critical to human development are provided outside the market – but these are being squeezed by the pressures of global competition. There is a fiscal squeeze on public goods, a time squeeze on care activities and an incentive squeeze on the environment (*ibid*, 2).

In the *Plan of Action* presented at UNCTAD X in Bangkok in 2000, UNCTAD, like UNDP in 1999, again presents both sides of the globalization case. The positive aspects for developing countries are seen as the opening up of market opportunities for their exports, promoting transfer of information skills and technology, and increasing the financial resources available for investment in physical and intangible assets. One of the negative aspects is seen as the fast pace of financial liberalization which has in some cases significantly delinked finance and investment from international trade. This has led to high volatility of capital flows and "weakened the capacity of some developing countries to manage effectively their integration into the world economy" (UNCTAD, 2000a: 6).

The World Bank also acknowledges that there are negative as well as positive sides to globalization. It describes how it is praised "for bringing new opportunities for expanded markets and the spread of technology and management expertise which in turn hold out the promise of greater productivity and a higher standard of living" but how it is also "feared and condemned because of the instability and undesired changes it can bring" (World Bank, 1999: III). The instability and undesired changes are brought "to workers who fear losing their jobs to competition from imports; to banks and financial systems and even entire economies that can be overwhelmed and driven into recession by flows of foreign capital; and, not least, to the global commons, which are threatened in many ways with irreversible change" (*ibid*).

Given this acknowledgment that globalization, however defined, has costs as well as benefits and produces losers as well as winners, it is not surprising that the declared objective of these international development organizations is to ensure that globalization works for all people, especially the poor. The objective is stated in fairly similar language by all of them: "to ensure that globalization becomes a positive force for all the world's people" (Secretary-General of the United Nations at the Millennium Assembly 2000); "The challenge is . . . to ensure that globalization works for people – not just for profits" (UNDP, 1999: 2); "To make globalization an effective instrument for the development of all countries and all people" (UNCTAD, 2000a: 5); "The forces of global integration and technological advance can and must be harnessed to serve the interests of poor people" (World Bank, 2000: v); "I see the IMF as an active part of the workforce to make globalization work for the benefit of all" (International Monetary Fund, 2000: 303).

The ways in which the general objective of "making globalization work for all" is translated into specific proposals for action clearly reflect the individual interpretations of globalization held by the various international organizations. While their proposals normally reflect their own individual mandates, most of them are not averse to providing advice for their sister institutions.

Because UNDP defines the process of globalization in a multidimensional way ("a process integrating cultural, technology and governance"), it also attempts to design an "agenda for action" that is also multidimensional. However, it ignores cultural factors and is heavily biased toward governance issues relating to reform of international institutions, especially the IMF, the World Bank, and the WTO. At a general level, UNDP calls for an improvement in the quantity and quality of official development assistance, more and faster debt relief, building a more coherent and more democratic architecture of global governance (including strengthening the United Nations, building a world environment agency, and a world criminal court with a broad mandate for human rights). More specifically, it wants the WTO to promote "free and fair international trade". It sees the need for the WTO's mandate to be extended to include global competition policy and a code of conduct for TNCs and calls for its trade-related intellectual property (TRIPs) agreement to be reviewed. It also wants the voting patterns of the World Bank and the IMF to be reviewed.

UNCTAD identifies the need for a rather similar list of socio-economic and governance reforms if all countries are to be effectively integrated into the international trading system and if globalization is to work for all. They include: improving supply capabilities; overcoming the debt problem; strengthening the commitment to social development; ensuring women's political, economic and social participation; generating adequate financial flows for development, including addressing the declining trend of ODA and its effective use; undertaking institutional reforms; reducing financial volatility; and enhancing the technological capabilities of developing countries (UNCTAD, 2000b: 2). In order to ensure that the benefits of globalization are accessible to all on an equitable basis, it demands "more inclusive, transparent and participatory institutional arrangements for international economic decision-making". Reflecting its definition of globalization with its focus on international flows of trade, finance and investment, UNCTAD calls for "improved market access for goods and services of particular interest to developing countries, resolving issues relating to the implementation of WTO agreements, fully implementing special and differential treatment, facilitating accession to the WTO by developing countries, and providing technical assistance to enable them to cope with the demands of WTO membership" (*ibid*, 3).

The World Bank has a very broad development mandate but because it confines its definition of globalization to "the continuing integration of the world's economies and collective action to address global environmental problems", its call for action "to harness global forces to help poor people" is also focused on economic and governance issues. They include: expanding market access in rich countries for developing countries" goods and services, reducing the risk of economic crises, encouraging the production of international public goods that benefit poor people, and ensuring a voice for poor countries and poor people in global forums (World Bank, 2000: 179).

The World Bank rightly criticises the governments of industrialised countries. It acknowledges that many developing countries have already undertaken reforms in their trade sectors. But it claims that the reason why these developing countries have not yet benefited in full from the globalizing world economy is because their reforming efforts have not been matched by reforms in rich countries (*ibid*, 180). The Managing Director of the IMF made the same point at the Board of Governors meeting in September 2000: "Many industrial countries have not yet developed enough of a sense of urgency to deliver *their* part of structural change to make globalization work for all. This includes, crucially, that industrial countries recognize that it is both in their own interest and in the interest of the global economy to take a strong lead in opening their markets" (IMF, 2000: 304). Although the World Bank praises the IMF for having developed standards on financial data dissemination, financial sector soundness, and fiscal, monetary, and financial transparency, it implicitly criticises the Fund when it states that very little progress has been made in setting up early warning devices that could alert the international community to impending crises. The Bank also states that international institutions – especially the WTO – need to take the lead in helping developing countries to strengthen their capacity to analyse issues and represent their interests at international negotiations.

In its advice to international organizations in general, it calls on them to "place a premium on transparency, accountability, and effectiveness" so that "all parties have a seat at the table" (*ibid*, 181). No doubt this is in response to the increasing number – and growing aggressiveness – of demonstrations that now take place on the occasion of the joint World Bank/IMF meetings. The WTO was the first international organization to be targeted by protesters in what is now being described as the "backlash" against globalization. At the Third WTO Ministerial meeting held in Seattle in December 1999, at which a new round of multilateral trade negotiations was to have been launched, a diverse group of development NGOs, environmentalists and trade unionists mounted demonstrations in the streets outside the meeting. These protests marked the beginning of a new chapter in the debate around globalization broadly defined. The fact that a new trade round failed to be agreed at the meeting was presented by the protesters as support for their case and, at the annual meetings of the World Bank and IMF held in Prague in September 2000, the backlash against globalization gathered momentum as 10,000 demonstrators took to the streets to protest against the policies of these two institutions in particular and against globalization and capitalism in general. It has now become the norm for all major meetings of international organizations to be accompanied by such "anti-globalization/anti-capitalist" protests.

Initially, the reaction of the international organizations as well as many sections of the media to these demonstrations and to protests by NGOs like Greenpeace against scientific testing of the safety of genetically-modified crops was dismissive. Demonstrators were described as "playing on popular fears of globalization and Luddite yearnings …(while) they owe much of their impact to two of globalization's most potent tools, television and the internet" (*Financial Times*, 29 July 1999). Many IMF and World Bank delegates described the Prague protesters as "naive and unpopular" (McCaughan, 2000).

Yet, the mood was already shifting and international organizations have begun to take them into account. In its issue of 27 November 1999, *The Economist* stated that "for all the gains that globalization brings [the demonstrator's] concerns should not be dismissed". Less than a year later it argued that "it would be a big mistake to dismiss this global militant tendency as nothing more than a public nuisance, with little potential to change things". It claimed that it had already has changed things, citing the "scuttling" by protesters, working through the internet, of the OECD's planned Multilateral Agreement on Investment, the success of the Jubilee 2000 campaign on debt relief, and anti-sweatshop campaigns dedicated to improving working conditions in third world factories. On the other hand, while noting that the UNDP now has an advisory board of NGOs, it also raised the issue of a code of conduct for NGOs themselves given that they are "unelected, unaccountable, and very often unrepresentative" (*The Economist*, 23 September 2000).

The 1999 annual report of the WTO defended the organization claiming that "sweeping pronouncements" on its future and on that of the multilateral trading system in the wake of the "disastrous Seattle meeting" had proved unfounded. Nevertheless, while it claimed that "The WTO is not lost and it is not discredited" it accepted that the demonstrations may "prove salutary" describing them as "a wake-up call" (WTO, 2000a). The Chair of the WTO used the same term and gave some ground when he acknowledged that "we need to address the perennial problem of how to ensure in the decision making process of the WTO the right balance between transparency, democracy, inclusiveness and representativity among the entire membership of the organization on the one hand and efficiency in reaching an agreement on the other" (WTO, 2000b). In the wake of the demonstrations in Prague in September 2000, the IMF's new Managing Director stated that the IMF "should show respect for the cultural and historical traditions of its member countries and should not lecture" (IMF, 2000: 304). The UK government's White Paper summed up the changing mood when it stated that there are legitimate public concerns about the impact of globalization on people's culture, the environment, inequality within and between countries, and the effect on the world's poorest people. Echoing the sentiments of O'Rourke and Williamson, DFID warned that "if democrats and internationalists do not address these concerns, then those who advocate narrow nationalism, xenophobia, protectionism and the dismantling of multilateral institutions will gain in strength and influence with disastrous consequences for us all" (DFID, 2000: 15).

Some Implications for Key Actors and for Research

What are the implications for human security of what is being described as the "globalisation" of much activity in the world today, and the relentless competition among globalizing actors? Does globalization imply that national governments are powerless to act in the global arena, or even in the national arena on international issues? Will non-governmental organizations (NGOs) play a major role in filling any policy vacuums? Do the main international economic organizations need further reform to enable them to fulfil their mandates? Finally, what are some of the main research challenges facing academics today on the topic of globalization?

This article began by presenting the multidimensional concept of human security together with its various aspects (economic, food, health, environmental, personal, community, and political) and the various insecurities that threaten each of them. The two concepts of competitiveness and globalization were then examined. While there is agreement that firms compete, some would deny that nations do so. Yet, many policy initiatives implemented by national governments (upgrading physical infrastructure and human capital, investment in high-tech skills, promoting the flexibility of markets) are clearly designed to improve national competitive advantage in global production and trade. Globalization, and its many definitions, were examined next. While its economic aspects have received most attention to date, it is increasingly being described as a multidimensional concept. Because it is defined differently by so many of its users, there are many different opinions regarding its implications for human security. It is essential to be clear about definitions in the debate about globalization because it is from an understanding of the process that one's interpretation of its implications for human security arise. It is helpful to distinguish between the concepts of "shallow" and "deep" integration when considering the arguments of some economists who doubt that the world economy is globizing or at least globalizing in any significantly new way.

The study of globalization should be linked with that of competitiveness. It is clear that the type of aggressive competition that defines the activities of many global corporate actors today is the fundamental characteristic of "deep" integration, or globalization, in today world economy. It is also the main reason why the globalization process exacerbates, and in many cases is the prime cause of, major disruptions and insecurities at national, community, and individual levels. There are many negative links between competitiveness and human security: in a number of instances, what might be considered as a positive contribution to human security (job security, guaranteed old age pensions, and a comprehensive welfare programme) is considered a threat ("inflexibility" of labour markets and "social costs") to national competitiveness in a globalizing national economy. Of course, aggressive competitiveness is facilitated by the globalization process. But, in turn, this type of competitiveness facilitates the globalization process, and the promotion of insecurities that arise from it.

Because there is insufficient attention paid by many commentators to the nature of the two-way links between competitiveness and globalization in today's world economy, over-optimistic conclusions are often drawn about the implications for human security of the globalization process. This is evident even in the statements of international economic organizations whose mandate is focused on development and poverty eradication. Despite the fact that they acknowledge the process has costs as well as benefits, winners as well as losers, they tend to claim that it can "work for all." However, in saying this they are probably defining globalization in the "shallow" sense of increased internationalisation, especially within a liberalized trade environment. Many policy reforms also need to be implemented at global and national levels, and many reforms need to be introduced within international organizations before globalization can benefit all the world's peoples. Practical assistance is also needed to help developing countries, especially the least-developed (LDCs), to minimize the negative and maximize the positive impacts of globalization. Studies carried out over the past few years suggest that the main export-related constraints faced by LDCs include poorly-developed physical and institutional infrastructure, inefficient production systems, low labour force skills, and a general absence of business culture. An initiative called the Integrated Framework (IF) for least-developed countries (LDCs) was in 1996 to help increase the effectiveness and efficiency of trade-related technical assistance to them and ensure that it is demand-driven. The participating institutions are the WTO, UNCTAD, the WTO/UNCTAD International Trade Centre, the World Bank, and the IMF (LDCs, 2001).

Distinguishing between "shallow" and "deep" integration is helpful when considering whether national governments still have the capability to intervene in the global arena in a globalizing world – or indeed in the national arena on international issues. If it is agreed that the world is still only shallowly integrated, then there is no argument about the capacity of governments to intervene via policies and institutions. If, on the other hand, it is agreed that at least some parts of the world, either territorially or in relation to specific sectors or both, are "deeply" integrated, then there may be some constraints on the ability of individual governments to make policy interventions. This is particularly true of small and poor countries. It is not true in the case of powerful countries especially those in the Triad. Of course, it is in the interests of some global actors (especially the TNCs) to promote the myth of governmental policy impotence.

In any case, the existence of "constraints" is quite a different thing from an incapacity to act. Moreover, if governments act in concert, using (reformed) international, regional, and inter-governmental institutions, then all governments have the capacity for policy interventions. And, whatever the similarities or differences between the current period of globalization and the earlier one, it is important to acknowledge that governments still played a large role in the pre-1914 period. Even the Gold Standard did not operate as "automatically" as is often claimed. As Bairoch and Kozul-Wright put it: "The dynamic processes that underlie investment and innovation are neither abstract nor spontaneous, but channelled and shaped by particular institutional arrangements and policy interventions" (*ibid*). Hirst and Thompson come to much the same conclusion when they state: "There are real potentialities for developing regulatory and management systems (and) the international economy is by no means out of control" ...[but]... "the political will is lacking at present to gain extra leverage over undesirable and unjust aspects of international and domestic economic activity" (*ibid*, 17). Or, finally, as Wolf puts it: "Policy matters. On their own or together governments can do a great deal. The debate should be over what they should do, not over whether they can do anything at all" (*Financial Times*, 13 February 1996, 22). What is needed is the political will – and further reform of the existing global institutional framework.

At a national level, one of the most important policy initiatives that governments of all countries, developing and industrialised alike, could take in the interests of promoting human security would be to incorporate into national policies all the relevant elements of the "20-20 compact" agreed at the Social Summit in Copenhagen in 1995, as well as those agreed at the Alma Ata ("Health for All by 2000") held in 1978, the Jomtien Conference ("Education for All") in 1990, the UN Environment Conference in Rio in 1992, the UN Women's Conference in Beijing in 1995, the Global Climate Change Conference in 1998, and the UN Millennium Summit in 2000. Already the Development Assistance Committee (DAC) of the OECD has established "policy markers" to help to track the compliance of DAC donors with the commitments they made at Rio, Copenhagen and Beijing.

Another area where national governments need to act in a liberalising and globalizing world economy is in relation to regulation. As privatisation expands and the state reduces its role as producer and provider, its role as protector becomes even more important and necessary. Stephens (1996) argues that the world has become very complex and even "mystifying" for most people, such that "scientific advance leaves us ignorant of how our food is produced, technology has injected permanent insecurity into our working lives (and) the pace of change leaves most of us unable to evaluate the risks" (*Financial Times*, 30-31 March 1996). Consequently, government must interpose itself so that "the state as provider is replaced by the state as regulator" (*ibid*]). Moreover, as governments trim down the size of the public sector through privatizations, the need for regulation increases.

Although not *directly* involved in policy making, the private sector (corporations, farmers, professional organisations) expends significant resources in all countries trying to influence government decisions and policies affecting their individual activities. In order to make the private sector (especially one operating in an environment that is increasingly privatized and deregulated) more accountable to people, increases in other forms of regulation are necessary. As noted earlier, there are some moves afoot to persuade the corporate sector to become more accountable, not just to their employees and shareholders, but to the wider public. The corporate sector, and especially TNCs, must become more responsible and sensitive to human security concerns. But increased regulation and government pressure will almost certainly be necessary if such accountability is to be effected. The failure to date of (especially powerful) governments to agree to wide-ranging and strong Codes of Conduct for TNCs is a discouraging reminder of the continuing differences between the power and interests of OECD and developing countries (and governments) in this regard. Never-theless, the issue will have to be revisited inside relevant international institutions as part of the agenda of global governance reform.

The role played by NGOs in relation to global issues has been evolving in new ways since the late 1990s. Their work spans the list of issues relating to human security concerns. Up until the late 1990s, their views tended to be taken into account by the UN organizations only when they are *planning* global conferences, as witness the "parallel" NGO conferences at Rio, Copenhagen and Beijing. But because these groups tended to be dispersed, disconnected and fragmented, their successes tended to be limited at the post-conference stage, largely because of lack of leverage at the stage when agreed resolutions are being considered (or ignored) in terms of implementation. As already noted, the use of more aggressive protests by some NGOs in the vicinity of meetings of international organisations (ironically, as a result of their becoming globalized through the internet) since the late 1990s has already led to some changes of attitude and approach within the international organizations.

It remains to be seen how the behaviour of some of the more aggressive NGOs impacts on the activities of all NGOs and on their relations with the international organizations in the years to come. There is a potential danger on the horizon. Demonstrations against the ways in which international organizations conduct their business could turn into demonstrations against the essence of that business itself. Protesters against the WTO are already calling into question the whole rules-based (in contrast to the pre-GATT/WTO power-based) system of international trade – and sometimes even against international trade itself. Indeed, *The Economist* implies that the NGOs can be the unwitting instruments of both anti-liberal governments and of TNCs. It states that it is natural for NGOs to focus their efforts on the World Bank, the IMF and the WTO "those handmaidens of today's specifically international species of capitalism" thereby "attacking the liberal order at its weakest point". It goes on to state that once NGOs go international, they can expect to gain allies among rich-country governments and, no less among rich-country corporations which, it claims, have "a political or economic interest in embracing varieties of 'social responsibility' that offer protection against competition from producers in the developing countries" (*The Economist*, 21 October 2000).

There is a huge research agenda waiting to be tackled on the implications of globalization in both its shallow and deep forms. One topic relates to its distributional implications: in what ways does it lead to convergence and in what ways to divergence between rich and poor both within countries and between them? Many implications of globalization need to be researched using multidisciplinary approaches because of the multidimensional nature of the process in which economic and political factors interact with social and cultural factors. According to RAWOO, such approaches should be used in order to assess local capabilities and responses to globalization. It identifies a number of actors which merit priority for research. They include manufacturing industry, exporters, small rural and urban producers, privatized industries, and women and youth and their organizations. For a proper understanding of the effects of globalization on developing countries, RAWOO argues that research on local processes cannot ignore the interaction between processes at all levels: local, national, and regional.

Under the heading of convergence/divergence, the costs (and benefits?) of marginalization call out for investigation. In 1996, the South Centre questioned whether African economies suffered from being marginalized from the international economy – and whether they need to rectify the situation. It argued that the economies of south-east Asia, whose success was attributed in many quarters to moderate government involvement and the openness of their economies, instead implemented vigorous state-directed industrial policy and "instead of close and unfettered integration with the world economy, these countries only integrated to the extent and in directions in which it was beneficial for them to do so, pursuing …. strategic integration" (South Centre 1996, 4). In the aftermath of the crisis that hit the south-east Asian economies in 1997, most analysts – even in the international financial institutions – would argue that financial liberalization and integration into the global economy needs to be managed carefully and in a phased and regulated way in a globalizing and increasingly competitive world.

References

Bairoch, Paul and Richard Kozul-Wright. (1996). "Globalization Myths: Some historical reflections on integration, industrialization and growth in the world economy", UNCTAD *Discussion Papers*, No. 113, March.

Business Week. (1996). "The Business Week Global 1000: The globetrotters take over", 8 July 1996, pp. 47-84.

Cook, Paul and Colin Kirkpatrick. (1996). "Globalization, Regionalization and Third World Development", mimeo, University of Manchester and University of Bradford.

Day, George and David Reibstein. (1996). "Keeping ahead in the competitive game", *Financial Times*, Mastering Management No. 18, 1995-96.

DFID. (2000). "Eliminating World Poverty: making Globalization Work for the Poor", *White Paper on International Development*, www.globalization.gov.uk.

The Economist. (1996). "The C-word strikes back", 1 June, p. 84.

The Economist. (2000). "Anti-capitalist Protests: Angry and effective", 23 September.

Financial Times. (1996). "Outlook for jobs remains poor, says OECD", 16 July.

Financial Times, 1999, "Uncivil society" (Leader), 29 July.

Friedman, Thomas. (1996). "Revolt of the Wannabes: Globalisation suffers a backlash", *New York Times*, 7 February.

Fortune. (1996). "The Fortune Global 500: A bigger richer world", 5 August, pp. 71-121.

Galtung, Johan. (1976). "Towards new Indicators of Development", *Futures*, June.

Griffin, Keith and Azizur Rahman Khan. (1992). "Globalization and the Developing World: An Essay on the International Dimensions of Development in the Post-Cold War Era", UNDP, Human Development Report Office, Occasional Papers, No. 2.

Hirst, Paul and Grahame Thompson. (1996). *Globalization in Question*, Cambridge, Polity Press.

Homer-Dixon, Thomas. (2001). "A world that turns too fast", *Financial Times*, 2 January.

International Council for Canadian Studies. (2001). "Status Report on the Transculturalism Research Project", Ottawa.

International Institute for Development Management. (1996). *The World Competitiveness Yearbook 1996*, Geneva, IMD.

International Institute for Development Management. (2000). *The World Competitiveness Yearbook 2000*, www.imd.ch/wcy.

International Monetary Fund. (2000). *IMF Survey*, Vol 29, Number 19, October 9.

Kapstein, Ethan B. (1996). "Workers and the World Economy", *Foreign Affairs, Vol. 75, No.3*, May-June.

LDCs. (2001). www.ldcs.org.

McCaughan, Michael. (2000). "Globalization has a long way to go", *Sunday Tribune*, Dublin, 1 October.

Oman, Charles. (1994). *Globalization and Regionalization: the Challenge for Developing Countries*, OECD, Paris.

O'Neill, Helen. (1993). "The Atlantic as a Moat: Are Europe and America Building Fortresses in a Regionalizing World Economy?", Paper presented at an international conference on the North American Free Trade Area, Cormier Centre, Bishops University, Canada, 30 April.

O'Neill, Helen. (1997). "Globalization, Competitiveness and Human Security", in Cristobal Kay (ed), *Globalization, Competitiveness and Human Security – Papers from the Vienna Conference of EADI 1996*, London, Frank Cass.

O'Rourke K and Williamson, J. (1999). *Globalization and History: The Evolution of a Nineteenth-Century Atlantic Economy*, MIT Press.

Porter, Michael. (1990). *The Competitive Advantage of Nations*, Macmillan, London.

Prouse, Michael. (2000). "Playing happy families? No, we're working", *Financial Times*, December 16/17, XXIV.

RAWOO (National Development Research Council) (2000). *Coping with Globalization; the Need for Research Concerning the Local Response to Globalization in Developing Countries*, The Hague.

Robertson, R. (1992). *Globalization*, London, Sage.

Rosenau, James. (1990). *Turbulence in World Politics*, Brighton, Harvester Press.

Schwab, Klaus and Claude Smadia. (1996). "Start Taking the Backlash Against Globalization Seriously", *International Herald Tribune*, 1 February.

South Centre. (1996). "Liberalization and Globalization: The Issues at Stake for the South and for UNCTAD", *South Letter*, Vol. 1, No. 25.

Stephens, Philip. (1996). "The dangers of deregulation", *Financial Times*, 30-31 March.

Suzman, Mark. (1996). "Europe gets inclusive", *Financial Times*, 17 June.

Thurow, Lester. (1996). *The Future of Capitalism*, Nicholas Brealey.

United Nations. (1993). *World Investment Report*, New York, UN.

UNCTAD. (1995). "Environment, International Competitiveness and Development: Lessons from Empirical Studies", Report by the UNCTAD Secretariat, TD/B/WG.6/10, 12 September.

UNCTAD. (1996). *Globalization and Liberalization*, Report of the Secretary-General to the Ninth Conference.

UNCTAD. (1999). Report of the Secretary-General of UNCTAD to UNCTAD X, New York and Geneva, United Nations.

UNCTAD. (2000a). *Plan of Action*, UNCTAD X, TD/386, 18 February.

UNCTAD. (2000b). Bangkok Declaration: Global Dialogue and dynamic Engagement, TD/387, 18 February.

UNDP. (Annually since 1990). *Human Development Report*, Oxford, OUP.

Wolf, Martin. (1996). "The global economy myth", *Financial Times*, 13 February, p 22.

World Bank. (1999). *World Development Report 1999/2000*, Washington, DC.

World Bank. (2000). *World Development Report 2000/2001*, Washington, DC.

World Economic Forum. (1996). *The Global Competitiveness Report 1996 and 2000*, Geneva, World Economic Forum.

World Trade Organization. (2000a). *Annual Report*, Geneva.

World Trade Organization. (2000b). *Focus Newsletter*, No. 44, January-February.

Chapter Six

Interrogating Globalization: Emerging Contradictions and Conflicts

by Elaine Coburn

There can be little doubt that the world political economy is increasingly integrated. World trade is expanding approximately twice as fast as the rate of growth of world production (Mussa 1993, p.373). Foreign exchange turnover, much of it speculative, now amounts to over a *trillion* dollars per day (Held, 1998: 15-16). Over 1160 bilateral investment treaties have been signed, two-thirds of them in the last ten years (Clarke and Barlow, 1997: 24). Since it was founded in 1995, the World Trade Organization has launched successive, ambitious negotiating rounds encompassing new, ostensibly "trade-related" fields like intellectual property rights and services. The increase in world trade and financial capital flows, the proliferation of bilateral and multilateral treaties, and the growing scope and power of bodies like the International Monetary Fund, the World Bank and the World Trade Organization bear testimony to an increasingly, if unevenly, integrated global political economy.

As the world political economy becomes more integrated, national autonomy is correspondingly limited, if not eliminated. Indeed, the intention of many free trade and investment treaties and world financial bodies is precisely to circumscribe the decision-making power of nation-states in the name of "market reform," free trade or increased foreign investment. Ironically, free trade, investment agreements and the like must be formally negotiated and signed by states, so that nations are important agents facilitating the constraint of their own autonomy. In this sense, states act as the ultimate guarantors of a neoliberal economic system that paradoxically limits the political space for distinctive national policy making. Even in the absence of free trade, investment treaties and structural adjustment plans, however, a new era of "global capitalism" (Ross and Trachte, 1990) has arguably reduced many of the nation-state's legislating options in the wake of the increased clout of mobile capital (about which more later). Neoclassical economists have spent considerable energy sketching out trends towards the globalization of capital (see, for example, Bhagwati, 1990; Krueger, 1992: 111-114; Riveria-Batiz and Xie, 1992: 422); Marxists have likewise documented economic liberalisation with an added emphasis on the impact of capital mobility on the state and labour.

While political economists are trying to understand the globalization of the market economy and its ramifications for the nation-state and other parties, social movement theorists have centred much of their research effort on understanding a shift in the locus of political protest to include not simply the local or national level but also the regional or international arena (Marks and McAdam, 1996). Even if local and national protest is not diminishing, they point out that there appears to be increasing activity directed at international-level bodies (see Imig and Tarrow (2000), for example, on the rise of political contestation targeting the European Union).

There is an increase in what some social movement theorists are calling "transnational social movements" (TSMs) or "transnational advocacy movements" (Keck and Sikkink, 1998). Such protests include the sort of international opposition that successfully terminated the negotiation of the Multilateral Agreement on Investment (MAI) at the level of the Organisation for Economic Cooperation and Development (OECD) and commanded international attention at the dramatic protests against the World Trade Organisation (WTO) in Seattle Washington in December 1999. TSMs also include joint actions by organisations like the United States based "50 Years is Enough" "Global Exchange" and "United Students Against Sweatshops", which have collaborated to support labour campaigns against the Gap, Disney, Nike and other transnational corporations exploiting low-wage workers in developing nations. If one face of globalization is the spread of the market economy, the other aspect of this process is the emergence of anti-corporate and sometimes anti-capitalist protest at the supranational, as well as the state and local, levels.

A more holistic picture of globalization as a somewhat contradictory process is needed, in which at least two distinct sets of actors, associated with different organizations and ideologies, struggle to define the future world political economy. Globalization is a conflicted, not uniform, process rooted within the changing dynamics of capitalism. While this assertion has much in common with traditional Marxist approaches, it is new insofar as it recognizes that capital is not solely or even essentially opposed by labour.

Labour as such is only one aspect of the emergent challenge to capitalism. As Ratner observes (1997), there are "many Davids" that comprise a potentially counterhegemonic social movement opposed to the single "Goliath" of (global) capitalism.

Power is shifting from the state towards capital and world financial institutions and arbitrating bodies, in several important policy areas. Partly in response, there has been an expansion in the terrain of protest to include the transnational. "Protest follows power" and the dynamics of global capital (i.e., the spread of markets world-wide) cannot be separated from the dynamics of global social movement activity. Local power spawns local protest, regional power is opposed by regional protest, and now (alongside other factors) the global power of capital has helped engender transnational protest, as well as new forms of local and national activism.

The novelty of the new international-level opposition should not be underestimated. For the first time since the Cold War, "capital" and sometimes even "capitalism" is squarely on the political agenda.

Globalization From Above: Transnational Corporations in the Global Economy

Ross and Trachte (1990) point out that changes in communications and transportation technologies have made both financial and manufacturing capital more mobile than ever before.[1] Contingent historical factors like the 1970s oil shocks, the collapse of the gold standard and "stagflation," have combined with these new technologies to create new competitive pressures amongst capital, this time on a global scale. Seeking to maintain profit margins amidst this growing international competition, corporations scan the globe for regions where wages, labour standards and other costly legislation (i.e., environmental protection laws) are less stringent or less rigorously enforced. To put it in more classical economics terms, competitive pressures combine with technical possibility to foster a "slicing up" of the value chain. Industrial production is decomposed into different stages that may then be carried out in multiple nations in order to obtain production cost and tax system benefits (Krugman cited in Chen and Hule 1998: 10). Since many more goods are now tradeable due to technological innovation (Held 1998:15), there is good reason to believe that the set of corporations that may feasibly relocate in more "attractive" sites is growing larger.

In presenting this argument, I do not mean to suggest that companies cease to consider other factors, like economies of scale, a skilled workforce, and an adequate infrastructure, when they are assessing the attractiveness of a new site for production (see Krugman, 1987). Nor do I mean to understate the extent to which the threat of capital flight varies by sector.

For example, in an earlier paper, I pointed out that private sector manufacturing workers are most directly vulnerable to capital flight, while private and public sector workers are less (directly) vulnerable (Coburn, 2000). However, some companies do choose to relocate in areas that offer reduced labour and environmental costs and so – other things being equal – higher profits. Even in cases where capital chooses not to relocate, however, the *credible threat* of capital mobility remains, giving capital a new "lever of exploitation" in its relations with workers and the state (Ross and Trachte, 1990). If workers in vulnerable sectors are overly adamant in resisting the demands of the employer or if states seek to impose new costs on capital, capital can threaten to withdraw (such a threat was dramatically realized, for example, in the case of Mitterand's first reform attempts in France in the 1980s).

The argument here is that a new era of "global capitalism," enabled by technological changes and fostered by new competitive pressures, is shifting the balance of power towards capital, away from the state and labour. This shift in power turns on the fulcrum of the new credible threat of capital flight amongst manufacturing capital. Although Ross and Trachte do not focus on investment capital, there is every reason to think that investment capital operates similarly, since nations seeking to attract foreign investment also have incentives to create "favourable" investment climates. In the developing world, nation-states may even have "attractive" investment environments designed for them, formalized and implemented as structural adjustment plans that are required as a conditionality of International Monetary Fund or World Bank loans.

Under this new regime of liberalised trade and capital flows, many transnational corporations have attained unprecedented economic clout. In a poster prepared for various non-governmental organizations, Gray (1999) offers some startling illustrations of the new weight of TNCs in the global political economy by comparing the revenues of individual corporations with the budgets of nation-states. He points out that Exxon-Mobil has revenues of $182 billion, which surpasses the national budget of Sweden, Spain, Canada and Australia (among other nations). Along similar lines, Shell Oil's $128 billion in revenue is over twenty billion greater than the national budgets of Norway and Israel combined. Indeed, of the top one hundred organizations ranked by revenue/budget, sixty-six are corporations not nations. The individual and combined economic power of these TNCs is clearly substantial, rivalling and even surpassing that of many nation-states.

Ross and Trachte anticipate that, over time, the increased relative power of mobile capital will become taken-for-granted, appearing to be a "natural force" akin to the weather (1990). Arguably, it is this sense of the inevitability of increased capital mobility that is – paradoxically – fuelling efforts to institutionalise wide-ranging rights to capital mobility. Indeed, organized transnational capital, represented by groups like the Canadian Business Council on National Issues (which includes Canadian branch-plants of American companies) or the United States Council for International Business, capitalizes on the notion that *There Is No Alternative* (TINA) as it seeks treaty protection of capital mobility and other liberalisation measures. Orthodox economists who see support for liberalisation and free trade as "a badge of professional integrity" (Krugman, 1993: 362) have not hurt their cause.[2] An environment in which liberalised trade and capital flows are seen as inevitable and/or desirable has helped foster regional trade and investment accords, as well as comprehensive multilateral trade and investment agreements. An obvious example of the latter is the negotiations aimed at concluding a Multilateral Agreement on Investment at the level of the OECD and more, recently, the WTO.

The creation of institutions facilitating world-wide capital flows is not limited to the negotiation of investment and free trade agreements. Rather, nation-states specifically delegate arbitration authority to new supranational bodies. In the case of the MAI, the treaty would have granted supranational powers to international agencies charged with resolving national (and investor-nation) disputes and enforcing the terms of the agreement. A supranational tribunal already makes binding decisions regarding the interpretation of the North American Free Trade Agreement and the European Court makes rulings that are respected by the member nations of the European Union. Similarly, the creation of new international bodies like the World Trade Organisation with its mandate to increase global trade is symptomatic of the growth of institutions intended to constrain national authority and foster the liberalisation of trade and capital flows.

In sum, the capitalist economy has entered a global era. This new epoch is characterised by increased capital flows and the attendant credible threat of capital flight. The main effect of the credible threat of capital flight, which is enabled by technological innovations and furthered by liberalizing trade and investment accords, is to reduce the autonomy of the state in important policy areas and weaken labour in its negotiations with capital. In this way, economic power has expanded from nationalist capital fractions to include mobile global capital. At the same time, political power has expanded from (and not infrequently at the expense of) nation-states towards supranational arbitrating bodies like the WTO. These trends are supported at the ideological level both by a sense of resignation that increased capital mobility is inevitable and by an economic orthodoxy that sees trade and increased global investment as desirable if economic growth is to be achieved.

I have focussed here on the political economy of the developed world, but there is good reason to suspect that the pressures for nations-states in the developing world to conform to liberalised trade and investment regimes are equally great, if not greater than in developed countries. As noted, the liberalisation of trade and the privatisation of public services are often formally required of developing nations as a condition of international loans. Moreover, the weak bargaining position of developing nations, who may have few areas in which to offer concessions in exchange for counter-benefits, often combines with a lack of technical resources to make it difficult for the developing states to challenge liberalising free-trade and investment negotiations that are already in progress. Finally, developing nations frequently have neither the economic nor technical resources necessary to challenge unfavourable rulings by supranational dispute resolution bodies (see, for example, Das Gupta, 1998; Lal Das, 1998).

Consequently, developing nations have a marginal influence on formal negotiations that institutionalise liberal regimes. Moreover, they are subject to intense financial pressures (in the form of conditional loans) to accept and implement packages of neoliberal reform. Finally, they are in a weak position to resist decisions and interpretations handed down by supranational juridical bodies, i.e., the WTO dispute resolution body. In an era of global capitalism, the autonomy of developing nations is, if anything, more constricted than in the developed world.

Globalization from Below: Transnational Social Movements in the Global Economy

Tilly (1984) has linked the rise of social movements with the emergence of the nation-state. Applying this observation to the era of global capitalism, or rather more particularly to the emergence of regional political bodies, notably the European Union, Marks and McAdam (1996) ask:

> "If, as many observers believe, integration is slowly shifting power away from the nation-state, should we not also be able to discern corresponding changes in the locus and form of social movement activity?" (p.118).

Given the preceding claims about the institutionalization of the power of transnational capital in trade and investment agreements as well as in supranational arbitrating bodies, this question takes on particular relevance. If power is shifting from national capitalist fractions and the nation-state – in important respects – to include supranational bodies and multinational treaties protecting the interests of international capital, should there not be an increase in social movement protest aimed at these new organizations and agreements?

Neo-Marxist scholars Ross and Trachte (1990) are pessimistic about the possibility of international opposition confronting an increasingly powerful capitalist class.[3] They suggest that labour remains divided by regional wage and labour standards competitions. Furthermore, their own study of mobilisation in the United States (prior to the 1990s) suggested that most protest against the growing power of mobile capital would be local in nature. Ross and Trachte argued that such local protests failed to pose a real challenge to capital since they could not address power shifts that were literally global in scope.

McAdam and Marks are more hopeful than Ross and Trachte that some non-capital groups will be able to mobilise successfully to protect their interests internationally. For example, they are optimistic about the possibilities for coordinated international action by environmentalists. Like Ross and Trachte, however, they are pessimistic about the prospects for labour. They suggest that organised labour is deeply rooted in distinct national histories that render coordinated international action difficult. Ultimately, they argue that labour faces particular problems in mobilising at the international level beyond the formation of nominal federations (pp. 104-108).

The pessimism of these authors, emerging mainly from the experience of labour in the United States in the 1980s, may be unwarranted. Wariness about the mobilising potential of labour may be unjustified in nations with quite different working class histories than the U.S. Moreover, a narrow emphasis on the role of organized labour in opposing the growing power of capital may be misplaced in an era when environmentalists and other activists are questioning the primacy of production for profit. Finally, there is reason to believe that local and national movements that are critical of corporate power and capitalism *do* offer important challenges to global capitalism, particularly insofar as locally-rooted activism self-consciously assesses the systemic logic underlying local symptoms of neoliberal globalizing processes. Indeed, Naomi Klein's best-selling book *No Logo* (2000) is just such a description of the ways in which local movements may begin with immediate issues (i.e., opposition to anorexic fashion models in Western advertisements) and spread to become whole-scale confrontations with the corporate commodification of culture and the exploitation of labour in the developed and developing worlds.

In any case, questions about the likelihood of international mobilisation against the growing power of capital ceased to be a theoretical issue when unions and nongovernmental organisations of all types (feminist, environmentalist, nationalist, indigenous) started staging multinational protests. Organisations as varied as Uruguay's World Rain Forest Movement, the Pennsylvania Fair Trade Campaign, the Africa Groups of Sweden, the

United Kingdom's Abantu for Development, Japan's Osaka YMCA and the Hungarian Traffic Club have become involved in struggles around free trade, environmental protection and the safeguarding of human rights.

In fact, a number of "international" protests have been regional rather than global in scope, taking place at the level of the European Union. This was the case when unionists from France, Belgium, Spain and elsewhere mobilised in Brussels against the closing of a Renault factory in 1997 (Imig and Tarrow, 2000). Similarly, opposition against the Canada-United States Free Trade Agreement in 1988 and then NAFTA in 1994 spawned supranational regional opposition, as coordinated forces in Canada, the United States and later Mexico waged a battle over free trade and highlighted their concerns about potential job losses, as well as increased dependency on and loss of sovereignty to the United States. Although many groups cut their teeth on regional struggles, these same organizations have frequently gone on to form international ties as well. This is the case with the Council of Canadians, for example, a nationalist group formed to combat free trade that has since expanded its mandate to issues of global concern, including the need to redress power imbalances between developed and developing nations in forums like the World Trade Organization.

One of the first truly multilateral coalitions emerged in the (provisionally) successful mobilisation against the Multilateral Agreement on Investment in 1997. This movement, including organizations like the Manitoba Federation of Labour, the Sierra Club, and the American Workgroup for People's Health and Rights, was centred mainly in the developed world. However, it was subsequently reactivated with significant participation from NGOs in developing nations in the spectacular international demonstrations against the World Trade Organisation in Seattle in December 1999. This new transnational coalition has since made its presence felt a third time at protests in Washington against the World Bank and the International Monetary Fund held in April 2000. Other recent transnational social movements include campaigns to ensure that water is exempt from status as a commodity in future trade negotiations, as well as boycotts of the World Bank's bonds and movements to cancel Third World debts. If, as Tarrow (1983) argues, protests occur in cycles, a new "protest cycle" has apparently begun, oriented towards the functioning of international organisations as well as the activities of nation-states.

Several social movement theorists have begun to describe the dynamics motivating the new "transnational" social movement protest (i.e., Smith, Chatfield and Pagnucco, 1997). Keck and Sikkink, for example, suggest that the same changes in technology that have enabled global capital mobility are helping to foster global actions in the name of environmental protection, human rights and the like. They point out that decreasing transportation costs, particularly airfares, have made face-to-face meetings of national organisations interested in coordinating efforts across borders more feasible. At the same time, new communications technologies from faxes to the internet to email have allowed information to flow much more rapidly and in some cases to reach areas that were previously inaccessible (1998: 220-221, 226). The sharing of information, organisational and leadership experiences and the monitoring of relevant developments in nations without the need for recourse to "official" media, have all helped to further cross-national ties and actions.

Similarly, Moghadam has written about transnational feminist networks. She argues that the women's movement has had a new dynamic since the 1980s. In that decade international women's movements began to be supplemented by transnational movements, which Moghadam suggests are unique insofar as they are characterized by "a conscious crossing of national boundaries and a superseding of nationalist orientations" (2000: 60-61). Enabled by changes in technology, an increasingly large group of educated, employed and "politically aware" women have created supranational feminist organizations that seek to cope with the changing and often harsh economic environment.

This last point of Moghadam's is an important one. The mobilisation of transnational organisations and movements is not simply the contingent result of changes in technology, conducted along parallel lines to economic liberalisation. Instead, many of these transnational movements are arising *as a response to* the globalization of markets and a perceived increase in the power of capital and international arbitration bodies like the World Trade Organisation over states. Indeed, transnational activists often frame their struggles in this way, arguing, for example that they want to "Globalize Liberation! Not Corporate Power" (from an advertisement for the San Francisco May Day Protest held in 2000 "in the spirit of Seattle").

Not all reactions to neoliberalism take this form. Some organizations may focus on local attempts to replace privatised public services with private non-profit charities while others may reject neoliberalism by turning towards religious fundamentalisms. Still others may focus on the inconsistencies within neoliberal ideology or its inconsistent application. A frequent complaint of activists in the Third World, for example, is that "liberalisation" is practiced unevenly, so that developing nations are forced to open their borders while developed nations keep theirs resolutely closed (i.e., especially in agriculture). In emphasizing human-rights based responses I am therefore focusing on a part, not the whole, of anti-neoliberal opposition.

Similarly, in suggesting that the new phase of global capitalism has helped foster international and supranational protest, I am only pointing out one factor, not all of the causes of the upsurge in transnational social movement activity. For example, the current wave of transnational activism would likely not have transpired in the absence of such broad historical events as the advent of the modern, active citizen, self-consciously endowed with the ability to shape the world according to his (or more recently her) ends (see, for example, Meyer 2000: 235-239; Touraine, 1992). The recent sustained and determined upsurge of transnational activism may partially depend upon a quintessentially modern sense of agency. It is in concert with such developments that I make the claim that "protest follows power" and argue that the emergence of transnational social movements (TSMs) can be seen, not just distinct from, but as a response to, the increasing strength of capital via regional and international trade and investment agreements.

It is worth emphasizing that this shift in power from states towards capital and international arbitrating authorities is not absolute: the state's autonomy has been limited, not eliminated. States continue to play an important, even expanding role in a range of activities. For example, nations vigorously police borders. The heavily armed Mexico-United States border, among others, is a vivid reminder that states and state lines continue to matter, at least for unskilled workers. Internally, states embracing neoliberal economic policies often actively survey the "undeserving poor", notably those on welfare and in prison. Prison rates in the United States, for example, are increasing even though crime rates are decreasing (Western, Beckett and Harding, 1998). Nations can and do exercise authority in non-trivial jurisdictions.

In those areas of economic and social policy where state activity *is* explicitly restricted, notably through binding trade and investment agreements, the state is a necessary – and sometimes willing – partner in the process. (Recall, for example, the Canadian government's enthusiastic pursuit of the Canada-United States Free Trade Agreement under Prime Minister Brian Mulroney) Once such agreements are entered into, further state cooperation is required for the actualization of neoliberal reforms. As Polanyi (1944) reminds us, markets do not simply "happen": they must be created and they often require elaborated rules and enforcement mechanisms. The state plays a significant role in elaborating the institutions of markets agreed upon at the international or global level within their national jurisdiction, although this task may be undertaken more or less willingly (see, for example, Adams, Dev Gupta and Mengisteab, 1999). In this sense, the decline in the autonomy of the state associated with global capitalism and the attendant threat of capital flight – not to mention the limitations on state activity imposed by binding international treaties – may mean a *re-direction* of state energies rather than a "hollowing out" of state capacities. In the developed world, national laws and policies must be reconfigured to conform to international agreements. Similarly, states in the developing world may be required to direct considerable energies towards implementing and upholding neoliberal reforms, not infrequently against the threat of popular unrest.

TSMs are self-consciously responding to the decline in the state's autonomy, if not its "hollowing out", by insisting on the democratic rights of peoples, by emphasizing the right of states to determine national policy, and by demanding that supranational adjudicating bodies be made accountable to "civil society" as well as corporations. The International Forum on Globalization, for example, bluntly condemns declining state autonomy and the ways in which state energies have been redirected so as to advance the interests of transnational companies:

> "For the past two decades, governments have transferred much of their sovereignty to the hands of global corporations. We advocate a shift from governments serving corporations to governments serving peoples and communities" (1999:2).

While they cannot match the economic clout of transnational corporations, TSMs such as the International Forum on Globalization are not without resources as they seek to halt the progress of neoliberal globalization – including the restructuring of the state in ways that more closely ally it with corporate interests – and develop alternative globalization models.

The mobilisation of TSMs derives legitimacy from a set of global institutions and treaties distinct from the liberalising bodies associated with "globalization from above." As Soysal and others have pointed out, the Universal Declaration of Human Rights, the International Covenant on Civil and Political Rights and a host of other human (and now environmental and state) rights "have been elaborated and regularized through a complex of international treaties, conventions, charters and recommendations" (1994: 145). Transnational activists frequently evoke these treaties when attempting to legitimate their claims. In contrast to trade agreements, the majority of these conventions "do not for the most part entail formal obligations or enforceable rules" (p.149). Nonetheless, combined with supranational authorities like the United Nations such charters provide legitimating resources to organisations demonstrating against the growing power of capital. An ideology of rights for persons, the environment, and the state underlies the activities of transnational social movements. Importantly, TSMs do not simply passively invoke such rights to validate their struggles, but are actively engaged in defining and expanding the scope of human rights and environmental protection against the rights of capital.

In recent negotiations at the Organisation for Economic Cooperation and Development, for example, Mexico resisted the formal adoption of (non-binding) corporate commitments to fair labour practices and environmental standards. Mexico argued that the normative import of these voluntary clauses would embolden human rights and other external "watchdog" organizations to publicly humiliate companies operating in Mexico. Ultimately, Mexico suggested this would undermine the comparative advantage conferred by cheap Mexican labour (Crane, 2000). Along similar lines, the national chief of the Assembly of First Nations, Matthew Coon Come, promised to fight for a share of national resources on First Nations land "by exerting international pressure through the United Nations" (Bailey, 2000). Clearly, provisions in the United Nations and other voluntary charters upholding labour, human and other rights can provide social movements, including transnational social movements, with an important strategic resource as they seek to legitimate their claims.

In short, then, processes of the specifically neoliberal form of dominant economic globalization have their shadow in a series of transnational mobilizations by social movements. If the central actor in "globalization from above" is mobile capital, the central actors in "globalization from below" are diverse transnational social movements. The power of capital is being institutionalised in a series of trade and investment treaties, guaranteed and enforced by supranational trade tribunals and economic organisations like the World Bank. Such institutions may weigh even more heavily on the developing nations than the developed states. In contrast, the legitimacy of transnational social movements, which arise precisely to oppose the growing power of capital, is supported by agreements like the Charter of Human Rights and legitimised through world bodies like the United Nations. Organized labour, the traditional opponent of capital, has new allies as it seeks to shape the emergent global political economy.

A Tale of Two Globalizations: A Dialectical Schematic of Globalization Processes

I have argued that it is not enough to discuss either international political economy *or* transnational social movements. Instead, I have suggested that these two literatures must be understood as describing two somewhat contradictory aspects of the process of globalization, each associated with distinct actors, institutions and motivating ideologies. I summarize the dual face of globalization in Table 1.

Table 1. Actors, Institutions and Ideologies of Globalization "From Above" and "From Below"

	Globalization from Above	Globalization from Below
Actor	Transnational Capital e.g. Business Council on National Issues, United States Council on International Business, Trilateral Commission	Transnational Social Movements e.g. Amnesty International, Greenpeace, Council of Canadians, Global Exchange
Institutions	Free trade and investment agreements WTO, IMF, World Bank, etc.	Charter of Human Rights, Rio Summit Charter United Nations
Ideology	Neoliberalism	Human, environmental and state rights

Globalization from above is primarily driven by the interests of transnational capital, which is coping with new competitive pressures by seeking out areas with lower costs (i.e., lower wages, more "relaxed" environmental standards etc.). Transnational corporations use the credible threat of capital flight to threaten nations and labour organizations that do not offer a "competitive" business environment. Transnational capital frequently collaborates to pursue its interests in larger lobbying bodies like the Canadian Business Council on National Issues or the American United States Council of International Business. These lobby groups, along with some intellectuals (mainly American economists), have elaborated a neoliberal ideological agenda that emphasizes both the inevitability and desirability of liberalised trade and investment. Somewhat paradoxically, this sense of inevitability is helping to fuel the institutionalization of markets and the rights of capital in elaborate free trade and investment agreements. These agreements are part of an institutionalized framework of market-driven policies that includes pro-liberalisation supranational organizations like the World Trade Organisation, the World Bank and the International Monetary Fund. Such organizations weigh even more heavily on the developing nations than the developed ones, because of the formers' dependency on international financial aid.

I have tried at various points to emphasize that the declining autonomy of the state is not synonymous with an elimination of state power altogether. Indeed, the state continues to exercise important disciplining and policing functions, both internationally (as with border patrols) and domestically (as with increasingly elaborated penal systems). Moreover, the decision to entrench the rights of capital in trade agreements and through newly-created bodies like the WTO is an active *political* decision. There may be few measures that are currently available to stem capital flight by individual corporations. However, the decision to enhance capital mobility by entering into binding trade and investment agreements is a political act concluded by nation-states. To clarify the difference between these two situations, it need only be pointed out that a simple "No" from France ultimately felled negotiations around the Multilateral Agreement on Investment. No such option was available to Mitterand after the capital flight from France in the 1980s. The point is not that there are *no* means available to stem the threat of capital flight and the loss of state autonomy that frequently results. Nor can extensive liberalisation be upheld without the involvement of states, as Polanyi reminds us. Indeed, precisely because the process of *institutionalizing* liberalisation norms requires the explicit consent of states, this process of institutionalization may be especially vulnerable to social movement protest (and state opposition).

In addition to trends towards the transnationalisation of capital just noted, a shift that is ultimately possibly because of state's active participation, are trends towards the transnationalisation of social movements. These movements, including organizations like Amnesty International, the Sierra Club, the Council of Canadians and other human rights, environmentalist and nationalist groups, draw on an expanding repertoire of human and environmental rights to legitimate their causes. The voluntary Charters that institutionalize these rights are not always new, as with the United Nations Charter of Human Rights. Nonetheless, the scope and vigour with which they are invoked does appear to be unprecedented. Transnational social movements contrast human, environmental rights and nation-state rights in the UN and other charters with the "capital rights" or "corporate rights" protected by free trade and investment agreements. Despite some common ground, including a shared commitment to liberal individualism or what Marx called the "bourgeois" freedoms of individual rights and security, transnational social movements have succeeded in turning the ideological antagonism between this "human rights" doctrine and neoliberal policy into one of the major axes of contention in the new global political economy.

The intent of the schema outlined above is to bring together two sets of literatures that have too often talked past each other. Theories about the political economy of globalization have rightly pointed out the increased power of mobile capital vis-à-vis labour and, often, the nation-state. Moreover, neo-Marxist accounts of this process of globalization have correctly pointed out the neoliberal ideological commitments that are fuelling the political act of institutionalizing capital mobility and market-oriented policies more generally. However, this tradition has tended to be (unrealistically) pessimistic about the potential for mobilization around alternative (non-market) norms.

The collapse of the Multilateral Agreement on Investment at the level of the OECD and the failure to conclude the Millenium Round of negotiations of the WTO at Seattle suggest that normative pressure linked to human rights and environmental protection can have important political and economic repercussions. Similarly, the decision by Nike to raise the age of its overseas labourers to eighteen years and allow some independent monitoring of overseas manufacturing plants, as well as the recent move by Starbucks to sell "Fair Trade" coffee after a coalition of activist organizations threatened an anti-Starbucks campaign, suggest that human rights claims can sometimes successfully counter the hegemonic neoliberal commitment to the unfettered market. Transnational social movements may not have the same amount of power as transnational corporations in the emerging global capitalist order but it would be a mistake to conclude that activists cannot wield legitimating human rights and environmental protection norms that are institutionalized in voluntary international agreements to political effect.

In short, social movement theorists correctly point out that there is a growth in transnational social protest. Moreover, neoinstitutionalists like Soysal have highlighted an important legitimating resource available to these social movements, namely United Nations and other voluntary Charters that affirm the rights of individuals to certain democratic freedoms and a modicum of economic security and the right of the environment to some protections. Although these charters do not have the binding power of most free trade and investment agreements, they can be used to exert normative pressure on transnational corporations, national governments and international bodies like the World Trade Organisation. It is not enough, however, to conceptualize these transnational actors as emerging in isolation. Rather, they must be seen, in part, as a conscious challenge to the increase in the power of transnational capital and the hegemony of neoliberalism.

An Illustration: The Multilateral Agreement on Investment (MAI)

I have written a more complete account of the origins and demise of the OECD-level MAI elsewhere (Coburn, 2000). Here, my intention is not to detail a comprehensive history of the MAI, but simply to offer a cursory illustration of the way in which the dialectical schema of globalization that I have sketched might be used to highlight the contradictory but linked dynamics of globalization from above and globalization from below.

Transnational Capital

Elements of transnational capital acted in a remarkably cohesive and class-conscious manner when they initiated and then attempted to consolidate the MAI. In 1991, the Organisation for Economic Cooperation and Development (OECD) established a working group to examine the feasibility of a Multilateral Agreement on Investment (Larson, 1996). In 1992, the Business and Industry Advisory Committee (BIAC), which represents 32 national industry and employer organisations in the (then) 29 OECD nations, released a statement saying that it considered a MAI to be the OECD's "most important endeavour in the field of investment". By 1995 the BIAC had submitted a report outlining, "how business would like to see various elements treated in an MIA [Multilateral Investment Agreement]." This report listed all the major provisions of the final MAI draft, including: the most-favoured nation principle, which holds that foreign investors must be treated no less favourably than investors of any other signatory nation; binding subnational commitment to the MAI; compensation for investors in a wide range of instances of investment losses; free movement of key personnel across national borders; prohibition of national performance requirements; and investor to state binding arbitration. In addition, the proposal objects to any sector carve-outs for culture and any inclusion of voluntary or binding environmental, labour, cultural or other protections (BIAC, 1995). The negotiating text of the MAI incorporated all of the suggestions outlined in the BIAC proposal. In essence, organized transnational capital, as represented by the BIAC, wrote the draft text upon which the MAI negotiations were based.

Transnational capital was not only instrumental in initiating the key elements of the accord, but lobbied hard afterwards to conclude the agreement. In the United States, the United States Council for International Business (USCIB) was particularly active. The USCIB has a membership of over 300 transnational corporations, businesses and law firms. Among its Officers and Board of Trustee members are the former Vice President of General Electric, the CEO of Shell Oil, the Chief Financial Officer of Coca-Cola, the Chairman of Disney/ABC, the Chairman of Proctor and Gamble, the CEO of Phillip Morris and the Vice-Chairman of Ford Motor Company (USCIB, 1999; USCIB, 1999a). The Council's mandate is to "advanc(e) the global interests of American Business both in the US and internationally" (USCIB, 1999b). Representatives of the Council wrote numerous letters to then President Clinton and Ambassador Charlene Barshevsky (among others) emphasizing the importance of ratifying the agreement. The USCIB was particularly opposed to provisions reaffirming labour rights and environmental protection, since they feared that such considerations might restrict the rights to capital mobility that the MAI was designed to protect.

In a letter to Clinton dated January 13, 1997, for example, USCIB Chairman and Vice-President McCormick and Katz outlined the USCIB position. The Council's demands are presented in stark terms:

> "Complete the negotiation in the OECD of the Multilateral Agreement on Investment (MAI), providing for maximum liberalisation of investment regimes and high standards of investor protection; and begin to educate the American public on the advantages of such an agreement" (McCormick and Katz, 1997).

The letter goes on to emphasize that the USCIB is opposed to the incorporation of protections for labour and the environment. "We believe," McCormick and Katz conclude, "that legislation should not be encumbered by labour and environmental objectives. We would oppose *any* implication that trade agreements should provide for the use of trade sanctions to enforce labour or environmental objectives" (italics added). In a separate letter to Charlene Barshevsky dated July 11, 1997, the USCIB restates these concerns but suggests that, given growing opposition to the MAI, the organization "probably could live" with non-binding provisions to protect labour and the environment in order "mollify" anti-MAI activists (Katz, 1997).

Transnational Social Movements

Transnational social movements, particularly the nationalist Council of Canadians and the French Observatoire de la mondialisation, did not remain quiet around the MAI negotiations. The first task of the opposition was to "leak" the draft text of the MAI onto the internet in early March 1997. It quickly became apparent that key officials in the potential signatory nations knew nothing of the agreement. In 1997 in France, for example, the president of the National Assembly's Commission for Foreign Affairs, Jack Lang, angrily declared *"Nous ignorons qui négocie quoi au nom de qui"*[4] (Wallach, 1998). International actions against the MAI were coordinated, including an April 28, 1998 "Forum on Globalization" that coincided with a MAI negotiating round in Paris at the OECD headquarters. More than fifty organizations, including unions, environmental groups, cultural groups and others attended or made presentations.

At the same time, anti-MAI books were published, including two in Canada. Petitions against the agreement were formulated and a "citizen's alternative" to the MAI was drafted in consultation with community groups. The critique offered by these groups centred on the "unbalanced" nature of the agreement and suggested that the rights of investors and capital were enshrined in the MAI at the expense of the rights of citizens and workers.

A petition signed by over 500 international non-governmental organizations in over 60 nations, for example, criticized the agreement for "elevat(ing) the rights of investors far above those of governments, local communities, citizens, workers and the environment" (NGO statement on the MAI 1998). The petition concluded its substantive section by objecting to the MAI's central purpose:

> "The MAI is explicitly designed to make it easier for investors to move capital, including production facilities, from one country to another, despite evidence that increased capital mobility disproportionately benefits multinational corporations at the expense of most of the world's peoples" (ibid).

Globalization as a liberalisation project is presented here as an affront to popular rights of "peoples." A second petition, signed by over 50 unions and other organizations, makes this point emphatically, concluding with the slogan, "Against neo-liberal aggression, for Human Rights and the Rights of Peoples" (l'Observatoire de la mondialisation 1998).

Ultimately, the MAI negotiations at the OECD level collapsed. The French government commissioned a study to examine the growing objections by what it termed a "new civil society" (Lalumière, Landau and Glimet, 1998). Concluding that the MAI could not be fundamentally altered to take into account the concerns expressed by this new civil society, the French government withdrew from the negotiations. Because accords can only be ratified by consensus at the OECD, the MAI was effectively dead – although its proponents quickly began to advocate for a more comprehensive MAI to be concluded among the member nations of the WTO. Transnational social movements thus secured a surprising – if provisional – victory over organized transnational capital.

Discussion and Conclusion

Academics and activists seeking a world founded on economic and social justice, rather than market logic, have good reason to be concerned about the unfolding contradictions of the "globalization" process. Through lobbies like the USCIB, transnational capital is demonstrating remarkable class-consciousness and aggressively pursuing its interests in a world of liberalised trade and minimal respect for labour, human rights and environmental protections. Moreover, the hegemonic ideology – neoliberalism – is being institutionalized as binding policy in over 1,100 bilateral (and now multilateral) investment and trade treaties.

At the same time, however, social justice activists have some reason to hope. The hegemony of neoliberalism and the power of transnational capital are facing important new challenges from a human and environmental "rights" centred discourse. Transnational movements cooperate across borders seeking to change the practices of individual corporations. They are vigorously opposing nation-states' decisions to negotiate and sign agreements like the MAI. In this struggle, non-binding charters like the UN Charter of Human Rights offer an important legitimating resource for social movements. The "human right" to refuse child or prison labour, for example, can be held up in contradistinction to capital's right to pursue profit. Voluntary charters, despite their non-binding nature, can be used strategically by TSMs to buttress their calls for protection from the fallout of unfettered market activity.

The consistency of neoliberal theory and practice is probably overstated. Activists from the developing world frequently complain that in practice "liberalisation" is uneven, with developing nations forced to open their borders while developed nations retain protective barriers in precisely those areas where the developing world is competitive (notably agriculture). TSMs may be able to exploit such inconsistencies, as well as contradictions between, for example, "liberalisation" rhetoric that is supposed to apply to goods but that is not supposed to apply to the movement of (working and middle class) peoples. TSMs have multiple points of leverage in their struggle against neoliberal forms of capitalism.

The ideological movement against neoliberalism's identification of market rules with social progress and democracy is, however, in danger of co-optation. The World Trade Organisation has taken great pains since the "Battle of Seattle" to re-make its image as an organisation primarily committed to alleviating poverty and dedicated to open, democratic processes. It is very likely that transnational social movements will be invited to participate in future trade discussions and investment treaties, not only by the WTO but by the OECD and a host of other organisations. Securing meaningful participation is going to be difficult if TSMs adhere to a liberal individualist critique.

In particular, the sharp criticism of the power of *capital* offered by Canadian social movements needs to be turned into a more telling critique of the system of capitalism that is the guarantor of that power.[5] Without a more structural analysis of the capitalist economic system and the extent to which market freedoms undermine, rather than support, democratic principles like equal representation, it will be difficult for TSMs to convincingly argue that their involvement in structures like the WTO must include more than a nominal seat at the table. An analysis of the institution of the market and of production of profit, not simply the power of individual corporate actors, is both a central theoretical challenge and a political necessity if co-optation is to be avoided. Otherwise, TSMs face the possibility of achieving formal democratic representation with little substantive input.

The *individual* right to freedom and economic security must be expanded to include notions of *collective* freedom of expression and welfare. "Human rights" is not a uniform concept, but instead encompasses (to use T.H. Marshall's classic formulation) civil, political and social rights. Any one "type" of right might be championed to the exclusion of the others. Basic civil-legal protections and the political opportunity to participate in government are clearly important. However, unless these rights are predicated upon a modicum of socio-economic equality, they risk being what Marx called "bourgeois freedoms" – that is, formal rights without real substance. The right to organize and the right to a modicum of economic and social security are necessary if civil and political rights are to have meaning. The struggle to secure these "social" rights must therefore be given a central place in the emerging conflict between TSMs and transnational capital.

There are some encouraging developments in this respect. The preliminary report by a task force for the International Forum on Globalization (1999), for example, begins by emphasizing that "(t)he "free market" paradigm is anything but free...And, the "free market's" beneficiaries are increasingly few" (p.1). The Task Force goes on to highlight the UN Universal Charter of Human Right, quoting its commitment to "a standard of living adequate for...health and well-being..., including food, clothing, housing and medical care, and necessary social services, and the right to security in the event of unemployment" (p.3). The final report is still forthcoming. It remains to be seen if the Task Force will clearly contrast market norms and institutions that underlie capital power with a call for broad areas of social protection outside of the market. Nonetheless, this kind of analysis at least begins to address both the question of the inequality built into markets and the need for broad social and economic, not simply legal and political, rights.

The implication of securing collective, rather than simply individual, social rights is quite radical. The notion of social *rights* suggests that many goods and services are to be supplied irrespective of participation in the market. Rights are granted universally and are not predicated upon being a workforce participant (or, indeed, upon any other criteria beyond "human-ness"). The more comprehensive and high quality the supply of "social rights" like health care, social security and the like, the more serious are the alternatives to what Esping-Anderson (1990) calls the "cash nexus" of the market. Collective social rights shrink the domain of the capitalist market place, since they allow individuals to meet needs without recourse to participation in the market.

Combined with an emphasis on the realization of democratic rights – in the formal "political" arena but also in local communities and workplaces – transnational social movements have a strong ideological base from which to challenge neoliberal hegemony and ultimately the structured inequalities of global capitalism. The legal and institutional framework that guarantees the functioning of markets and the rights of capital can thus be challenged by a legal and institutional framework that protects the civil and political "human rights" of individuals. Moreover, collective "social" rights to a modicum of socio-economic well-being can potentially be held up to challenge the liberal individualistic contracts that underlie market transactions.

David Held (1998), among others, sets out the conditions for democratic participation in a globalizing world, a programme that he calls "cosmopolitan democracy". In arguing for new democratic institutions at the supranational level to complement (not replace) state structures, he calls for a mixture of market, state and "civil society" organizations. His aim is to propose workable structures that allow citizens maximum autonomy within the context of profound recognition of local, regional and supranational inter-connections and dependencies. He argues that such recognition is necessary to protect locally and globally vulnerable populations and to ensure international cooperation for global problems (whether the issue is inequality or the deterioration of the ozone). Debate of such models for progressive change is yet another potentially important venue for building the counter-hegemonic challenge to neoliberalism.

Who will undertake these debates and begin the long struggle against neoliberalism? Transnational social movements, championing causes as diverse as aboriginal rights to environmental protection to national autonomy, are currently at the forefront of the struggle. Labour is no longer the sole protagonist in the struggle against capital. Marxists in particular need to begin to theorize the role of these social movements in an era of global capitalism. At the same time, social movement theorists need to recognize the anti-capital stance of much of "new" social movements and seek to place their development within the changing dynamics of a market economy. "Old" labour is joining new anti-capital forces; "new" social movements are often grappling with "old" labour dilemmas related to labour rights, capital rights and the need for protection from the functioning of the market. The emerging relationships between these groups offer fruitful ground for theoretical debates between, not simply among, Marxist and social movement theorists.

If labour is now one of many groups, substantial fractions of transnational capital have arguably never been more united. Theorists who have argued that "class is dead" ought to take a closer look at the cohesive class-conscious behaviour of international capital. Organizing in associations like the Business and Industry Advisory Councils, these leviathans wield tremendous economic clout, individually and collectively controlling hundreds of billions of dollars. Moreover, they are actively seeking to transform that economic advantage into political capital through serious lobbying efforts. So far, they have been remarkably successful in setting up new world institutional frameworks designed to protect and further capital's ability to profit. Neoliberalism may reflect (U.S.) neoclassical economists' training, but neoclassical economists' ideas are only holding sway because of the determined backing of organized capital.

Clearly, new challenges to capital are occurring at the world level. Transnational social movements are cooperating to "take on" the practices of individual transnational corporations as well as the anti-democratic processes and neoliberal policies of organisations like the International Monetary Fund and World Bank. However, national governments remain important targets, especially insofar as international liberalising and trade agreements are concluded in the name of nation-states. The *institutionalisation* of neoliberalism requires the explicit political consent of member nations. Consequently, that process of institutionalisation remains vulnerable to national protest and political influence, as was the case with the MAI. Local and national arenas of contestation – with global implications – remain important loci of struggle alongside the novel emergence of transnational protest.

Clearly, many questions remain. How much of globalization is really "Americanization" in economic, cultural and ideological terms? Are neoliberal ideology and practice consistent and if not, can these inconsistencies be fruitfully exploited by progressive oppositional groups? Is North-South cooperation destined to founder on questions about the "universality" of Western conceptions of "human rights" and the implications of the comparative advantage of low-wage workers in the South? How united are *nationalist* capitalist fractions likely to remain with their international capitalist counterparts, given the seemingly objective protectionist interests of the former? What is the relationship between "progressive" transnational protest and right-wing protectionism in the United States – and how troubled should "progressive" transnational social movements be by their presence? Can TSMs themselves be democratized, so that their representatives do not become an autocratic "cosmopolitan elite" (Held, 1998: 14)?

It is realistic to be hopeful about the potential of emerging transnational social movements, particularly if the current developments are contrasted with the ideological climate that prevailed during the Cold War. The importance of the emergence of this new anti-capital (and sometimes anti-capitalist) transnational movement should not be underestimated, either in pragmatic political or academic and theoretical terms. For the first time, at least since the Cold War, capital and capitalism is squarely on the political agenda. The central axis of concern is not whether the Soviet Union will succeed in taking over other nations, but how to control an increasingly powerful capitalist class. Symptomatic of this shift is a new preoccupation with the disjuncture between capitalism and democracy, particularly how to negotiate the conflict between the profit motive and the realization of individual, and perhaps collective, rights. During the Cold War, capitalism was identified with democracy. Now, market structures are seen as opposing or undermining democratic, human and environmental rights. The collapse of the Soviet Union has forced capitalism itself out of the shadows and onto the world agenda. Ironically, the domination of capitalism has (potentially) provided a common basis for mobilization to previously disparate progressive activists. Did the "Battle of Seattle" mark the high point of the struggle – or only the beginning of the movement?

Notes

1. Ross and Trachte write within the Marxist tradition. It is worth noting, however, that traditional economists have made similar arguments to those presented here. Neoclassical economists like Anne Krueger, for example, argue that "the world economy has unquestionably become increasingly integrated as transport, communications, and other costs of international transactions have dropped sharply" (1992). Irwin (1996), remarking on increased global competitive pressures on firms, suggests that by 1980 the United States had experienced "a vast increase in the exposure of tradable goods industries to international competition". Bhagwati (1994), noting the mobility of capital in several manufacturing industries, concludes that "more industries than ever before are 'footloose': the number of industries that are 'shiftable' due to someone else gaining a new small advantage seems to have swelled" (239). In short, these economists suggest that the 1980s and onwards have been marked by increased international competition and the growth of mobile capital enabled by changes in communication. Ross and Trachte's story is unique insofar as they consider the implications of these changes for the power relationships among capital, labour and the state. The neoclassical economic approach to the same subject tends to bracket questions about the implications of capital mobility for power relations among these actors, or at least not to theorize these relations very explicitly.

2. Indeed, it is worth noting that many economists who see increased trade and capital flows as not just inevitable but desirable hold important positions within international boards regulating trade and investment. For example, Michael Mussa, cited earlier, is both the author of the *American Economic Review* article "Making the Practical Case for Free Trade" and a researcher in the International Monetary Fund's Department of Research.

3. In contrast, classical Marxist accounts are much more optimistic about the potential for the emergence of an international opposition to globalizing capital. In *The Communist*

Manifesto, for example, Marx and Engels argue that, "The need of a constantly expanding market for its products chases the bourgeoisie over the whole surface of the globe. It must nestle everywhere, settle everywhere, establish connexions everywhere" (1985: 83). As capital is globalized, they argue, the contradictions of the capitalist system are writ large and class struggle takes the entire globe as its platform—hence the famous exhortation, "Workers of the world, unite!". In the classical Marxist tradition, then, it is not surprising that the global capitalist system has engendered a transnational social movement against capitalist exploitation. What *is* interesting, within this paradigm, is the *form* of that opposition. Labour – or at least labour organized *as* labour – appears as only one of several interests (i.e., nationalist, human rights, and environmental movements) that are emerging to counter the growing power of transnational corporations. Neo-Marxist accounts must grapple with the new forms that political struggle against capital (and sometimes capitalism) is assuming.

4. "We were ignorant of who was negotiating what in the name of whom."

5. There is interesting cross-national variation in this regard. The Council of Canadians, for example, criticizes the power of capital and corporations, but frequently re-affirms its basic commitment to capitalism and its opposition to socialist and communist alternatives. The Observatoire de la mondialisation through *Le monde diplomatique* and other media has been much more critical of capitalism, i.e., arguing that the obvious adversaries for TSMs are financial capital and more broadly "les marchés" [the markets] (Cassen 1999: 11). The position of non-governmental organisations in the developing world and the former Communist states are likely to exhibit further variations.

References

Adams, Francis, Satya Dev Gupta and Kidane Mengisteab. (1999). "Globalisation and the Developing World: An Introduction." Pp. 1-13 in *Globalisation and the Dilemmas of the States in the South.* Edited by Francis Adams, Satya Dev Gupta and Kidane Mengisteab. London: MacMillan Press.

Bailey, Sue. (2000). "Activist Coon Come Wins Native Leadership." P.A2 in *The Toronto Star.* July 13, 2000.

Bhagwati, Jagdish. (1994). "Free Trade: Old and New Challenges". Pp. 231-246 in *The Economic Journal.* Volume 104:423.

Bhagwati, Jagdish. (1990). "Departures from Multilateralism: Regionalism and Aggressive Unilateralism". Pp. 1304-1317 in *The Economic Journal.* Volume 100:403.

Business and Industry Advisory Committee. (1995). *The OECD Multilateral Investment Agreement: BIAC Views on Specific Elements of an Eventual Instrument.* Committee Submission: International Investment and Multinational Enterprises. <http://www.biac.org/ Textes/ BIAC?FINVIEWMNES95.html> Last accessed 11/20/1999.

Cassen, Bernard. (1999). "Comprendre et agir avec ATTAC." Pp. 9-12 in *Attac: contre la dictature des marches.* France: VO éditions.

Chen, John-Ren and Richard Hule. (1998). "Globalization of Economic Activities and Its Effects". Pp. 9-30 in *Economic Effects of Globalization.* Edited by John-Ren Chen. Sydney: Ashgate Press.

Clarke, Tony and Maude Barlow. (1997). *MAI: The Multilateral Agreement on Investment and the Threat to Canadian Sovereignty.* Toronto: Stoddart Publishing.

Coburn, Elaine. (2000). *Solidarity Forever? Labour Fissions and Labour Fusion in an Era of Global Capitalism*. Presented at the Society for Socialist Studies meetings at the Canadian Sociology and Anthropology Association meetings in Edmonton, Alberta. May.

Crane, David. "OECD Okays Guidelines for Multinational Firms". P.E5 in *The Toronto Star*. June 28, 2000.

Dasgupta, Biplab. (1998). *Structural Adjustment, Global Trade and the New Political Economy of Development*. London: Zed Books.

Esping-Andersen, Gøsta. (1990). *The Three Worlds of Welfare Capitalism*. Princeton: Princeton University Press.

Falk, Richard. (1995). *On Humane Governance: Towards a New Global Politics*. Cambridge: Polity Press.

Gray, Charles. (1999). *Corporate Cash: Few Nations Can Top It*. Poster. For further information contact W.E.P., P.O. Box 5896 Eugene, OR 97405, USA.

Held, David, (1998). "Democracy and Globalisation." Pp. 11-27 in *Re-Imagining Political Community*. Edited by Archibugi, Daniele, David Held and Martin Köhler. Cambridge: Polity Press.

Imig, Doug and Sidney Tarrow. (2000). "Political Contention in a Europeanising Polity." In *West European Politics*. Volume 23.4.

International Forum on Globalisation Task Force. (1999). ""Beyond the WTO: Alternatives to Economic Globalisation-A Preliminary Report". San Francisco: International Forum on Globalisation.

Irwin, Douglas A. (1996). "The United States in a New Global Economy? A Century's Perspective". Pp. 41-46 in *The American Economic Review*. Volume 86:2

Katz, Abraham. (1997). *Letter to Ambassador Charlene Barfshevsky*. July 11. <http: www.imex.com/uscib/policy/mailtr.htm>. Last accessed 11/22/1999.

Keck, Margaret E. and Kathryn Sikkink. (1998). "Transnational Advocacy Networks in the Movement Society." Pp. 217-238 in *The Social Movement Society: Contentious Politics for a New Century*. Edited by David S. Meyer and Sidney Tarrow. Oxford: Rowman and Littlefield Publishers.

Klein, Naomi. (2000). *No Space, No Choice, No Jobs, No Logo: Taking Aim at the Brand Bullies*. New York: Picador.

Krueger, Anne O. (1992). "Government, Trade and Economic Integration." Pp. 109-114 in *American Economic Review*. Volume 82: 2.

Krugman, Paul. (1993). "The Narrow and Broad Arguments for Free Trade." Pp. 362-366 in *The American Economic Review*. Volume 83:2.

Krugman, Paul. (1987). "Is Free trade Passé?" Pp. 131-144 in *The Journal of Economic Perspectives*. Volume 1:2.

Laclau, Ernesto and Chantal Mouffe. (1985). *Hegemony and Socialist Strategy: Towards a Radical Democratic Politics*. London: Verso Press.

Lal Das, Bhagirath. (1998). *The WTO Agreements: Deficiencies, Imbalances and Required Changes*. Penang: Third World Network.

Lalumière, Catherine, Jean-Pierre Landau and Emmanuel Glimet. (1998). *Rapport sur l'Accord multilateral sur l'investissment (AMI)*. Paris: Conseiller référendaire à la Cour de Comptes.

Larson, Alan. (1996). "The Multilateral Agreement on Investment: Origins and State of Play." Pp. 5-9 in *OECD Working Papers: MAI State of Play as of July 1996*. Volume 4: 90.

Marks, Gary and Doug McAdam. (1996). "Social Movements and the Changing Structure of Political Opportunity in the European Union." Pp. 95-120 in *Governance in the European Union*. Edited by Gary Marks et al. London: Sage Publications.

Marx, Karl and Friedrich Engels. (1985). *The Communist Manifesto*. London: Penguin Classics.

McAdam, Doug. (1998). "Conclusion: The Future of Social Movements". Pp. 229-245 in *From Contention to Democracy*. Edited by Marco G. Giugni, Doug McAdam and Charles Tilly. Oxford: Rowman and Littlefield Publishers.

McCormick, Richard D. and Abraham Katz. (1997). *USCIB Recommendations to the Clinton Administration on International Economic Issues*. February 13.

McCulloch, Rachel. (1993). "The Optimality of Free Trade: Science or Religion?" Pp. 367-371 in *The American Economic Review*. Volume 83:2.

Meyer, John et al. (1997). "World Society and the Nation-State." Pp. 144-181 in *The American Journal of Sociology*. Volume 103:1.

Meyer, John. (2000). "Globalization: Sources and Effects on National States and Societies." Pp. 233-248 in *International Sociology*. Volume 15:2.

Moghadam, Valentine M. (2000). "Transnational Feminist Networks: Collective Action in an Era of Globalisation." Pp. 57-85 in *International Sociology*. Volume 15:1.

Mussa, Michael. (1993). "Making the Practical Case for Freer Trade." Pp. 372-376 in *The American Economic Review*. Volume 83:2.

NGO Statement on the MAI. (1998). Pp. 319-337 in *Dismantling Democracy: The Multilateral Agreement on Investment and Its Impact*. Edited by Andrew Jackson and Matthew Sanger. Toronto: CCPA/Lorimer.

L'Observatoire de la mondialisation. (1998). "Pour un NON definitive à l'A.M.I. (accord multilateral sure l'investissement." Petition. April 28.

Polanyi, Karl. (1944). *The Great Transformation*. Beacon Press.

Ross, Robert J. S. and Kent C. Trachte. (1990). *Global Capitalism: The New Leviathan*. Albany: State University of New York Press.

Ratner, R.S. (1997). "Many Davids, One Goliath". Pp. 271-286 in *Organizing Dissent: Contemporary Social Movements in Theory and Practice*. Edited by William K. Carroll. Toronto: Garamond Press. Second Edition.

Riveria-Batiz, Luis A. and Danyang Xie. (1992). "GATT, Trade and Growth." Pp. 422-427 in *The American Economic Review*. Volume 82:2.

Smith, Jackie, Charles Chatfield and Roan Pagnucco. (1997). *Transnational Social Movements*. Syracuse: Syracuse University Press.

Soysal, Yasemin Nuhoglu. (1994). *Limits of Citizenship: Migrants and Postnational Membership in Europe*. Chicago: University of Chicago Press.

Tarrow, Sindney. (1983). "Struggling to Reform: Social Movements and Policy Change During Cycles of Protest." Cornell University. Western Societies Paper #15.

Touraine, Alain. (1992). *Critique de la Modernité*. Paris: Fayard.

Tilly, Charles. (1984). "Social Movements and National Politics." Pp. 297-317 in *Statemaking and Social Movements: Essays in History and Theory*. Edited by Charles Bright and Susan Harding. Ann Arbor: University Of Michigan Press.

United States Council for International Business. (1999). *Officers*. <http: www.uscib.org/whoweare/officers.htm> Last accessed 11/20/1999.

United States Council for International Business. (1999a). *Trustees*. <http: www.uscib.org/whoweare/trustees.htm> Last accessed 11/20/1999.

United States Council for International Business. (1999b). *Global Network*. <http: www.uscib.org/global/global.htm> Last accessed 11/20/1999.

Wallach, Lori. (1998). "Le nouveau manifeste du capitalisme mondial." P.22 in *Le Monde Diplomatique*.February.

Western, Bruce, Katherine Beckett and David Harding. (1998). "Système pénal et marché du travail aux États-Unis." Pp. 27-35 in *Actes de la recherche en sciences sociales*. Paris: le Centre de sociologie européene du Collège de France and collaborators.

Part IV Politics of Alternatives

Chapter Seven

Women and Globalization in the Economic North and South

by Ann Denis

Introduction

Globalization is not a new phenomenon (Mies, 1986), but by the latter part of the twentieth century its impact had become increasingly significant and had taken new forms which undermine the autonomy of national governments (Mishra, 1999) in what Hoogvelt has described as "a period of 'unembedded' liberalism" (1997: 135). Moreover, consciously or unconsciously, this is a gendered phenomenon, both in its practices and outcomes: women, collectively, control fewer economic resources than men, and their relative economic status has, at best, remained stable or else has deteriorated during the emergence of the present phase of globalized capitalism (Ward, 1990; Backer, 1994; Sen, 1994; Moghadam, 1999). Two societies with British roots are examined in this chapter. One, Canada, is an advanced capitalist society, while the other, Barbados, a small island nation, is less economically developed, yet both are experiencing shifts in economic and social policies which are informed by the neo-liberal orthodoxy of globalization.

Feminism's Conceptual Contributions to the Analysis of Globalization

Globalization and its consequences are gendered phenomena. This is a fundamental, but often overlooked, contribution that feminism has made to the analysis of globalization. Four more specific theoretical and conceptual contributions by feminist approaches to the analysis of globalization, particularly to the analysis of its impact for women, are discussed in this chapter:

- the broadening of the concept of work to include "productive" and "reproductive" activities, and within "productive" work to include informal as well as formal sector activities;
- the introduction of the concept of "sexage," which includes both the individual and the collective appropriation of women;
- the recognition of the interaction among gender, social class and race/ethnicity, which underlines that "women" is not a homogeneous category;
- the recognition that resistance (including women's resistance) to oppression, even to appropriation, can take a variety of forms, both individual and collective.

The Concept of Work

Since industrialization, "work" has mainly been conceptualized as a paid activity, usually carried out away from home.[1] "Work" occurs in the "public" sphere and is thus (potentially) subject to state regulation. Since the 1970s Western feminist theoreticians[2] have questioned the separation of the "public" and "private" spheres and, consequently, the principle that only paid activities are "work," a principle, they argue, that obscures the contribution to the national economy (and to the profits of capitalists) of free (unpaid) activities which women, including wives, do in their own homes. This has led some feminists to use, instead, the concepts of "productive" and "reproductive," "market" and "nonmarket" or "paid" and "unpaid" work. Reproductive (or nonmarket) work includes unpaid activities which provide material, social and emotional support within the family, as well as the bearing and socialization of children. When such tasks are done for pay and categorized as "service" occupations, the wages are typically low, whether the employer is an individual, a business or the State. Furthermore, such jobs are typically done by women. Explanations of the gendered nature of work, and of women's lower pay are often framed in terms of the concept of patriarchy – the domination of women by men – or of capitalist patriarchy – the domination of women and most men by a minority of men (Juteau and Laurin, 1988; Fox, 1988). Volunteer activities outside the home, including the participation in community activities, constitute another type of unpaid work which is often completely ignored in analyses.

Whereas Western feminists, primarily concerned with industrialized societies, have stressed the importance of acknowledging (and measuring) unpaid domestic work (Luxton, 1997), it has been development specialists (both men and women) who have denounced the fact that work in the informal economy is hidden by the current systems of national accounts (Rogers, 1980; Ward, 1990). Even when work in the informal sector is included, its gendered nature is not necessarily integrated conceptually. As a result women's economic participation and the impact of economic changes on them are often obscured. Whereas, for men, participation in the informal economy is frequently a strategy for social mobility, for women, it is more often "simply" a strategy for survival (Ward, 1990).

The Concepts of Individual and Collective Appropriation

"Appropriation," a fundamental concept in Colette Guillaumin's (1995)[3] materialist feminist analysis, is defined as "the relation in which it is the producing material unit of labour power which is appropriated and not just labour power" (181), in short, "the reduction of [members of the dominated class in a social relationship] to the state of appropriated material units" (179). The forms this appropriation takes vary depending on the society and the era. In this type of power relation, of which slavery and sexage[4] are examples, the dominant group uses selected "natural" markers, which are often somatic, in order to oblige members of the dominated group to do some things and forbid them doing others (148-9), socially constructing sets of apparently inescapable constraints. Within sexage, Guillaumin distinguishes individual and collective appropriation. The former refers to the appropriation of one woman by one man within marriage, while the latter refers to the appropriation of the class of women by the class of men within a society. According to Guillaumin, women's low salaries are one manifestation of collective appropriation. Another is the expectation, and the fact, that it is largely women who, on a voluntary basis, look after both members of society who cannot fully care for themselves and healthy men. This unpaid work will be considered in our analysis.

Women as a Non-homogeneous Category:
Intersectional Analysis

Since the mid 1970s much Western feminism has integrated the intersection of social class and gender in its analysis, recognising that women's gender oppression is experienced differently depending on their class location. Critiques, mainly by black feminists and feminists of colour, have been articulated since the 1980s of the ethnocentrism of "white" (or Anglo-Saxon) feminism (Anthias and Yuval-Davis, 1983; Bannerji, 1993; Denis, 1981), of the homogenisation of "third world women" when they *were* considered as a separate category, and of the uncritical (often normative) use of Eurocentric models and definitions (Barriteau, 1995). Intersectional analysis therefore posits that it is essential to analyse the interaction among women's positionings in terms of such factors as social class, race/ethnicity and economic and geographical location (Stasiulis, 1999) in order to adequately understand the complexities of women's experiences of gender oppression, including mitigating and exacerbating factors. We will highlight some instances of this complexity in our analysis.

Women's Resistance to Oppression

For some it is unduly pessimistic to identify the fact of women's appropriation without, at the same time, pointing out the forms of resistance they practise. Identifying these forms requires broadening the concept of "forms of resistance." The most widely recognized forms are those which have characterized men: trade union activity; participation in formal political processes, by voting or standing for elected office; pressure group activity; the use of physical violence. Later in this chapter we will consider some of the individual and collective practices of women which have been or could be analysed as forms of resistance. It is in order to incorporate the concept of women as agents rather than as victims that I have entitled this chapter "women and globalization" rather than "the impact of globalization on women."

Having now presented conceptual contributions of feminism that can be used in the analysis of globalization and women, we will introduce the concept of globalization and then consider how the political economies of Canada and Barbados have responded to its challenges.

The Concept of Globalization

Moghadam defines globalization as "a complex economic, political, cultural, and geographic process in which the mobility of capital, organizations, ideas, discourses, and peoples has taken on an increasingly global or transnational form" (1999: 301). The "globalization" of capital and technology occurs concomitantly with the integration of markets: thus national economies become parts of a global capitalist economy. According to Joekes and Weston (1994), the reduction or even the elimination of trade barriers is one of the factors which speeds up this process, leading to the concept of a "world market factory" in such industries as the manufacture of textiles, clothing and electronics components. Hoogvelt identifies three significant features of what she calls "global regulation": global market discipline (which reduces national autonomy), accumulation through global webs "in which many discrete fabrication activities and services are brought in for the short term" (Hoogvelt, 1997: 127), and the politics of exclusion. The privatisation of space and services and the neo-liberal emphasis on self help and reduced dependence on the state illustrate these politics (Hoogvelt, 1997: 148-9). In short, "national governments adjust their economies to globalization by regulating for deregulation" (Hoogvelt, 1997: 139). As a result, a three-tier categorisation exists within societies: the unemployed (or excluded), those in economically insecure jobs and those who are structurally secure either from jobs or incomes from capital investments. Thus core and periphery have come to describe social relations rather than spatial ones, although the percentage in each category varies with the country's level of "development" (Hoogvelt, 1997: 147). Mishra also highlights the threat of relocation of capital, resulting in organised labour's weakened leverage, and the role played by such intergovernmental organisations as the IMF and the WTO in directly or indirectly promoting deregulation, commodification, the privatisation of economic activity and the downsizing of government, including the scaling down of social protection (1999: 6-8).

Critics of globalization also note the contradictions of "rising levels of protectionism and the growing marginalisation of large numbers of Third World economies in the world market" (Watson, 1993: 2). In fact the costs and benefits of globalization – whether conceptualized in purely monetary terms or also in social terms – have become increasingly unevenly distributed between societies and within societies (Hoogvelt, 1997; Mishra 1999). Structural adjustment measures articulate the neo-liberal capitalist orthodoxy of debt reduction, deregulation, privatisation and the scaling down of social protection. Whether imposed by such international organizations as the World Bank or the International Monetary Fund, or adopted by societies in order to avoid being placed in trusteeship by these organizations or blacklisted by international credit rating organisations, they reinforce the burden experienced by much of their population, especially by the women. This is as evident in the North as in the economic South, but, because of the initial conditions, the consequences are worse in the South.

The Impact of Globalization on the Political Economies of Canada and Barbados

Both are relatively fragile economies, which have historically been based on the primary sector – agriculture and the extraction of natural resources – with the products exported after little or no transformation. Because of the relatively small size of the population, internal markets for manufactured goods have been small, which has limited the possibility of economies of scale in the production of goods for domestic consumption. Protectionism has played an important role in economic strategy. Much investment has been of foreign origin, first from Great Britain (especially during the colonial periods), then from the United States, and now, to some extent, from Asia, and from multinational corporations, which, increasingly, do not have clear national affiliations. In both cases policies of investment by invitation were intended to develop local manufacturing capacity, including the associated human resources. What has occurred instead, however, has been considerable development of branch plants, especially of American multinational firms, for production without investment in research and development. This trend is now exacerbated by short term purchase of many fabrication activities and services by transnational enterprises (Hoogvelt, 1997: 125-8). Moreover, these multinationals typically relocate when a sufficiently qualified, but cheaper labour force becomes available elsewhere or when they are offered better fiscal conditions, such as tax exemptions, elsewhere. Thus both societies have become incorporated as parts of a complex economic constellation whose boundaries are not within the confines of territorial nation-state. *Footloose multinational capital* could be a way of summarising these phenomena.

Changes since the 1980s in the philosophy underlying *trade agreements* are another consequence of globalization. Trade agreements, such as Lomé (between the European Community and the Caribbean), which were explicitly intended – at least in part as a measure of social justice – to give preferential opportunities for food export to the European market by Caribbean signatories are now threatened precisely because they are considered inimical with the neo-liberal orthodoxy of trade liberalisation. CARIBCAN (between Canada and the Commonwealth Caribbean) and CBI (between the United States and the Caribbean), trade agreements which were also, in part, intended to promote development within the Caribbean, involve rules which promote export markets for the more dominant partner and/or retain the more skilled components of the manufacturing process in the dominant society (Watson, 1994; Girvan, 2000). Similarly FTA and NAFTA have involved a power imbalance from the start. In all these cases, the economic dominance of one of the partners (the United States in FTA, NAFTA and CBI, and Canada in CARIBCOM) has resulted in that partner having a greater impact on the ostensibly neutral rules, which it often succeeds in fashioning to its own benefit (Watson, 1994; Bakker 1994 and 1996; Benn and Hall, 2000). These rules can undercut national sovereignty, pressuring the weaker partner to modify domestic social and economic policy. Canada has experience as both a stronger and weaker partner, while Barbados has only been a weaker partner, although this will change when the CARICOM Single Market and Economy, an agreement for the free movement of people and goods within CARICOM (a Caribbean regional grouping) takes effect early in the twenty first century. The advent of the FTAA and the need for harmonization of the various trade agreements with the free trade terms of the WTO constitute additional pressures toward trade liberalization (Bryan, 2001; Benn and Hall, 2000) in both societies.

Obligatory harmonization and remaining an attractive locale for investment can be achieved by deregulation of the economy. *Deteriorating labour standards and a more flexible labour force* can be outcomes of deregulation.

Although capitalist societies, Canada and Barbados have also both implemented policies informed by social democratic philosophy in such fields as health, education, old age security, public transportation and communications. During the past fifteen years, however, the level of their respective national debts, combined with the international economic climate, has resulted in governments in Canada and Barbados being "obliged" to adopt, formally or informally, structural adjustment policies, including *privatisation, and other means of reducing State expenditures.*

Women have borne the brunt of these various measures. We will now highlight some of the ways in which this has occurred, first considering Barbados and then Canada.

Barbados[5]

Women and Footloose Capital

The strategy of investment by invitation in Barbados, with its associated fiscal benefits in the form of serviced industrial parks, exemption from tariffs and taxes on imported materials, exported goods and profits, opened considerable employment opportunities for women in Barbados, both in semiskilled assembly work in the manufacture of garments and semiconductors, and in service occupations in the hotel industry and in data entry jobs for offshore firms. Multinationals benefit from fiscal concessions which may not be available to local firms.[6] For some women, with limited education, who had previously been agricultural labourers, maids in private houses or unemployed, the jobs in garment manufacturing which opened in the 1970s represented opportunities, at least in the short run, for some training, improved wages – though these were the lowest wages within manufacturing (Green, 1994) – and better working conditions. Opportunities for advancement have, however, been limited. For seamstresses, whose market has been undercut by cheap, imported clothing, such manufacturing jobs clearly entailed deskilling. During the 1980s there was a sharp decline in EPZ garment manufacture: as limited-term tax holidays ended, the attraction of lower wage rates and new concessionary fiscal packages drew much of the foreign capital elsewhere, a trend subsequently reinforced by the introduction of NAFTA, in that case, to the advantage of Mexico. Similarly, the EPZ firms assembling semiconductors, after offering an important source of employment for women during the 1970s and 1980s, were either downsizing or departing by the end of the 1980s, in part due to a glut on the market, in part to more attractive conditions elsewhere (Green, 1994; Watson, 1994). In both sectors of the manufacturing industry, the average wages of the few men who were employed were higher than those of women, and opportunities for women to extend their skills or develop transferable skills have been minimal (Jayasinghe, 2001).

Data entry jobs are another important source of EPZ women's jobs. Although not necessarily better paying than assembly jobs, the nature of the work and the working conditions offer a certain cachet, which makes them more popular (Freeman, 2000). Recognising its relatively high labour costs, Barbados markets itself on the basis of its skilled labour force. The needs of foreign capital in this field have recently been changing. With some data entry now being done mechanically by scanning, it is in software design and other technologically sophisticated tasks that expansion in Barbados seems to be occurring, the very jobs for which men, rather than women, have obtained qualifications (Barbados Industrial Development Corporation 1998). The more routine data entry jobs are being relocated elsewhere, to reduce labour costs and to avoid unionisation (Social Partners, 1998, quoted in Barbados Workers' Union, 1998: 5-6).

A third important growth area of employment for women has been in service, clerical and administrative jobs in hotels and restaurants, which are, increasingly, owned by international chains and other foreign investors. This is, however, a seasonal industry, very dependent on exchange rates, price, the 'fashionable' destination of the day, in short externally controlled factors (Enloe, 1990). Thus jobs in this industry are frequently unstable, with the service jobs being poorly paid, although the wages are better than those for maids in private houses. Existing research does not permit an assessment of the gender, class, race and nationality (local or expatriate) of those in the clerical, administrative or managerial jobs, nor of their conditions of employment and ease of finding re-employment.

Women and Trade Agreements

Those trade agreements which have included a development component have given preferential access to Northern markets for agricultural products, mainly sugar in the case of Barbados, and for light manufactured goods, such as garments and semiconductors. As sugar cultivation has become increasingly mechanised, women's employment in agriculture has diminished substantially, since it has been men who have obtained the new, more qualified jobs, while women continue to work in the fields for low wages, in a sector of declining importance due to world competition from alternative products. Women are also indirectly influenced in their reproductive roles because of rising male unemployment, as the viability of exporting sugar continues to decline, due to the elimination of preferential markets and of existing subsidies from the Barbados government which the WTO will be imposing.

The effect on women is more direct in the case of EPZ light manufacturing – and eventually data entry and other services – as now NAFTA and ultimately FTAA and WTO require the overriding of trade agreements inconsistent with their terms (Watson, 1994; Hall and Benn, 2000; Benn and Hall, 2000). The elimination of protective tariffs which WTO requires is already undermining manufacturing for the domestic market: late in 2000 both soft drink bottling and chicken processing plants closed, due to the influx of lower priced competing products. Bottling is a predominantly male sector, and chicken processing a predominantly female one. Similarly, the expansion of supermarkets, and the increasing importance of American food products is undermining the traditional marketing businesses of women with limited education. Some of these vendors of regional produce (fruit, vegetables, fish) sell the surplus from their own land, or that of their neighbours. Others have larger scale, often inter-island businesses. On the other hand, opportunities to work as sales persons in stores in the modern sector are increasing, and are now open to more educated black women. In addition, as consumers, women have access to more diverse, and sometimes less costly, merchandise.

Women, Labour Standards and the Flexibilization of the Work Force

The Social Partnership of government, business and trade unions was formalised in Barbados in 1990 to deal with the crisis of the threat of externally imposed structural adjustment measures (SAPs), and the agreement has been renewed, in modified forms, three times. Initially a prices and incomes policy, which included a voluntary reduction in wages at all levels in the public sector, and voluntary price increase restraint, it also contains undertakings by the social partners to work cooperatively to increase productivity and to incorporate union participation in decision-making about job cuts. Recently the economic climate has allowed for the gradual reinstatement of the earlier wage cuts (Barbados Workers' Union, 1998, 2000).

Consistent with the ILO Conventions it has ratified, Barbados' labour legislation is quite comprehensive, relative to such matters as maternity leave, hours of work, holidays with pay, the right to free association. There is, on the other hand, no overall minimum wage, only wage standards within particular industrial sectors, while occupational safety and health regulations are embryonic and sexual harassment legislation is nonexistent. Research on the informatics sector (Dunn and Dunn, 1999; Freeman, 2000) indicates that the high production quotas can be a cause of both physical and mental stress for women, particularly when combined with ergonomically inappropriate work stations, as is the case in some enterprises. The high level of turnover, particularly in the data entry work in which women are concentrated, suggests that problems exist. A Barbados Industrial Development Corporation's profile of the sector seemed to imply that it was thanks to the high turnover that the health related problems were not greater (BIDC, 1998).

An additional problem that Dunn and Dunn (1999) noted in some companies was that, although overtime or additional shift work is formally optional, there is implicit pressure to do it, in part in order to earn enough to meet financial responsibilities for one's family. That many of those who do not work overtime for their formal employer do additional informal sector work is indicative of the relatively low wage rates, both in data entry and female dominated areas of manufacturing. Apart from the public service, the average wages for women are systematically and significantly lower than those for men. Typical informal sector work by women includes sewing, cooking or baking, hairdressing and "suitcase" trade reselling of goods purchased abroad.

Unionisation in offshore companies has been the exception rather than the rule, although it is quite widespread in other parts of the private sector and very prevalent in the public sector. It is unclear whether, until recently, there was an implicit agreement that the unions would not try to organise in the EPZs.[7] In the late 90s there were, however, documented cases of offshore companies objecting to legitimate attempts at unionisation, with one offshore data entry company choosing to relocate instead of accepting unionisation, alleging that the voluntaristic labour relations practised in partnership by the government, unions and the private sector constituted an unacceptable form of labour relations (BWU, 1998). If taken at face value, rather than simply as a pretext for rejecting unionisation, this reaction could be seen as indicative of a lack of respect for the indigenous cultural practices. Other evidence (Dunn and Dunn ,1999) suggests that such a lack of respect can extend to the workers themselves, their working conditions and the challenges that women, in particular, experience, often as single parents, in coping with the demands of their productive and domestic responsibilities.

While multinational firms seem to hire a predominantly local, black, female work force, management, and even supervisory positions, have tended to be filled either by men or by foreigners, whether men or women. Differential salaries and benefits received by local and expatriate managers and professionals (Dunn and Dunn, 1999), resulting in a two tiered system of remuneration are another cause of social (and economic) strain. Related to this have been the increases in the cost of housing, the introduction of gated communities and the development of conspicuously exclusive resorts, all of which both widen and emphasise the gap between the wealthy and others, impacting negatively on community dynamics.

Women, Privatisation and Reduced Public Services

As is the case for many societies which became independent during the second half of the twentieth century, the public service has been an important employer in Barbados, employing about one fifth of the male and one fifth of the female labour forces in 1990 (Barbados, 1994), and contributing to the realisation of a social democratic project of economic development and increasing equity and social justice. The substantial migration of well-educated women from Barbados to Canada and the United States since the 1960s reflects the obstacles to employment they experienced at home, and, to some extent, continue to experience. In fact, the public sector (which includes most education and some medical service) has been more open than private sector enterprises to the hiring of blacks, whether men or women, and to the hiring of women in professional, management, and office jobs. It has also been a relatively well paying source of employment, especially for women, and the only one where their salaries are approximately equal men's: in 1990 only 20% of each sex earned less than $200B a week, in contrast to the labour force as a whole where 22% of men and 50% of women earned less than $200B a week (Barbados, 1990). Since 1990, salary reductions, layoffs and reductions in operating budgets and privatisation have been introduced in the public sector as part of the tripartite Social Contract, justified by the threat of structural adjustment measures imposed by international agencies. The resulting loss of jobs, increasing expectations at work (having to do more with less), and lower incomes have had a particularly deleterious effect on women, due to the concentration of the best paid women within this sector and its importance as a means of occupational mobility for black women. We could anticipate, on the basis of past practices within the large scale enterprises of the private sector, that, in the newly privatised organisations, women's opportunities for advancement, particularly those of black women, will decrease.

Some of the government austerity measures, introduced to counter the threats of SAPs, affect women, not just as employees, but also because of their family responsibilities. Thus, not only do most women earn less for their paid work, but, thanks to fiscal and monetary policies (elimination of price controls on basic food stuffs, introduction of VAT), they have to manage their household needs with less money. Furthermore, if their male partner becomes unemployed (and male unemployment has also been rising), it becomes even more difficult to manage financially (Black, 1997). The cutbacks in some services (public transport, medical care) and the privatisation of others (telephone) substantially increases the stress women experience, resulting in such problems as deteriorating health. It is women who continue to have informal responsibility for the care of elders and the infirm, and child care in the face of insufficient provisions for such care by the State. Although its extension has been among the objectives of the Barbados Development Plans, implementation has been curtailed by these external constraints on government spending. In summary, these "invisible" negative effects of globalization and structural adjustment policies tend to weigh more heavily on women than on men (Antrobus, 1989; Barriteau, 1996; Massiah, 1990a, and 1990b).

Resistance by Barbadian Women to Negative Effects of Globalization

Women's resistance to the negative effects of globalization take two forms: individual coping mechanisms and strategies whose objective is the promotion of social change. One form of individual resistance has been to invest in further training in order to be able to obtain jobs which offer greater autonomy. Another is for those with salaried, typically full-time, employment to take on a second or third job, often establishing micro-enterprises in the informal sector. These could involve the sale of fruit, eggs or preserves, for instance, or the provision of tutoring or day care: this is a strategy used by professionals as well as those with clerical, manufacturing or service jobs. Although this strategy entails an additional source of stress, it also provides a way for women (and men) to maintain the standard of living they had achieved ten or twenty years ago and which they now see slipping away. The sharing of housing by three generations, by adult siblings and their families, or by unrelated nuclear families reduces the cost of housing and may, at the same time, facilitate child care.

Barbadian women's collective resistance to the negative effects of globalization has primarily taken non-confrontational forms – research, lobbying and public education through NGOs at the local, regional and international levels, often working in collaboration with sympathetic bureaucrats within the government and international organisations (Antrobus, 1989; Barriteau, 1995; Massiah, 1990a, and 1990b; Reddock, 1998). The preparatory work for the Beijing Conference and follow-up activities are examples of this strategy, as are various activities of Women's Forum, NOW, the Centre for Gender and Development Studies and WAND (all local), CAFRA (regional) and DAWN (international). Other women's organisations continue to support social welfare-type work which helps to fill the gaps in the social safety net: on the one hand these activities meet a clear community need, but on the other, they facilitate the State's disengagement, the preferred policy of the proponents of the neo-liberal globalization. Women have also become active in unions, as paid officers, elected leaders and rank and file members, participating both in the social partnership negotiations and in demonstrations when they feel there have been infringements of their rights as workers.

Canada[8]

Women, Footloose Capital and Trade Agreements

Much of the analysis of U.S. branch plants in Canada discusses a period that predates the recent phase of globalization, and that relates to the types of manufacturing in which the majority of the labour force is male. Transformations to the east coast fishery from the 1980s, caused by technological change and over fishing, are an exception to this generalization. In this case some of the women's fish packing jobs have moved from smaller to larger plants, while others have been replaced by new technology (MacDonald, 1994).

The vulnerability of women's jobs in clothing and electric assembly, due to the risk of the companies' relocation to countries with less constraining labour legislation, has been acknowledged since the 1980s (North-South Institute, 1985). The loss of the women's jobs associated with the movement of capital has been, however, primarily linked first with the FTA (1989) and subsequently with NAFTA. Declines in women's employment in manufacturing by the early 1990s, after the advent of the FTA have been documented, particularly in clothing and electrical production (Cohen, 1994), effects that Cohen (1987) had anticipated while the FTA was still under discussion (1987). The increasing use of outwork, another cost-cutting measure, is discussed below in the section on labour standards. Immigrants, particularly women of colour, who make up the overwhelming majority of the female labour force in manufacturing, have borne the brunt of these changes (Gabriel and Macdonald, 1996) in a sector which, for women, has been characterised as racist, imperialist and offering very poor pay and working conditions (Ng 1999; Das Gupta, 1996).

Writing in 1987, Cohen predicted that jobs in services would also be affected by the trade agreements. As it became technologically possible and lucrative to offer such services as banking electronically or by telephone, staff could be concentrated remotely, in a lower wage area. New Brunswick, an economically depressed province, has become an important locale for such call centres, and we have seen in the earlier section how such data processing has entered – and then left – Barbados.

Women, Labour Standards and the Flexibilization of the Work Force

Another consequence for Canada of globalization, this time related to the movement of people as a result of poor economic prospects in their home countries, has been the continuing availability of women recruited from overseas under special Canadian government programmes as live-in care-givers or domestic servants. In general, women admitted under these programmes have not enjoyed the same rights as those admitted as landed immigrants, in particular the right to choose their place of residence, the length of time they must wait and the conditions they must meet before they can apply for citizenship.[9] Many have come from the economic South, initially from the Commonwealth Caribbean, and more recently from the Philippines. It was only as a result of extensive lobbying, primarily by women's groups and immigrants' groups, that the government agreed to allow them to apply for landed status at the end of their contract, without having to leave Canada to do so, and also allowed them to change employers during their initial contract. The exceptional constraints placed on women entering under these programmes combined with the demanding working conditions which these "second class" immigrants often experience has led some scholars (*Canadian Women Studies*, 1999; Calliste, 1989; Silvera, 1989; Bakan & Stasiulis, 1997; Daenzer, 1993) to analyse the situation as the result of a racist and imperialist policy. This indicates the negative impact of globalization on the working conditions of some domestic workers in Canada. In addition, that there is an unsatisfied market for the services of live-in domestic servants reflects the benefits that some Canadian households are deriving from the current economic situation, coupled with the unappealing working situation of live-in caregivers and the inadequacy of state provision of care for children and for others requiring home support.

Turning now to the majority of Canadian women, who do not have live-in positions, one notable consequence of globalization has been the deterioration in working conditions, in particular the increasing prevalence of non-standard work and of homework. Although both may ostensibly make it easier to reconcile productive and reproductive responsibilities, in fact they are more likely to result in the employee experiencing social isolation, increased stress and a shift in costs from employer to herself. Non-standard work refers to work which is part-time, contractual, on a flexible schedule, including split shifts, or based on piece work. The advantage for the employer is having a flexible work force, which can be shifted from one section to another, called in as needed and, depending on the nature of the worker's contract and/or hours of work, may not have to be paid benefits. Particularly common now in retail stores, including supermarkets, and in fast-food restaurants (Barndt, 1999), this strategy of flexibilization is also increasingly evident in clerical work, in various nursing jobs within hospitals and long term care facilities, and in other professional, technical and managerial fields. Women are more likely to be employed in "low end" flexible occupations, while men are more likely to be found in the "high end" ones where lucrative fees are charged.

The prevalence of home work, once confined to garment making and other types of assembly work in light manufacturing, has been increasing (Ng, 1999) and the activities diversifying, mainly into clerical work (Menzies, 1997). Although it is often assumed that child or elder care can be done concurrently with home work, in fact the latter is typically done when those being cared for are not at home or are asleep: time spent on paid work is fragmented, and may exceed usual employment standards. Women working from home also find they are less likely to get "help" with domestic tasks from other family members than when they go out to their paid jobs, clearly underlining the continuing private and collective appropriation of women's time informed by the assumption that unpaid domestic work is women's responsibility and that what is done at home is not "really" work. The noise of sewing machine or staple gun, having to keep the telephone line free during one's shift in order to receive and transmit pizza orders are examples of ways in which women's outwork impinges on their families' – and their own – lives (Barndt, 1999). Furthermore, it is the women, rather than their employers, who pay overhead, from renting or buying equipment and supplies to additional electricity costs.

Issues of employment and pay equity have been a preoccupation of the Canadian women's movement since the 1970s and, following the Abella *Report* of 1984, had begun to be addressed, particularly in the public sector. Job cutbacks, salary and hiring freezes, privatisation and deregulation, all phenomena associated with globalization, have seriously restricted advances on this front (Briskin and Eliasson, 1999).

Women, Privatisation and Reduced Public Services and Entitlements

As in Barbados, the public service is one of the best employers for Canadian women, in terms of pay and employment equity. The cutbacks, hiring freezes and wage freezes which characterised the 90s as cost-cutting measures to reduce the national debt and maintain a good national credit rating have therefore weighed particularly heavily on women. Privatisation and outsourcing can have similar effects.

Changing rules for (un)employment insurance (EI), family allowances (which were formerly paid directly to women) and the old age pension, all associated with liberalisation and/or government cost cutting, have had a more deleterious effect on women's entitlements than on men's. In the case of EI, the period of employment required for eligibility has increased, to the disadvantage of women, since they are more likely to work part time or have interruptions in their employment history. The exclusion of cases of resignations from eligibility for EI restricts women's use of this strategy to deal with notoriously difficult-to-prove cases of sexual harassment. The claw-back of old age security on the basis of *family* income and the replacement of family allowances by child tax credits, also based on family income, have removed autonomous entitlements to revenue from women.

Cutbacks in state funding of child care subsidies, home care, and Medicare offload responsibility for care to the family, more specifically to women, a fact that is rarely acknowledged in official pronouncements or in the media. Increased responsibilities expected of women range from assisting their aging relatives to providing convalescent care to providing unpaid child care for grandchildren to having unemployed children (and their families) returning home to live. The silence about the ways in which changes in public and para-public services increase women's unpaid work can be treated as an indicator of the strength of patriarchy within Canadian society, while the expectations, in themselves, illustrate women's collective (and individual) appropriation.

Resistance by Canadian Women to Negative Effects of Globalization

Holding multiple jobs is an individual strategy, known to be used particularly by women who are involuntary part time workers, but its prevalence is inadequately documented. It does seem to be less widespread in the middle and upper-middle income groups than in Barbados, an indication, no doubt, of a somewhat wider margin of discretionary income. The establishment of small businesses by women could be interpreted as a form of resistance to the work place stresses and constraints to which globalization has contributed.

Forms of collective resistance seem to be more diverse in Canada than in Barbados. Women continue to be a crucial part of the volunteer work force (in hospitals, seniors' residences, for Meals on Wheels). Various groups within the women's movement, notably NAC, have been voluble critics of trade agreements, beginning with FTA. They have produced documents, lobbied and demonstrated, either alone or in collaboration with like-minded groups on this and other public policy issues arising from globalization, through pay equity to the promised national child care strategy (Briskin and Eliasson 1999). Their research has helped demonstrate, among other things, the deleterious effects of NAFTA, of programmes of economic restructuring and of the destruction of the social safety net (Bakker, 1996; *Canadian Woman Studies, 1998, and 1999*). Cooperatives in which women are involved (housing, shared food preparation, non-profit food buying, day care) offer alternative, more socially supportive, types of social organization (Barndt, 1999). Organizations, such as INTERCEDE, are lobbying for improved working conditions for their members who are immigrant domestic workers (Knocke and Ng, 1999), while others, such as the National Organization of Immigrant and Visible Minority Women (1998-9) are lobbying for more satisfactory retraining and re-certification processes for professionals with overseas qualifications. All these forms of intervention underline the complex lines of cleavage among women on the basis of social class and race and the diverse preoccupations to which globalization has given rise.

Internationally, the Canadian and Québécois women's movements have played leadership roles in international networks, including the Women's March, Beijing and post-Beijing activities, and in other coalitions related to specific issues (Barndt, 1999; Briskin and Eliasson, 1999).

Conclusion

This admittedly selective overview has demonstrated the effects of specific aspects of globalization on women's paid and unpaid work in Barbados and Canada. That it has been possible to provide more detailed analysis of the effects on paid work than on unpaid work suggests the continuing marginality of the latter. We have, however, been able to identify ways in which women's unpaid work has been affected by globalization. There is striking similarity in this respect between the two societies, and the effects are mainly negative ones which increase women's unpaid work, often without acknowledging that this is being done.

Overall, apart from a brief period of improvement during the 1970s in Barbados, globalization has been associated with deteriorating working conditions for most women, as many have become part of the excluded or those with economically insecure jobs (Hoogvelt, 1997). Although the fact of deteriorating working conditions is a commonality for the two societies, the details differ, reflecting the relatively more privileged starting position of most Canadian women in terms of social programs, wage levels and economic options and, arguably, a less conservative dominant ideology about gender relations. Will the effects of flexibilization which currently preoccupy Canadian women come to the fore in Barbados in the future?

At the moment, despite daunting odds, it seems as if the political will to oppose negative effects of globalization on social policy is stronger in Barbados than in Canada, as witness the Social Partnership, the success in maintaining tuition free post-secondary education (where the majority of the students are women), and the recent, albeit limited, introduction of home care.

On the other hand, women's strategies for coping and resistance in Barbados seem to be primarily individual or as part of mixed groups, whereas in Canada the women's movement has played an important leadership role in opposing globalization – a difference in culture or in strength (Scott, 1985)?

Women's individual and collective appropriation remains evident in both societies, often implicitly reinforced by the neo-liberal policies and pressures in the public and private sectors. These pressures, in fact, constitute a backlash against gains that women had gradually, if unevenly, been making. Finally, this overview also highlights, in a very summary manner, the fact of the diversity of women's experience due to differences in training, in race or ethnicity, in social class, and in nationality. The ways in which women therefore live the effects of globalization vary in form and severity, but, for most, they share two common threads – of being difficult and of being faced actively, not passively.

Notes

1. As a result of the recent development of telework, and the increasing importance (or at least the increased visibility and formality) of home-based businesses, this aspect of the concept of work must be revisited (Menzies, 1997).

2. See, for example, Armstrong and Armstrong (1990) and Siltanen (1994) for an overview of this literature. Mies (1986), Rogers (1980), Blumberg (1978) were among the early feminist authors who applied this critique specifically to societies of the economic South.

3. During the 1970s Colette Guillaumin began publishing her materialist analyses of racism and of women's appropriation in relations of sexage. Several of these articles have been translated from French and published in Guillaumin (1995).

4. By using this neologism, Guillaumin underlines the fact that the concept of "sexage" entails the same principle of appropriation as "esclavage" (slavery), except that it applies to relations between men and women.

5. See Denis (2001) for a more detailed account of women's work in Barbados.

6. A young entrepreneur in Barbados explained to me that, in his business of picture framing, because of tariffs which he had to pay on his imported framing materials, but from which international hotels were exempted, his production costs were higher than theirs (Denis, 1994).

7. This was both suggested to me, and denied, in the course of my research in Barbados in 2000-2001, but was not a focus of systematic investigation on my part.

8. See Armstrong and Armstrong (1994) for a more detailed account of women's work in Canada.

9. The rules governing these programmes have changed a number of times: during some periods it was necessary to leave Canada on completion of the domestic service contract in order to apply for landed immigrant status, at other times eventual landed status was impossible (Daenzer, 1993).

References

Abella, Rosalie. (1984). *Report of the Royal Commission of Equality in Employment*. Ottawa: Supply and Services.

Anthias, Floya and Nira Yuval-Davis. (1983). "Contextualising Feminism – Gender, Ethnic and Class Divisions," *Feminist Review*, 15: 62-75.

Antrobus, Peggy. (1989). "Structural Adjustment. Cure or Curse? Implications for Caribbean Development." Presented to the *Outreach Programme of the Caribbean Development Bank*. Mimeo.

Armstrong, Pat and Hugh Armstrong. (1990). *Theorizing Women's Work*. Toronto: Garamond.

Armstrong, Pat and Hugh Armstrong. (1994). *The Double Ghetto*. 3rd ed. Toronto: McClelland & Stewart.

Bakan, Abigail and Daiva Stasiulis (ed.). (1997). *Not One of the Family*. Toronto: University of Toronto Press.

Bakker, Isabella. (1994). *The Strategic Silence*. London: Zed Books with North-South Institute.

Bakker, Isabella (ed). (1996). *Rethinking Restructuring: Gender and Change in Canada*. Toronto: University of Toronto Press.

Bannerji, Himani (ed). (1993). *Returning the Gaze*. Toronto: Sister Vision Press.

Barbados. (1994). *1990 Population and Housing Census*, I, Bridgetown, Barbados: Statistical Service.

Barbados Industrial Development Corporation. (1998). *The Informatics Sector*. Unpublished report. Bridgetown, Barbados: BIDC.

Barbados Workers' Union. (1998). *57th Annual Report*. Bridgetown, Barbados: Barbados Workers' Union.

Barbados Workers' Union. (2000). *59th Annual Report*. Bridgetown, Barbados: Barbados Workers' Union.

Barndt, Deborah (ed.). (1999). *Women Working the NAFTA Food Chain*. Toronto: Second Story Press.

Barriteau, Eudine. (1995). "Postmodernist Feminist Theorizing and Development Policy and Practice in the Anglophone Caribbean: the Barbados Case." Pp. 142-158 in Marianne Marchand and Jane Parpart (eds)., *Feminism/Postmodernism/Development*. London & New York: Routledge.

Barriteau, Eudine. (1996). "Structural Adjustment Policies in the Caribbean: A Feminist Perspective," *N.W.S.A. Journal*, 8, 1: 143-156.

Benn, Denis and Kenneth Hall (eds.). (2000). *Globalisation. A Calculus of Inequality*. Kingston, Jamaica: Ian Randle Publishers.

Black, Jan Knippers. (1997). "Responsibility Without Authority: the Growing Burden of Women in the Caribbean," *Review of Social Economy*, LV, 2: 235-242.

Blumberg, Rae Lesser. (1978). *Stratification: Socioeconomic and Sexual Inequality*. Dubuque: William C. Brown.

Briskin, Linda and Mona Eliasson (eds.). (1999). *Women's Organizing and Public Policy in Canada and Sweden*. Montreal and Kingston: McGill-Queen's University Press.

Bryan, Anthony T. (2000) "Caribbean International Relations: A Retrospect and Outlook for a New Millenium." Pp. 347-381 in Kenneth Hall and Denis Benn (eds), *Contending with Destiny*. Kingston, Jamaica: Ian Randle Publishers.

Calliste, Agnes. (1989). "Canada's Immigration Policy and Domestics from the Caribbean: the Second Domestic Scheme." Pp. 133-165 in Jessie Vorst et al. (eds) , *Race, Class and Gender: Bonds and Barriers*. Toronto: Between the Lines.

Canadian Woman Studies. (1998). Special issue on 'Women and Work'. 18, 1.

Canadian Woman Studies. (1999). Special issue on 'Immigrant and Refugee Women'. 19, 3.

Cohen, Marjorie Griffith. (1987). *Free Trade and the Future of Women's Work: Manufacturing and Service Industries.* Toronto: Garamond.

Cohen, Marjorie Griffith. (1994). "The Implications of Economic Restructuring for Women: the Canadian Case." Pp. 103-116 in Isabella Bakker, *The Strategic Silence.* London: Zed Books in association with the North-South Institute.

Daenzer, Patricia. (1993). *Regulating Class Privilege. Immigrant Servants in Canada, 1940s-1990s.* Toronto: Canadian Scholars' Press.

Das Gupta., Tania. (1996). *Racism and Paid Work.* Toronto: Garamond.

Denis, Ann. (1981). "Femmes: Ethnie et occupation au Québec et en Ontario 1931-1971," *Études ethniques au Canada*, 13, 1: 75-90.

Denis, Ann. (1994). *A Follow-up Study of Participants in the People of Tomorrow Programme, WAND, Barbados.* Ottawa: CBIE.

Denis, Ann. (2001). *Whither Work? A Comparative Analysis of Women and Work in the Commonwealth Caribbean and Canada in the New Era of Globalization.* Working Paper No. 6 . Cave Hill, Barbados: Centre for Gender and Development Studies.

Dunn, Leith L. and Hopeton S. Dunn. (1999). *Employment, working conditions and labour relations in offshore data service enterprises: Case studies of Barbados and Jamaica.* Multinational Enterprises Programme, Working Paper No. 86. Geneva: ILO.

Enloe, Cynthia. (1990). *Bananas, Beaches and Bases.* Berkeley, Los Angeles: University of California Press.

Fox, Bonnie. (1988). "Conceptualizing 'patriarchy'," *Canadian Review of Sociology and Anthropology*, 25, 2: 163-182.

Freeman, Carla. (2000). *High Tech and High Heels in the Global Economy.* Durham N.C. & London: Duke University Press.

Gabriel, Christina and Laura Macdonald. (1996). "NAFTA and Economic Restructuring: Some Gender and Race Implications." Pp. 165-186 in Isabella Bakker (ed.), *Rethinking Restructuring: Gender and Social Change in Canada.* Toronto: University of Toronto Press.

Girvan, Norman. (2000). "Globalisation and Counter-Globalisation: the Caribbean in the Context of the South." Pp. 65-87 in Denis Benn and Kenneth Hall (eds.), *Globalisation. A Calculus of Inequality.* Kingston, Jamaica: Ian Randle Publishers.

Green, Cecilia, (1994). "Historical and Contemporary Restructuring and Women in Production in the Caribbean." Pp. 149-171 in Hilbourne Watson (ed.), *The Caribbean in the Global Political Economy.* Boulder, Colorado & Kingston, Jamaica: Lynne Rienner Publisher & Ian Randle Publishers.

Guillaumin, Colette. (1995). *Racism, Sexism, Power and Ideology.* London & New York: Routledge.

Hall, Kenneth and Denis Benn (eds.). (2000). *Contending with Destiny.* Kingston, Jamaica: Ian Randle Publishers.

Hoogvelt, Ankie. (1997). *Globalization and the Postcolonial World.* Baltimore: Johns Hopkins University Press.

Jayasinghe, Daphne. (2001). "'More and more technology, women have to go home': changing skill demands in manufacturing and Caribbean women's access to training," *Gender and Development*, 9, 1: 70-81.

Joekes, Susan and Ann Weston. (1994). *Women and the New Trade Agenda.* N.Y.: UNIFEM.

Juteau, Danielle and Nicole Laurin. (1988). "L'évolution des formes d'appropriation des femmes," *Canadian Review of Sociology and Anthropology*, 25, 2:183-207.

Knocke, Wuokko and Roxana Ng. (1999). "Women's Organizing and Immigration: Comparing the Canadian and Swedish Experiences." Pp. 119-146 in Linda Briskin and Mona Eliasson (eds.), *Women's Organizing and Public Policy in Canada and Sweden*. Montreal and Kingston: McGill-Queen's University Press.

Luxton, Meg. (1997). "The UN, Women and Household Labour: Measuring and Valuing Unpaid Work," *Women's Studies International Forum*, 20, 3: 431-439.

MacDonald, Martha. (1994). "Restructuring in the Fishing Industry in Atlantic Canada." Pp. 91-102 in Isabella Bakker (ed.), *The Strategic Silence*. London: Zed Books in association with the North-South Institute.

Massiah, Joycelin. (1990a). "Economic Change, Structural Adjustment and Women in the Caribbean." Revised version of a document submitted to the *Commonwealth Caribbean Regional Meeting on Structural Adjustment, Economic Change and Women*, Cave Hill, Barbados: Institute for Social and Economic Research, University of the West Indies.

Massiah, Joycelin, (1990b). In Search of Social Equity: Women as Social Partners in Caribbean Development. Cave Hill, Barbados: Institute for Social and Economic Research, University of the West Indies, Mimeo.

Menzies, Heather. 1997. "Telework, Shadow Work: The privatization of work in the new digital economy," *Studies in Political Economy*, 53: 103-123.

Mies, Maria. (1986). *Patriarchy and Accumulation on a World Scale*. London: Zed.

Mishra, Ramesh. (1999). *Globalization and the Welfare State*. Cheltenham UK and Northampton MA.: Edward Elgar.

Moghadam, Valentine M. (1999). "Gender and Globalization: Female Labor and Women's Mobilization." *Journal of World-Systems Research*, http://csf.colorado.edu/wsystems/jwsr.html 5: 301-314.

National Organization of Immigrant and Visible Minority Women of Canada. (1998-1999). *Recognition and Accreditation of Foreign Qualifications: Case Studies of the Nursing, Teaching and Social Work Professions*. Ottawa: NOIVMWC.

Ng, Roxana. (1999). "Homeworking: Dream Realized or Freedom Constrained?," *Canadian Woman Studies*, 19, 3: 110-114.

North-South Institute. (1985). *Women in Industry. North-South Connections*. Ottawa: North-South Institute.

Reddock, Rhoda. (1998). "Women's Organizations and Movements in the Commonwealth Caribbean," *Feminist Review*, 59, 57-73.

Rogers, Barbara. (1980). *Domestication of Women*. London & New York: Tavistock Publications.

Scott, James C. (1985). *Weapons of the Weak*. New Haven and London: Yale University Press.

Sen, Gita. (1996). Gender, Markets and States: A Selective Review and Research Agenda, *World Development*, 24,5: 821-829.

Siltanen, Janet. (1994). *Locating Gender*. London: UCL Press.

Silvera, Makeda. (1989). *Silenced*. Rev. ed. Toronto: Sister Vision Press.

Stasiulis, Daiva. (1999). (Feminist Intersectional Theorizing.) Pp. 347-397 in Peter Li (ed.), *Race and Ethnic Relations in Canada*. 2nd ed. Toronto: Oxford University Press Canada.

Ward, Kathryn. (1990). "Introduction and Overview." Pp. 1-22 in Kathryn Ward (ed.), *Women Workers and Global Restructuring*. Ithaca, N.Y.: ILR Press, School of Industrial Relations, Cornell University.

Watson, Hilbourne. (1993). "The Changing Structure of World Capital and Development Options in the Caribbean." Pp. 1-46 in Hilbourne Watson and Folker Frobel, *The Future of the Caribbean in the World System. Two Contributions.* Kingston Jamaica: Friedrich Ebert Stiftung & University of the West Indies.

Watson, Hilbourne. (1994). "The United States-Canada Free Trade Agreement, Semiconductors, and a Case Study from Barbados." Pp. 127-146 in Hilbourne Watson (ed.), *The Caribbean in the Global Political Economy.* Boulder, Colorado & Kingston, Jamaica: Lynne Rienner Publisher & Ian Randle Pubs.

Chapter Eight

Two Faces of Globalization in Mexico: Maquiladoras and Zapatistas[1]

by J.L. Chodkiewicz

During the last decade observers and social scientists have pondered the implications of the increasingly dominant paradigm of neo-liberalism. This paradigm informs the policies of many countries, leading governments to slash social spending and destroy "safety nets" while privatizing public services and granting more freedom to international investments and international commerce. The debate is phrased in terms of "globalization" because of the growth of multinational corporations and the weakening of national sovereignty implied in international agreements such as the GAAT and NAFTA. Theorists emphasize the increased importance of such supranational institutions as the International Monetary Fund and the World Trade Organization. The tariff laws and trade restrictions that had regulated international trade and investment crumbled during the 1980s and 1990s accelerating the rate of international economic integration, further justifying the claim that a process of "globalization" was taking place.

I would suggest that most of the economic benefits and social costs that are the object of this debate result from neo-liberal economic policies of governments and continuing ecological problems of pollution, erosion and overpopulation, rather than a possibly mythical "Globalization." Nevertheless, changes in the global economy and how these affect poor countries, worry many observers such as Barry Coates (2000) who claims that

> Two important inferences can be drawn from the available information: firstly, there is no justification for the claim that globalization is delivering benefits for all, and secondly, there is ample evidence

showing that millions of poor and vulnerable people have been adversely affected.

My purpose here is to document this claim by describing and analysing some aspects of the social consequences of the internationalization of production, the "Structural Adjustments" and the neo-liberal policies of the Mexican government during the last decades, as it responded to the demands of the IMF and the United States government. I shall refer to the new factories mushrooming on the northern border of Mexico, and to the peasants of the southern border, in Chiapas, who represent the other, more traditional, face of Mexico. My main focus will be on the current effects of the neo-liberal economic policies of the Mexican government on these groups, and their future implications. Women constitute just over half of the 100 million population of Mexico, and are the group most affected by inflation, loss of social benefits and unemployment. It is therefore relevant to focus attention on their plight. I consider two examples: 1) women working in the maquiladoras (in-bond assembling plants); 2) Mexican peasants, many of whom are disenfranchised women unable to gain title to land, and left behind by their migrating husbands. I then discuss the Zapatista movement in Chiapas, the most successful reaction so far to the forces of globalization.

Mexico's "Liberalization"

The oft repeated lament "Poor Mexico, so far from God and so close to the United States" expresses well the ambivalence of the Mexicans for their neighbours to the North, who after confiscating nearly half of Mexico's national territory, became wealthy and politically powerful. This love-hate relationship is expressed in nationalistic pride and at the same time in the rapid acceptance of gadgets, fashions and many aspects of North American "mass-culture." Since the 1960s, Mexico tried to join the global market; this required greater commerce with the United States, enhanced by the General Agreement on Tariffs and Trade and by the creation since 1965 of the *maquilas* on the border with the United States. At the time, the Mexican government owned or controlled several sectors of the economy and practiced "ISI," a policy of Import Substitution Industrialization.

During the 1970s, national pride was supported in Mexico by newly discovered oil fields and by the rising price of oil. Frantic spending in the expectation of oil exports profits led to a drastic debt crisis exacerbated by the reinvestment in the United States of billions of "flight capital." "In 1976, under pressure from the International Monetary Fund (IMF) and other foreign lenders to stabilize the economy, the government devalued the peso by almost 100 percent" (Tiano, 1994: 21). This followed many years of growing unemployment and underemployment: the new crisis worsened the plight of many Mexicans and the situation became politically unstable. The chosen cure was as dangerous as the crisis itself, since "the government deflected urban unrest by placing price ceilings on basic foodstuffs, a policy that jeopardized the welfare of the rural population and ultimately led to the agrarian crisis of the 1970s." (Tiano, 1994: 21)

The nationalist agenda was advanced by President Echeverria, who expanded the role of state enterprises, and his successor President Lopez Portillo. Lopez Portillo spent billions in infrastructure and in aid to agriculturalists who received credit, machinery and chemicals so as to improve their productivity by imitating U.S. industrial agricultural practices. In spite of this emphasis on agribusiness, Mexican agriculture declined by half during that period, from 14% to 7% of Gross Domestic Product. Furthermore, a recession gripped the rich foreign buyers of Mexican products: the prices of Mexican exports fell. The price of oil plummeted in 1982, ruining Mexico in a few weeks (Beaucage, 1998: 15). The situation was made worse by the fact that "US$25 billions was taken out by wealthy Mexicans between 1978 and 1982" (Sinclair, 1995: 55). Mexico had to admit that it could no longer pay its huge foreign debt of more than one hundred billion U.S. dollars. Shortly after, Brazil also defaulted.

The default of such huge borrowers was a setback to many banks and financial institutions in the United States and Canada, and threatened political chaos in Latin America. The World Bank and the International Monetary Fund intervened and rescued the banks and Latin American countries. The cost to Latin American countries was a very bitter pill to swallow. They had to accept Structural Adjustment Policies (SAP) which required them to devalue their money, cut government spending on education, health and other social programs, privatize state enterprises, accept foreign investors, welcoming them with relaxed labour and environmental laws. These policies were based on the assumption that the debtor countries were the authors of the economic crisis, not the eager and imprudent bankers who had fostered their borrowing. The SAP were devastating to the poor, but they spared the banks of the northern countries from being inconvenienced. In Mexico, this resulted in wage freezes and inflated prices that badly hurt the poorer classes, notably the peasants, most particularly women. One of the visible effects of SAP was a sharp decrease in life expectancy, especially for children: child mortality increased 10% in Mexico following SAP (Shaw 2000). "The crisis and the structural adjustment measures designed to ameliorate it have had devastating consequences for the bulk of the Mexican population, for whom the 1980s has been called the "Lost Decade" (Tiano, 1994: 22).

The devastating character of this "Lost Decade" is succinctly illustrated with a simple statistic:

> The gap between rich and poor has grown wider and the living standards of large sectors of the population have plummeted. Extreme poverty has increased: according to the Economic Commission on Latin America and the Caribbean (ECLAC), by 1981 the percentage of Mexicans living in poverty had fallen to 46 percent. However, by 1988 it had once again risen to 60 percent, similar to the 1977, pre-oil boom level. (Tuñón Pablos, 2000: 106)

The Mexican economist L. Roman Morales (1999: 16) pointed out that after two decades of "Structural Adjustments" and liberalization of the economy, the danger of economic crisis has not diminished, taxes are not lower, low wages did not generate new employment, and corruption continues unabated.

The government of Mexico did not have economic policies, but rather reported to the International Monetary Fund. Turning away from the policies of his predecessor, President Miguel de la Madrid enacted with enthusiasm the bitter recipes of SAP: he devalued the peso, cut subsidies to food supplies and started selling or closing small or unprofitable state enterprises. The rationalization for these new policies was a new "neo-liberal" economic theory that had earlier inspired Pinochet's economic policy in Chile, well subsidized by the United States. That economic theory has since dominated the policies of all Latin American countries, although with significant local variations. Neo-liberal policies led these countries to compete for foreign investment by protecting foreign enterprises ruthlessly from zealous environmentalists and labour activists. One type of new enterprise is the maquiladoras, where in-bond materials are processed and assembled, then re-exported without duties at the border. To attract foreign investments low wages were guaranteed and pollution was officially ignored. Mexico was in many instances a winner of this "race for the bottom", i.e., the lowest wages, the most docile labour force and the greatest tolerance for pollution. Hence Lisa Shaw's description of NAFTA as a cow being fed in Canada, milked in the USA and polluting Mexico (Shaw, 2000).

The neo-liberal economic policies of Miguel de la Madrid cut by half the purchasing power of minimum-wage earners, and only the tight grip of the government party, the PRI, in power for sixty years, over the unions maintained an uneasy peace. However, the callous neglect of the victims of the 1985 earthquake in Mexico City caused unrest in the city and the peasants were becoming paupers. "Since 1982 the purchasing power of the minimum wage has dropped an average of 12 percent per year" (Tiano,

1994.) To deal with these problems, his successor, President Carlos Salinas instituted PRONASOL, a program of "National Solidarity" that funded roads, schools, and other small community projects as well as assistance to peasants, slum dwellers and the unemployed:

> This public-works program proved insufficient, however. Women suffered from the "feminization of poverty," as they were the most affected by declining standards of living. (Tuñón Pablos 2000: 107)

President Salinas continued the privatization of state enterprises. When he left office in 1994, the Mexican peso collapsed again, causing severe hardship for peasants and other poor people. This reinforced the determination of his successor, President Ernesto Zedillo, to increase foreign investments. One of the important ways to secure them was to multiply the maquiladora assembly plants.

The Mexican government had worked hard to obtain the North American Free Trade Agreement (NAFTA), which they conceived as a wide open door to Mexico's participation in a greatly expanded global economy. Six years after its implementation, many observers are less optimistic, and would support Selby's (1985: x) terse judgment:

> [...] NAFTA has been a disaster for the ordinary working Mexican aside from those who are fortunate enough to get a job in transnational corporations. Intermediate and small-scale industry in Mexico was crushed not just by NAFTA, but by the ideologically driven opening of the economy to foreign imports under the General Agreement on Tariffs and Trade (GATT).

To begin with, the Mexican government devalued the peso again in 1994, making Mexican labour still more attractive to foreign investors, actually cheaper than in South Korea, Taiwan, Hong Kong, Singapore, and Brazil (Sinclair, 1995: 56). For Mexican workers, the consequences were tragic as "wage increases that had previously been approved by the government were wiped out, so that wages fell further behind, and workers' real buying power dropped even more profoundly." (Kopinak, 1996: 197). The Mexican government was counting on the growth of numbers and production of the in-bond assembling and processing plants (the maquiladoras) to restore the balance of payments. It counted on the devaluation of the peso to tempt foreign investors with still cheaper Mexican labour. It was not disappointed, because maquiladoras multiplied at the rate of a new one every day, and produced a significant trade surplus. To understand the eagerness of Canadian and United States companies to create new maquiladoras in Mexico is not difficult, as Sinclair comments:

"The difference between low Mexican wages and what companies used to pay Canadian and American workers to produce the same products, is some $12 billion annually. This is a direct subsidy to global corporations from Mexican workers" (Sinclair, 1995: 175).

Alas, the prosperity of the state did not benefit most Mexicans. The government's attack on the standard of living of the workers, started with the devaluation of the peso, continued with setting the minimum wage very low and preventing wage increases, while it dismantled the safety net by lowering or cutting support for pensions, health, education and a variety of other social services. Women are among the most vulnerable of the vulnerable in Mexico, and do not feel thankful for the neo-liberal policies and the globalization dreams of their leaders. Many of those left in the countryside live in villages abandoned by men who went, legally or not, to the United States looking for work, scratching their meagre plots to make a living. Other women, especially young ones, are sent in increasing numbers by their families to earn a few pesos working at the maquiladoras.

Maquiladoras

Most of the maquiladoras (also called "maquilas") are located in a narrow strip along the Mexico-United States border. These are factories where clothing, furniture, chemicals, electronic goods and now automobile parts, are assembled and then shipped duty-free back to Canada or the United States. The borderland region where these maquiladoras are concentrated attracts migrants from central and southern Mexico, creating an overload on the region's urban infrastructure and its fragile ecology. The assembly plants blight the borderlands' environment through undisciplined and illegal disposal of their waste material. (Williams, 2000)

Raw sewage, toxic metals and solvents are dumped illegally in great quantities. The international press of the 1980s had sensational reports about birth defects and other adverse consequences of this environmental disaster on the health of the workers and their families. The growth of the electronics industry, which uses large quantities of powerful solvents, increases the danger of pollution of the water table. Mexico must compete with other Latin American countries to attract foreign investors who will start a new maquila only if they are guaranteed low wages, no unions and no environmentalists. Labour discipline is ruthlessly maintained (e.g. only one bathroom break in ten hours), and the wages are so low that it is advantageous for many firms to establish their plant within the Mexican border, rather than deal with union wages and environmental regulations in the United States or Canada.

The reason for the government's laxity in applying basic health measures and ecological rules, and its systematic curb on union activities and demands for higher wages becomes clear when one considers the contribution of the maquilas to Mexico's employment figures and balance of payments :

> With over 500,000 workers, the assembly plants account for about 25% of employment in the nation's manufacturing sector. […]In 1994, the industry earned Mexico nigh on to $6 billion in foreign exchange, well above tourism earnings and approaching petroleum export earnings of about $7 billion, long Mexico's primary earner of foreign exchange. (Williams 2000)

It is important to note that, even by Mexican standards, the wages of the maquila are low, and that only unemployment in the country justified accepting the strict conditions of work in a maquila: "Real wages paid in maquiladoras were about half of those paid in the non-maquiladora manufacturing sector in Mexico from 1975 to 1992" (Gambrill, 1994, see also Tiano, 1994: 21). The following table indicates the value of the wages of the workers:

Hours of Maquiladora Work Required to Buy Basic Necessities

Beans, 1 kg	4 hrs
Rice, 1 kg	1 hr, 26 mins
Corn Tortillas, 1 kg	40 mins
Chile Peppers, 1/8 kg	1 hr, 15 mins
Tomatoes, 1 kg	1 hr, 35 mins
Beef, 1 kg	8 hrs
Chicken, 1 kg	3 hrs
Eggs, 1 doz	2 hrs, 24 mins
Vegetable Oil, 1 ltr	2 hrs, 25 mins
Limes, 1 kg	1 hr, 20 mins
Milk, 1 gal	4 hrs, 17 mins
Toilet Paper, 1 roll	43 mins
Detergent, 1 kg	2 hrs
Diapers, Box of 30	11 hrs, 30 mins
Shampoo, 10 oz	2 hrs, 25 mins
Elementary School Uniform	57-86 hrs
Roundtrip Bus Fare	1-3 hrs
Cooking Gas, 1 tank	20 hrs
Aspirin, Bottle of 20	2 hrs, 25 mins

These figures are based on average prices in Tijuana for an assembly line worker earning 26 pesos a day ($3.57). (1 kg is equivalent to 2.2 lbs.) (Maria, 1996).

To put in perspective the purchasing power of maquiladoras, Kopinak gives the example of a young woman working in Nogales:

> She liked this job, but she wanted to be able to earn more money, since hers was the main income supporting herself, her brother, and mother. Her total weekly income, including bonuses, was 98,000 old pesos (US$33.00) [...] The three of them lived together in a small one-bedroom dwelling, which they rented for 100,000 old pesos ($25) a month. (Kopinak, 1996: 90-91)

Since their beginning in the 1960s, maquiladoras had recruiting practices that consistently led them to hire "young, single, childless women and [to] discriminate against older women, partnered women and women with children" (Tiano, 1994: 73). Avoiding the growing army of unemployed men whose possible union militancy they feared, the owners sought the stamina of young girls, and counted on their being as docile and submissive as they had been with their father and brothers (Tiano, 1994: 73). They subscribed to the view (enforced by law in Mexico until 1974) that married women and mothers should stay at home. The reasons for the women to work in the maquiladora were directly related to the unemployment of their father and brothers:

> Eleven percent lived in households with at least one unemployed adult male; another 79 percent lived with men who were marginally employed as street vendors, unskilled workers, or petty clerks. (Tiano, 1994: 54)

While they complained of the high turnover of their workforce, the maquiladoras avoided the payment of seniority bonuses by replacing employees with younger ones:

> [...]the average length of female employment in the maquiladora does not exceed five years. . Maquiladoras generally dismiss women older than twenty-five or thirty years of age and replace them with younger women, from whom greater productivity is anticipated. (Iglesias Prieto, 1985: 99)

The "young" maquila workers are often girls of 14 or 15 who have falsified papers to pretend that they are 16, the legal age to join the work force. These young girls are easy prey to thieves and sexual predators. (Recently, one such girl, thirteen year old Irma Angelica Rosales, was one of the most famous victims of crime in Ciudad Juarez, in the state of

Chihuahua, where possibly 200 women working in maquiladoras have been murdered (La Botz, 1999; Alicia Sepúlveda, 2000).) The hiring process includes such discriminatory practices as pregnancy tests: the owners do not want to pay for maternity leave, and they do not expect a young mother to keep her job, therefore they do not want to invest in training her (Kopinak, 1996: 162). This is illegal, but who will apply the law, and risk losing such good business and much needed foreign currency?

The "mucho macho" attitude is also evident in the lack of promotion opportunities for women, who are used as cheap, docile, unskilled labour:

> Jobs for which women are required were not spread randomly throughout the job hierarchy. [...] None of these jobs which management would prefer to be filled by women are in the skilled production or control categories, but almost 89 percent (475-535) are unskilled production personnel. (Kopinak, 1996: 83)

As a result of this guaranteed labour peace (supported energetically by the police and the army, ready to break any strike with harsh violence), the new maquiladoras, which multiplied at a startling rate during the 1990s, started employing more men; women lost their jobs in certain sectors. At the same time, employers radically changed their notion of the ideal worker, deciding that young women are too frivolous and undependable, choosing mothers instead. In interviews in 1990,

> Employers frequently said that children are an asset to women's successful job performance because the responsibilities of caring for children make women more reliable in all aspects of their lives (Tiano 1994: 92).

Women's job opportunities continue to be determined by the frame of mind of the men who manage the maquiladora, and their definition of the ideal worker. The women working in growing numbers in the maquiladoras still find little reward in the low pay, poor housing and job insecurity, and lack of any union to defend them from flagrant denials of their rights.

In spite of all these grievances, many women accepted the harsh work conditions in the maquilas because their family, living in the countryside, was poor and getting poorer. This was the result of the erratic agricultural policies of the Mexican government over several decades.

Mexican Peasants

Since the 1960s the Mexican government attempted to develop the economy through industrial growth and increasing exports. The main mechanism for implementing this policy are the maquiladoras, but this corresponded to a considerable neglect of the agricultural sector. This sector was further damaged by the attempt to deflect the social unrest resulting from low wages and unemployment in the cities by placing price ceilings on basic foodstuffs, a policy that jeopardized the welfare of the rural population and ultimately led to the agrarian crisis of the 1970s. Between 1965 and 1975, over two million hectares of farmland, which had originally produced most of the food staples for the cities, were abandoned because the rising costs of basic inputs such as tools and seeds outpaced the artificially stabilized prices for crops (Tiano, 1994: 21)

Another blow for the peasant communities came when in late 1991, President Salinas changed article 27 of the Constitution to stop agrarian reform and to transform *ejidos*[2] into communal lands to which individuals could gain title, so that they could rent or sell to outsiders, even to foreigners. (Barry, 1995: 117) In practice, it is still difficult for women, even if they are widows and heads of household, to claim rights to land. The privatization and opening to foreigners of what had been, since the Revolution, national land administered by local communities, has potentially disastrous consequences:

> The withdrawal of state regulation and institutions from rural markets will not result in free markets but ones in which a small circle of oligopolists, *caciques*, moneylenders, and coyotes hold sway. Although the state is not perfect or impartial itself, its capacity to moderate market distortions that leave people without food and growers subject to exploitative practices should not be so easily dismissed. In the Mexican countryside, the free market that neoliberalism envisions is more ideology than reality (Barry, 1995: 23).

Mexico's economic restructuring to regain economic stability and to bolster its position in the integrating global economy has left it without a coherent food and farm policy. "Trade liberalization, the reduction of government support, and the absence of an alternative farm policy have left corn producers extremely vulnerable to foreign competitors" (Barry, 1995: 114). Already now, many Mexican peasant women find themselves alone for many months, as their husbands migrate to Mexico City or to the United States, in order to (barely) support their families (Wiest, 1984). As subsistence farming decays further, entire families will have to abandon their villages. The cities are not, and will not be, ready to accept them and provide them with jobs. If, as some suggest, at least three million *ejidatarios* and their families join the ranks of the unemployed and fill the shantytowns, they will suffer dire poverty and the economy of the entire country will decline.

A Globalized Zapata

After several decades of emphasis on industrial development and misman-agement of agriculture, the Mexican government was confronted with a variety of peasant revolts. "Among the most marginalized and neglected were the indigenous populations, that became restless" (Tuñón Pablos, 2000: 107). The best known of the recent Mexican peasant uprisings is that of the Zapatista started January 1, 1994. Their base is in southern Mexico in the state of Chiapas, one of the richest and yet poorest states in Mexico. It is rich in hydroelectric power, mineral and agricultural resources, but the oppression of the majority of the population by a tiny aristocracy of PRI party members supported by police and judges, leads to extremes of rural poverty. Peasants from six Maya ethnic groups drew the attention of the world to the dangers of the admission of Mexico into the North American Free Trade Agreement for native peoples and the poor, choosing to start publicizing their plight on the day marking the start of the implementation of NAFTA. Far from succumbing to xenophobia and parochialism, the Chiapas rebels were, from the start, fighting not only for their own villages and land, but also for the interests of all peasants and indigenous populations of Mexico. This was well understood by the huge and enthusiastic crowds that welcomed them during their triumphant "Zapatatour" to the capital city in April 2001. As Collier and Quaratiello (1994: 7) note,

> [...] it is primarily a peasant rebellion, not an exclusively Indian rebellion, because although the Zapatistas are demanding rights for indigenous peoples, they are first and foremost calling attention to the plight of Mexico's rural poor and peasants, both indigenous and non-indigenous.

The Zapatista weapons were not guns or old-fashioned pitch-forks, but internet messages and media events – a revolution of the global age. Their use of the internet has become legendary (Rodriguez, 2000). Their web site allowed them to by-pass government-controlled press and radio, giving them access to a wide audience. The free and often humorous style of the news releases of Sub-Comandante Marcos gained them sympathy at home even from rather conservative elements, and kept a very wide international audience interested and committed to helping them. The many foreign journalists and television reporters they invited prevented the Mexican army from committing obvious atrocities and human rights violations. This peasant rebellion was waged on a global scale from the start, and most would agree that this is the only reason for the survival of the leaders and their supporters. The Structural Adjustment policies imposed on Mexico required improvements in democracy and human rights, thus preventing violence and too much intransigence from the federal government. While fighting "globalization" the Zapatistas cleverly used it for their own defence.

The Zapatistas have been innovative and global not only in their strategy, but in their objectives. Instead of restricting their rebellion to a fight about personal grievances and local issues, they organize and defend other ethnic groups, other disadvantaged peasants. The Zapatistas do not fight for themselves alone, and insist on including the demands of many other indigenous people in Mexico in their negotiations with the Mexican government. They have put indigenous people at the centre of political debate in Mexico, and mobilized them on an unprecedented scale. They organized in 1992, and again in 1996 a *National Indigenous Forum* that included five hundred delegates from thirty-two different ethnic groups. They changed the national politics significantly by forcing the Mexican federal government to abandon its policy of *indigenismo*, the forced integration of Indians into the Mexican cultural mould, and the denial of the cultural "otherness" of the native populations of Mexico. The Zapatistas made indigenous autonomy a national issue and considerably advanced the fight for indigenous rights and self-determination. This led to the unsatisfactory "Ley Indígena" of July 16, 2001, that will surely be amended in the years to come. This central emphasis of their campaign for multiculturalism and also for women's rights, reflects clearly globalizing cultural influences rather than own traditional culture and knowledge. While one should not pretend that the Zapatistas are a women's liberation movement, many women are very active participants and influential members of the Zapatista councils. Several reports confirm Tuñón Pablo's claim (2000: 107) that:

> The 1994 indigenous uprising in Chiapas has underscored the need to attend these groups' needs, particularly those of indigenous women, some of whom, in fact, hold key leadership posts in the rebel ranks. Zapatista women have proposed a Revolutionary Law for Women demanding important changes in their communities, including the right to chose their husbands, to limit the number of children they bear, and to not be abused by their spouses.

It is significant that when the Zapatistas made their peaceful march on Mexico in April 2001, becoming the first rebel army to enter Mexico City since 1915, and obtained the right to speak to the deputies and senators, Sub-Comandante Marcos did not speak. The leading and most influential speech was made by "Comandante Esther" who pleaded eloquently for the rights of Mexican peasants and most particularly for those of indigenous women.

In spite of these achievements, there is no indication that the Zapatistas or any other political force will be able to save communal lands from privatization, prevent the extension of agribusiness by foreign companies, prevent the massive import of corn and other basic foodstuffs from the United States and Canada, and the competition with small producers. The appropriation of the best land and water supply by foreign investors is likely to proceed rapidly in the next few years and cause a massive exodus of uprooted peasants to overcrowded cities. What are the likely consequences of such a process?

Conclusion

An important principle guiding neo-liberal economic policies is that large investments in infrastructure and facilities provided to large corporations will cause economic growth and will eventually benefit even the poor as a result of a "trickle down" effect in the form of jobs and other economic opportunities. In simple terms this is the paradoxical assertion that to help the poor we should give money to the rich. The problem with the "trickle down" economic process is that it is too slow, so slow that, by the standards of homeless, hungry and unemployed people, it never takes place. It appears instead that corporate welfare has replaced relief for the poor. As Collier and Quaratiello (1994: 154) suggest:

> Corporations pursue cheap labour and hefty profits on a global scale that escapes responsibility for conditions in any given nation. But concentrations of new wealth do not readily trickle down to the masses. In the final analysis, can modern economies and modern states afford societies in which so many people are losing their economic power as purchasers and consumers?

For the last three decades the government of Mexico has followed with enthusiasm the recipe for economic recovery imposed by the IMF in the name of free trade, minimal governance and austerity. In increasing numbers, the poor have paid for these policies with homelessness, unemployment, underemployment, sub-standard wages, poor health and hunger. The social safety nets provided by an appropriate minimal wage, free health and education services, pension funds (even for some women), subsidies for basic food items, and fair unions defending the rights of the workers, have all been abandoned by the Mexican government (Wilson and Whitmore, 2000: 40). This coincided with a total reorganization of Mexican industry and agriculture, multiplying the need for safety nets. Women employed at sub-standard wages in the maquilas, or left behind to care for the children by husbands who migrated to the United States, are the one who suffered most from the disappearance of the safety nets.

If we look at the economy of Mexico, not in dollars and cents but in terms of human satisfaction, we discover quickly that the glowing success of the economist's figures conceals the despair, increasing hunger, homelessness and poverty of tens of millions of Mexicans, rising infant mortality rates and lowered health standards. One can therefore sympathize with Collier's claim:

> But I am equally alarmed by the willingness of planners, in Mexico and in our own society, to shuck off responsibility for the impoverished for the sake of economic restructuring, especially when restructuring has actually swelled the ranks of the homeless, the unemployed, and those women and men who must work at multiple minimum wage jobs with no benefits just to survive. (Collier and Quaratiello, 1994: 153)

The explicit purpose of recent Mexican governments has been to integrate Mexico into the global economy. So far, the world has taken advantage of the very low wages and the protection from its own legislation offered by the Mexican government. Starting January 2001, a flood of goods from the United States, Canada and the maquilas is going to destabilize further several branches of the Mexican economy. What price integration? One is reminded of Mike Fleshman's (2000) exclamation: "Africans remained integrated into the world economy at the very bottom. And the bottom is falling!"

I have argued that one of the sectors that is threatened by new imports is the economic basis of the livelihood of nearly twenty million peasants, more than half of them women, who are threatened by imports of cheap wheat and corn mass-produced by the U.S. agribusiness[3]. This substitution of more expensive with cheaper grains may make apparent economic sense in the short term, but only in a very naive way. We already know how in 1986, under the influence the IMF, a flood of U.S. rice into Haiti destroyed its local agriculture (Pooley, 2000: 23). The destruction of the Mexican shoe industry, smothered under a mountain of cheaper imports, is a sad precursor to what is yet to come (Selby, 1985: x). The unrestricted importation of large quantities of grains, combined with the purchase of Mexican land by foreign-owned cattle-ranchers and agribusiness would make Mexico dependent on another country for its most essential staples. These staples will now be produced with the polluting, inefficient, oil-dependent and unsustainable technology of U.S. agribusiness. Given the lowering of aquifers, the rise in oil prices and the effects of global warming, the viability of this agribusiness is doubtful, and the prices of its products are sure to escalate steeply in a few years. Once the Mexican agricultural system is dismantled and becomes totally dependent on the United States for the supply of important staples, there is no guarantee that prices will remain low, especially as the price of oil is likely to rise and the available water supply of the United States is dwindling. Even without these disasters, one has to realize that the social fabric and the multicultural basis of Mexico would be torn apart by the mass migration of subsistence farmers to cities that are already short of water, choked by pollution and unable to cope with rising unemployment. As Coates (2000) puts it:

Campesino-based food production systems are probably structurally incapable of being competitive in the world market or providing the same standards of living enjoyed by those created by modern (unsustainable) agribusiness. Nonetheless, until the economy can provide other productive employment, the peasantry merits government support in its attempts to diversify production and increase self-provisioning. Without such a targeted farm policy that benefits the peasantry, Mexico faces accelerating urbanization, disintegration of rural society, and loss of cultural diversity.

Several Mexicans have commented that the picture presented in this chapter is too dark, that many Mexicans owe their higher standards of living to the neo-liberal economic policies of the government, and that the recent and very significant progresses in democracy were encouraged and required by the foreign partners of Mexico. I suggest, nevertheless, that Mexican economists and their IMF strong-armed advisors have forgotten that development is not necessarily growth. The purpose of "development" should not be outstanding "economic indicators" but rather human indicators, such as health, nutrition, employment and housing. On these criteria, Mexico has been losing ground, and may lose more.

The neo-liberal policies of the Mexican government have been so strongly imposed by the IMF, the World Bank and other global institutions, that a solution to this crisis cannot be found in Mexico alone. Like the proverbial tail wagging the dog, economic principles are allowed to prevail over moral principles and social responsibility. We must react to the obscene neo-liberal claim that the rules of the market should prevail over the social and moral rules of a society.

The recent history of poor countries is replete with examples of "stubborn peasants" whose technologies were proven to be more sound and sustainable than those of "well meaning" development specialists full of hare-brained schemes and locally maladaptive advice. As J. Bodley illustrates so well in the latest edition of his *Victims of Progress* (Bodley, 1999), these peasants benefit from a more holistic approach that, unlike the tunnel vision of our specialists, allows them to balance short-term economic gains with possible losses in social safety net or ecological sustainability. We could learn much from them on how to be human, instead of simply being economists.

Notes

1. I would like to thank Yildiz Atasoy and William K. Carroll for their very useful editorial comments, and several Mexican commentators on this essay. I remain responsible for any error and omission.

2. *Ejido*, which now means a land reform community, is a colonial term denoting public land (what in England is known as commons) attached to a settlement.

3. The yellow corn of the United States is not used to make the "tortillas" that are an essential part of the diet of most Mexicans.

References

Barry, Tom. (1995). *Zapata's Revenge: Free Trade and the Farm Crisis in Mexico.* Boston, South End Press.

Beaucage, Pierre. (1998). "The Third Wave of Modernization: Liberalism, Salinismo and Indigenous Peasants in México". Pp. 3-28 in *The Third Wave of Modernization in Latin America: Cultural Perspectives on Neoliberalism.* L. Phillips (ed.). Wilmington, NJ: Jaguar Books on Latin America, Scholarly Resources Inc.

Bodley, John. (1999). *Victims of Progress* (4th edition), Mountain View: Mayfield Publishing Company.

Coates Barry. (2000). "Globalisation, Development and Poverty: what do we know? Introductory thoughts to the on-line debate" "Globalization, E-Conference" <globalization@lists.worldbank.org>

Collier, George A. with Elizabeth Quaratiello. (1994). *Basta! Land and the Zapatista Rebellion in Chiapas.* Oakland: The Institute for Food and Development Policy.

Fleshman, Michael. (2000). "Africa and Globalization", "Globalization, E-Conference" globalization@lists.worldbank.org

Gambrill, M. (1994). "Maquiladoras and North American Integration" Paper presented at the Latin American Studies Association Conference in Atlanta, Georgia, March 10-12.

Iglesias Prieto, Norma. (1985). *Beautiful Flowers of the Maquiladora: Life Histories of Women Workers in Tijuana.* Translated by Michael Stone with Gabrielle Winkler. Austin: University of Texas Press.

Kopinak, K. (1996). *Desert Capitalism: Maquiladoras in North America's Western Industrial Corridor.* Tucson: The University of Arizona Press

La Botz, Dan. (1999). "Girl's murder sad symbol of corporate power, child labor, female exploitation on the border" *Mexican Labor News and Analysis,* March 2

Maria. (1996). "Blood, Sweat & Shears: Maquiladora Workers Demand a Living Wage". *Cross Border Connection,* Oct 1996, a publication of the Support Committee for Maquiladora Workers

Pooley, Eric. (2000). "The IMF: Dr. Death?: A case study of how the global banker's shock therapy helps economies but hammers the poor" *Time,* April 24.

Rodriguez, Leopoldo. (2000). "Globalization: What and for Whom?" Globalization E-Conference globalization@lists.worldbank.org

Roman Morales, Luis. (1999). *¿Que es el ajuste estructural?* Tlaquepaque (Jalisco) Mexico,

Instituto Tecnológico y de Estudios Superiores de Occidente.

Selby Henry. (1985). "Foreword" in Iglesias Prieto, Norma, *Beautiful Flowers of the Maquiladora: Life Histories of Women Workers in Tijuana.* Translated by Michael Stone with Gabrielle Winkler. Austin: University of Texas Press.

Sepúlveda Alicia. (2000). "Re: Women and poverty" "Globalization E-Conference" globalization@lists.worldbank.org

Shaw, Lisa. (2000). "Structural Adjustments and Third World Debt", Globalization conference, University of Manitoba, February 1.

Sinclair, Jim. (1995). *Crossing the Line.* Oshawa: The Alger Press

Tiano, Susan. (1994). *Patriarchy on the Line: Labor, Gender, and Ideology in the Mexican Maquila Industry.* Philadelphia: Temple University Press.

Tuñón Pablos, Julia. (2000). *Women in Mexico: A Past Unveiled.* Translated by Alan Hynds, Austin: University of Texas Press

Wiest, Raymond E. (1984). "External Dependency and the Perpetuation of Temporary Migration to the United States" pp. 110-135 in Richard C. Jones editor*: Patterns of Undocumented Migration: Mexico and the United States* Totowa, N.J.: Rowman & Allanheld.

Williams E. J. (2000). "The maquiladora Industry and Environmental Degradation in the United States-Mexican Borderlands." This revised edition of paper was presented at the annual meeting of the Latin American Studies Association, Washington, DC, September 1995.

Wilson, Maureen G. and Elizabeth Whitmore. (2000). *Seeds of Fire: Social Developments in an era of Globalism.* Halifax: Fernwood Publishing.

Winston Keith. (2000). Re: Trade, poverty and inequality" "Globalization E-Conference" globalization@lists.worldbank.org

Chapter Nine

Feminism and Resistance to Globalization of Capitalism

by Vanaja Dhruvarajan

Negative Impact of Corporate Sponsored Globalization

Neoliberal Policies and Practice

Over the years, particularly in the last two decades, one is confronted by disturbing headlines in newspapers and newscasts; "Common sense revolution sweeps Ontario;" "Famine spreads in Africa and ethnic strife is on the rise;" "Financial speculators scoop choice property in Thailand at bargain basement prices as property values are depressed after the stock-market collapse;" "Corporations make profits in unprecedented rates."

Terms such as efficiency, competitive advantage, and structural adjustment are heard repeatedly throughout the world as corporate sponsored globalization sweeps the globe. A constant preoccupation seems to be to cater to the demands of corporations. The fear is that if their demands are not met they might go to some other location where they can make a better deal. Thus, corporate agendas are becoming state agendas. Global economic organizations such as the World Bank (WB), the International Monetary Fund (IMF), and the World Trade Organization (WTO) are working diligently to enforce these agendas across the globe. New treaties are being negotiated in secrecy to give the transnational corporations (TNCs) unlimited access to world resources without accountability (McMurtry, 1998; Sinclair, 2000). The agreements with national governments are not binding on the corporations, as they can pack up and leave if they think their interests are not served, even if this destabilizes a national economy, causing tremendous hardships, loss of jobs and livelihoods.

These treaties have various clauses included that empower the corporations to sue sovereign states for lost future profits if they act in the national interest and choose to withdraw from the agreements. Laws of nation-states that make corporations accountable can be eroded by external challenges. For example, under the rules of WTO, European governments (serving their corporate interests) can challenge U.S. trade practices and vice-versa. Thus, through such friendly arrangements among corporations, the power of national governments to make corporations accountable to public interest is eroded.

Nation-states are forced to adopt structural adjustment policies to provide favourable business climate for corporations to the detriment of the welfare of the people, as cuts in health, education and social programs are made. The corporate goal is to harmonize the business environment across countries to create level playing fields for corporations to conduct their business. The contest among different countries and among different regions within countries to satisfy the unending demands of corporate interests is leading to a 'race to the bottom' by eliminating social supports to people who desperately need them (Mander, 1996). Thus, the needs of the homeless, the hungry and the poor are not considered pressing, and countries are not allowed to cater to the welfare of their citizens lest they antagonize the corporations.

The consequences of these policies of acquiescence to corporate interests have been devastating. Within Canada, this has meant disappearance of full-time jobs with benefits to be replaced by part-time or contract work without benefits. To obtain unemployment benefits rules are becoming more and more stringent, leading to undue hardship for those who lose jobs because of economic upheavals caused by corporate policies and practices (Bakker 1996). As Cohen (1999) has shown, the International Labour Organization (ILO), the champion of workers' rights over decades, instrumental in establishing the ground rule that "workers are not commodity," is gradually leaning towards satisfying the corporate interests. Cuts in spending on education and health care and downloading of work to families and communities are common. Environmental standards are dismantled and corporations continue to degrade, deplete, and pollute the environment in their greed to accumulate profits (McMurtry, 1998). Thus, democratically elected governments actively participate in implementing the corporate agenda and call it, as in Ontario, the "common-sense revolution."

Many former colonial countries, after relentless struggles, have gained political independence but are left with impoverished economies. With newly found freedom, these countries are struggling to develop their economies. The World Bank and the International Monetary Fund have been eager to provide loans, but with strings attached. A development model that has evolved in the west over several centuries is being imposed on these countries. Modernization, industrialization and urbanization are implicitly assumed to be the panacea for all the ills of Third World countries since that is the route the West has taken. This process has evolved in the West over centuries and their economies have grown and developed through various policies of state protection. But developing countries are not allowed to develop policies that are suitable to their economies, and in keeping with their histories and cultures. Instead, they are forced to accept terms and conditions developed by the global economic governance structures in place to serve the corporate interests of the North. Opposition to these prescriptions is dealt with violently as revealed by the case of Chile, among others, where enlightened leadership in the country tried to act in the national interest. The fledgling economies of the South are integrated with the robust economies of the North to create a level playing field to the TNCs. Third World countries are becoming open markets of the TNCs, to plunder with legal impunity.

The result has been new forms of bondage as these countries sink into ever-growing indebtedness and the international agencies use debt as a weapon to dominate and control these economies (Kumar, 1996; Khor, 1996). National policies are made in distant centres by creditors to serve their own interests and not the interest of the countries. These countries have lost the right to evolve policies and implement practices that serve their national interest. Thus the old colonial patterns are re-established as structural adjustment policies are imposed on these countries (Teeple, 2000). This has generally meant reduction in government spending on all social programs, including education and health; destruction of subsistence farming in favour of large-scale cash crops for export. Western food grains flood into the market, depressing the prices of local food grains. Water and fertile lands are earmarked for cash crops, and peasants are driven out of their meagre land holdings. The deliberate destruction of subsistence agriculture is undertaken. The result is that self-sufficiency in food is replaced by widespread shortage leading to dependence on foreign supply of food grains. Widespread poverty has resulted, as cash crops grown for debt servicing and subsistence farming is destroyed (Chossudovsky, 1997). In addition, in many parts of the world, as the social fabric unravels, disruption of community life has resulted as mindless consumerism spreads. Because of these disruptive policies, bonds between young and old and between neighbours break as bitterness and envy take hold and ethnic strife spreads (Appadurai, 1999). Local governments have lost control of their economies and have become too weak to govern as policies are made and imposed by the outside creditors.

In this new world order capital is given the right to unfettered movement. Money and bond speculators enter and exit the economies of various countries as they please. Any check, even in its mildest form, on such disruptive behaviour is resisted as it is interpreted as curtailment of freedom to do business (Friedman 2000). Devastating consequences for people's lives are completely ignored with the logic of "casino economics" (Barnet and Cavanagh, 1996). The single-minded purpose of this venture is to make as much profit as possible at any cost to people's lives. Since there are no limits to these expectations, speculators are always competing with each other to come out on top. This means the economies of various countries are just pawns in this game of profit-making. For reasons of their own speculators can start a trend by withdrawing capital investments from a given economy. This can become a contagion and spread, as it did in Asia in 1997. The result was the destruction of Asian economies, with decades of diligent efforts to build the economies wiped out in a matter of weeks. As property values plummeted, speculators with wads of money made through their speculations scooped up many lucrative properties such as steel mills and supermarket chains at rock bottom prices. Thousands of people lost their jobs, homes and their livelihood (Hahnel, 1999).

Discourse of Inevitability

These are just a few examples of the effects of corporate sponsored globalization. A discourse of inevitability surrounds this project. We are told over and over again that it is the only way. If such a discourse of inevitability is questioned, such a stance is often interpreted as lacking in common sense. Such people are often called globophobes, Luddites, and protectionists – all of which have intense negative connotations bordering on character assassination. The political clout of global economic organizations is gradually eroding the powers of the state across the globe. The governments are often set up to fulfil the corporate agenda. Most politicians occupying positions of power in various countries have been co-opted and have essentially become spokespersons to promote corporate interests (Nader and Wallach, 1996). Thus, neoliberal policies and practices are gaining hegemonic status, and, in fact, may already have established their hegemony (Friedman, 2000).

The corporate controlled media, instead of informing and educating the public as it should in a democratic society, acts to promote corporate interests (Chomsky, 1997). There is no integrated analysis to explain why, even though wealth in various countries is increasing at an unprecedented rate, there is still homelessness and poverty. Environmental pollution and degradation continues even when we know that it is bad for our health, well-being and for future generations. There is violent ethnic strife across the world, neighbours who lived peacefully for generations are killing one another. The media reports portray them as discrete events without analysing the connections, that are, in fact, due to profit-driven globalization (Mander, 1996).

One of the reasons for the popularity of such a discourse of inevitability is the widespread feelings of alienation and loss of control over their own lives experienced by people in general. Some are under the impression that markets operate on their own and fail to see the social basis of market operations. The markets are assumed to be objective and value-neutral, operating without human agency. The policies of democratically elected governments favouring corporate interests and their deliberate neglect of other needs has led to such feelings of helplessness and hopelessness for others (Hahnel, 1999).

Another important reason is the conviction that globalization is good not only for the corporations but for society at large. The general belief among some segments of the population is that if corporations are provided with all the concessions they demand, they will create more jobs and pay well because they need consumers to buy their products. But such a symbiotic relationship between capitalists and consumers is ruptured by borderless trade. The corporations do not care how and where they make their profit. If they cannot sell enough goods in one country, they move on to another, just as they move and relocate to regions where labour and environmental standards are low and the national governments have no clout to enforce control. Thus, the race to the bottom to provide competitive advantage to corporations does not result in sharing of benefits by all people. The often-stated slogan that "the tide will raise all the boats" has not come true (Mander, 1996). Only the corporations and their shareholders line their pockets. In Mexico, for example, under "free" trade, the agro-business is producing cash crops for export and has a competitive advantage in the world market. The North American consumers are getting quality agricultural products at a low price. But the workers do not receive a living wage, children are malnourished and live in unsafe, polluted environments. Clearly, globalization is not a good deal for these people. Similar trends are observable in many Third World countries under the influence of current styles of globalization (Hahnel, 1999).

In spite of these outcomes the project is implemented with religious zeal. There is a marked reluctance to critically evaluate these policies and practices. Instead, arguments are made that not enough has been done in terms of creating proper business climate. Thus more of the same policies – more structural adjustment policies, for example, is prescribed with more vigour. The inability or unwillingness to evaluate the effects of these policies by stepping outside the neoliberal paradigm is remarkable. Negative outcomes are dismissed as short-term effects and in the long run, with minor adjustments, it is argued that everyone will benefit (Friedman, 2000). No effort is made to define precisely what is meant by short or long term. Nevertheless, such conclusions are untenable on the bases of available evidence. The trend over the last two decades clearly establishes that the inequality of outcome is systemic and integral to the process. The pattern of outcome is consistent and the rules of the game are set up in such a way that only the rich and super-rich benefit from the outcome of these processes (McMurtry, 1998).

One of the problems with the paradigm adopted by corporate sponsored globalization is that it considers economic growth to be an end in itself. Thus all policies and practices privilege the economic aspect and consider all other aspects of life subsidiary. This orientation has become commonplace, reflected in the language used by experts in the field. For example, people are considered human capital or human resources (Sen, 2000). As we know, people are agents who actively participate in order to determine the direction of their lives. In the same way, the term 'externalities ' is used to refer to all aspects of life other than economic (McMurtry, 1998). As we know, the economic aspect is but one aspect, albeit an important one to enhance human capabilities. The economic aspect does not function independently, but is integrated with all other aspects of life. If all policies and practices reflect this integration, people will be considered agents and not as capital or resources to serve corporate interests. The satisfaction of social/cultural/spiritual aspects of life and environmental preservation and protection become an integral part of development policies and practices. It is only then people's health and well-being will be cared for, which, after all, should be the ultimate goal.

In spite of the arguments against it, careful scrutiny reveals there is nothing inevitable about this process of globalization. As Khor (1996) points out, to satisfy the insatiable greed, corporations have to be on the lookout for new frontiers. The developing countries provide rich resources in their biological and cultural commons developed through the efforts of a multitude of people over hundreds of years for the TNCs to plunder and appropriate. Thus the current style of globalization is taking place because corporate interests are deliberately planning and executing their agenda. Once we understand how policies are made and identify whose interests they are serving, these facts come to light. Because of the secrecy surrounding this venture, it is often difficult to know all the details. But, the fact that corporate interests are manipulating national governments and the media in a systematic way clearly reveals that if this process is inevitable there is no reason for such secret deliberations (Sinclair, 2000).

The main reason that corporate sponsored globalization has been able to create such havoc is that there are no structures in place that hold it accountable. A global market is being created without a global democratic structure empowered to monitor and control it (McMurtry, 1998; Hahnel, 1999). Meanwhile, corporate interests are playing one national government against another, forcing them to provide a favourable business climate under the threat of relocation. So far they have been able to get away with it because there is no unity among national governments to make decisions in the public interest and hold corporations accountable. It is important to realize that if there were no laws in the first place to enable corporations to have unfettered movement they would not be able to behave as they do. We also need to realize that if laws are changed, then corporations will not be able to behave as they do now (Grossman and Adams, 1996). The reason we ended up having free trade agreements such as NAFTA is because many elected politicians come from the ranks of the corporate elite and acted in their own interest rather than the public interest (Nader & Wallach, 1996). These agreements were made in spite of the fact that majority public opinion was solidly against such agreements.

Emergent Feminisms, Resistances, and Alternatives

Predicament of Women

Women bear the brunt of these changes everywhere, and it is overwhelmingly women and their dependents that suffer because of lack of access to resources needed to transcend poverty. This is because women are often solely responsible for caring for children, the elderly, the sick and those with disabilities. Even though it is the bedrock of an economic system, this work is neither valued nor remunerated. In mainstream economic theory and the UN system of national accounts, women's caring work is not considered productive. As Waring (1988) argues, this results in categorization of women as non-producers and dependents. Such status leads to devaluation of women as persons, and leaves them vulnerable to exploitation. For example, when women participate in paid work they are often paid less than men for the same and/or similar jobs. As policies and practices of globalization are superimposed on such patriarchal ideologies and social structures, the few gains that have been made after decades of feminist struggles in many countries are slowly eroding. For example, in the interests of competitive advantage for the corporations, extensive cost-cutting is implemented in areas of health and education, and this work is downloaded to families and communities. Debates regarding affordable quality childcare

are shelved. In all such cases, women in general are forced to assume these care giving responsibilities without any kind of recognition or remuneration. As full time jobs disappear, replaced by part time or contract work without benefits, women are filling the ranks. Employment equity programs have been shelved and discussions of equality and justice in the workplace have lessened as the ruling ideology of neoliberalism acquires hegemonic status (Cohen, 1999; Bakker, 1996).

Women are not a homogeneous group. Even though all women suffer from the legacy of patriarchy, there are class differences among women within societies, who therefore experience globalization differently. Upper class women benefit as members of affluent families. Some have money to invest and make gains as shareholders when corporations maximise profits. Access to education enables many women from middle and upper-middle classes to take better paying jobs and join the ranks of workers with skills relevant for the new economy.

There are also differences in women's experiences depending on the history of colonization and imperialism of their country of residence. Those women who live in the affluent North benefit from the exploitation of those living in the South. As Goldsmith (1996: 27) points out, "Mexican workers including children, have become world class competitors by sacrificing their health, lives and futures to subsidize the profits of investors." And again as Enloe writes, (quoted in Razack, 1998 : 13) , "The 'debt crisis' is providing many middle-class women in Britain, Italy, Singapore, Canada, Kuwait and the U.S. with a new generation of domestic servants. When a woman from Mexico, Jamaica or the Philippines decides to emigrate in order to make money as a domestic servant she is designing her own international debt politics. She is trying to cope with the loss of earning power and the rise in the cost of living at home by cleaning bathrooms in the countries of the bankers." Some women in the North are losing their livelihood as corporations relocate in free trade zones in Third World countries to cut labour costs and flaunt environmental standards to maximize their profits. Even though women in developing countries line up to work in these global assembly lines because they are desperately poor and need these jobs, the real benefici-aries are the corporations. These women are used as disposable commodi-ties, made to work in unsafe and unhealthy environments and not paid a living wage.

Thus women in the north suffer because of gender gap, while women in Third World countries suffer because of the gender gap and development gap. Feminization of poverty is a worldwide phenomenon. As the Vienna NGO Forum states "It must be recognized that there are deep contradic-tions in economic policies of restructuring and globalization. Current structural adjustment policies do not reduce poverty or create meaningful work for people and the detrimental impact on women is an inherent, not an accidental, feature of these programmes" (1994: 3). Thus the impact of globalization is felt by all women but experienced differently depending on their class position and country of residence. Women must therefore be very actively involved in resisting this process. It is important to realize that the feminization of poverty is not a "women's issue" as it is often made out to be. Such notions segregate the problems women face because of decisions made and implemented nationally and globally. Analysis of this problem must be contextualized within national and global politics.

Under structural adjustment policies, women in Third World countries suffer the most. Women are over-represented among those suffering from absolute poverty (Vickers, in press). Allocation of fertile land and water resources for cash crops has meant neglect of subsistence farming. Women in many African countries are the primary food producers. They form the majority of subsistence farmers dislocated by the imposition of cash crops for debt servicing. In addition, introduction of modern technology in some aspects of farming cash crops, such as sugarcane, has meant more work without remuneration for women. Men own the lands where cash crops are grown and pocket whatever income they get, but women are forced to work on these lands as a matter of duty within the patriarchal ideological context. This work is done in addition to all the caring work they have to do for their families. In other cases, men leave the villages in search of better opportunities and women are forced to fend for themselves and their dependents (Chpssudovsky, 1997).

Not all people suffer equally from the consequences when environments are degraded, polluted and depleted. In general, it is people at the lower socio-economic levels that suffer the most because they cannot afford to move to a better place. This is particularly true for women because they are tied by family obligations and are mostly poor. Women tend to be the preferred labour force because they are vulnerable and easy to exploit, and there are many stereotypes regarding women having nimble fingers and a compliant disposition that makes them suitable for routine, repetitive work. The work life of many of these women is very short as their health and stamina deteriorate because of work in unhealthy and stressful surroundings, and they are replaced by younger women in order to keep productivity levels high. The so-called "free" trade zones, controlled by TNCs (tax havens for the corporations, with concessions to pollute the environment and disregard labour standards) illustrate this problems vividly (Goldsmith, 1996).

There is a widespread conviction among development experts that population control is a prerequisite for economic development. Aid for economic development is often provided with the condition that these countries implement population control policies. This has meant forcing women to adopt chemical contraceptive devices without being told about side effects, and subjecting them to forced sterilization (Mies & Shiva 1993). There have also been cases where drug companies and doctors from North America have taken initiatives to implement these projects. In all of these instances, women in Third World countries are not treated as human beings capable of making choices but as dangerous wombs to be controlled by whatever means necessary.

There is an arrogant implication in all these efforts that what is good for the West is good for the rest, and Western experts know best. During the era of Western colonization of the Third World there was an unquestioned conviction that Western culture was inherently superior and Westerners had the "burden" or mission to civilize these people. This ideology continues and manifests itself in different forms. Imposition of Western models of development is considered natural and routine. This conviction is so strong that no other alternatives are considered. There is no awareness that economic systems are part of social systems. Societies with different histories and cultures devise economic structures consistent with their lifestyles and priorities. Imposition of an economic model that has evolved in the West without paying attention to the needs and aspirations of all people, is the cause of so much suffering in the world today. Homogenization of economic systems and imposition of a monoculture continue unabated (Shiva, 1997; Khor, 1996; Kumar, 1996).

Feminist Paradigms

Stemming the tide of this process is daunting, but a venture that must be undertaken before we reach a point of no return. An important first step in this project is the clear rejection of the discourse of inevitability that is debilitating any meaningful resistance. The role of intellectual and moral leaders in analysing this process and informing the public cannot be over-emphasized (Gramsci, 1987). Alternate visions for a better life are necessary in order to mobilize grassroots support to bring about social transformation. Nevertheless, these efforts provide only broad outlines, and precise solutions to this problem will be necessarily varied and must come from voices of experience in different localities.

The emerging feminist paradigms have an orientation that is life-affirming and life-enhancing and, therefore, offer useful frameworks to address these challenges. There is a remarkable convergence of broad principles underlying these visions. They include a way of life where there is harmony with nature, cooperation and mutual respect among people and a pervasive concern for justice and care of all people. Such visions promote a holistic, interdependent world-view and social relations that emphasize cooperation (Mies and Shiva, 1993; Lorde, 1984). They also recognize the finite nature of earth's resources and our own mortality and insist on taking these factors into account while organizing our lives (Gross. 1996).

Feminists inspired by the ideals of these emergent feminisms also offer insights to develop strategies to organize resistance. Some insist on our rights to preserve cultural diversity by resisting the imposition of monoculture (Shiva, 1996). The conviction here is that it is only under such circumstances that people are able to exercise their autonomy and self-reliance to have control over the direction of their lives. There are those that argue for redefinition of our values in such a way that they recognize the intrinsic worth of all people (Kerr, 1999). People, not profit, should come first. Material things are means, not goals, of life. True meaning of life is realized not by accumulating material things but by cultivating human values of caring, sharing, and developing a sense of community. Valuing people for doing life-sustaining and life-enhancing work is important. Therefore, developing feminist economics that take into account the reproductive and caring work for which women in general are responsible is considered important (Waring, 1988). Reclaiming our right to write our own histories and organize our lives on the basis of values cherished, particularly by people that have been victims of colonization and imperialism, is considered imperative (Spivak, 1990). Empowering communities through food self-sufficiency is considered an important way to resist corporate control (Barndt, 1999). The politics of food is too important to be controlled by outsiders with their own vested interests. Empowering communities through food self-sufficiency is an important way to resist corporate control. This also provides an enabling environment for people to preserve and protect their diverse ways of life.

In all these proposals a running thread of argument is the empowerment of women and people in general. The significant insight is that equal importance be given to means and ends. Creating conditions where daily life is lived in such a way that people feel they have control over determining the direction of their lives is considered essential. Providing an enabling framework for people to set their own priorities and organize their lives the way they see fit is considered a top priority. Construction of ideologies and social structures, implementing social practices that nurture people and provide for the satisfaction of survival needs including emotional, spiritual and social aspects in addition to economic ones, is considered necessary. All this necessarily implies that women must participate in decision-making structures and implementation of policies. There is a firm conviction that such meaningful participation on the part of women is very difficult, if not impossible, in circumstances where bureaucracies are large-scale and centralized in distant places, far from local and daily lives. This emergent

Feminist bias in general is to promote decentralization and local control of decisions. Preservation of diverse ways of life with attention to the unique needs of people, depending on their varied cultures and histories, is considered most important. This is the way to facilitate the creative expression of people in different localities in addition to promoting and perpetuating diverse ways of life.

Technology can help to remove drudgery in daily life and improve its quality. This can happen only when communities are able to choose the kind of technology they want to use to promote their own way of life. This requires control of decision-making powers by the people who are most affected. If decisions are made by those in charge of centralized bureaucracies far removed from local histories and cultures, they will only serve corporate interests, not the people concerned. In fact, under such circumstances, a monoculture will be imposed to the detriment of local histories and cultures.

By taking a holistic approach to life, this paradigm makes it necessary that we critically examine the way we live and the work we do, to assess their impact on other people, the environment and the world at large. Possibilities exist that an awareness of the devastating consequences of the way we live and the work we do can change us morally and spiritually, leading to the implementation of more positive alternative life arrangements. This awareness can motivate us to explore ways and means to become a part of the solution rather than being a part of the problem. This paradigm provides scope for such a possibility.

Such an analysis sheds light on the privileges we enjoy and the disadvantages from which we suffer, and helps us to understand that social life is complex and social hierarchies cannot be neatly arranged (Anderson & Collins, 1995; Dhruvarajan, in press) For example, a white middle-class woman living in North America is disadvantaged because of her gender hierarchy but at the same time enjoys privileges because of her race and class. Such awareness of our relational position in the social structure, revealing the costs and benefits of our lives on others, is necessary to facilitate coalition building.

Strategies for Resistance

The emphasis is on transnational alliances across differences – differences based on nationality, class, gender, race, ethnicity, sexual orientation, age, ability, to name but a few. Such a strategy is required under conditions where nation-states are handmaidens of corporate interests. Such alliances are imperative to dismantle global structures of governance set up to promote corporate interests. Building alliances is not an easy task. It requires patience and perseverance. Difficulties are often due to differences in power among groups due to the historical legacy of exploitation and domination. Kate Young argues (1988) that, when those who are in positions of domination and those who are in positions of subordination agree that it is in our strategic interests to stem the tide of environmental destruction, global poverty, consumerism and deterioration of quality of life, then development of solidarity across differences is possible. As bell hooks (1994) argues it requires a mass turning away from an ethic of domination inspired by an ethic of love and a shared vision of a better life for all. This can happen only when people come in touch with the spiritual aspects of their lives and consider moral and ethical issues an integral part of their day-to-day lives.

Transnational alliances among women/feminists across differences are useful to mount viable resistance to corporate power overlaid on patriarchal, colonial and imperial structures of domination and exploitation. Without such initiatives there is a real danger that resistance movements will focus on various dimensions of social inequality, but perpetuate gender inequality to the detriment of women around the world (Kaplan & Grewal, 1999). The impact of globalization differs, and therefore consequences vary in different localities due to differences in history and culture (Appadurai, 1996). The issues that confront people necessarily differ in different localities. For example, if addressing consumerism is necessary to cripple corporate control in developed countries, development of Collective Intellectual Property Rights (CIPR) is most urgent in developing countries to protect biodiversity and cultural diversity. In North America an advertising campaign was recently launched for cosmetic laser surgery to make people look younger. This was directed towards the aging "baby-boomer" generation. No one knows about the side effects of such surgeries, as it takes time to assess their effect. Corporate control over people's lives can only be resisted when people learn to accept aging as part of living, and refuse to succumb to the temptation of satisfying newly created, unnecessary wants, interpreted as needs. On the other hand, in countries like India, where 80% of the population depend on agriculture to derive their subsistence, corporate piracy of biological commons through patents is the major concern. In these communities relationships to the land, to other people and to one's inner-self are considered of fundamental importance. Thus, local solutions have to be arrived at for local problems faced due to oppressive regimes of globalization. Transnational alliances should support such struggles in different localities. Such alliances should focus on common goals and strategic interests

Coalition building with movements and with similar goals, such as the environmental movement, peace movement, labour union movement, in local struggles, is very important to gain broad-based support. The environmental movement is gaining momentum as more and more people around the world become aware of the problems of global warming, depletion and pollution of the environment. There is also a growing realization that a development model such as the one promoted by neoliberal ideology that defies the natural limits of the environment, and defies principles of economic and social equity is not viable. Feminist goals of living in harmony with the environment are shared by many activists in the environmental movement. The same applies to the peace and anti-nuclear movements. The Gandhian paradigm, amongst others, of aspiring to a simple but meaningful life marked by contentment and peace, has a very close affinity to the feminist paradigm. One of the biggest challenges facing humanity today is the spectre of the spread of violence and destruction across the globe. The diversion of earth's resources towards production and deployment of destructive weaponry is increasing, rather than decreasing. Instead of promoting peaceful co-existence and resolution of conflicts through peaceful means, confrontation is promoted. This is due to the promotion of an ethic of domination and control, and the interpretation of life as a zero-sum game. Such orientations are the hallmark of corporate capitalism. Such a framework brings out the worst in people rather than tapping into their best. Feminists working with peace and anti-nuclear activists can aspire to dismantle the hegemonic status of corporate sponsored capitalism, a hegemony it is acquiring at a very fast pace. Transnational alliances with labour movements are very important in a context where corporations are pitting one segment of workers against another, and workers in one country against another. Such alliances can also work towards strengthening and democratizing governments in different countries, to empower them to enact laws to limit the powers of corporations and make them accountable to people. Such immediate goals are worthy aspirations in order to realize the ultimate vision of self-directed communities across the world.

Conclusion

History is full of examples where those who have power and privilege are loath to give them up willingly. It is still necessary to continue to exert pressure on dominant groups, to make a relational analysis and understand how privileges are accrued, maintained and perpetuated. In addition, they must be made aware of the devastating impact of their behaviour on the well-being of all people and an appeal made to their humanity and sense of ethics and morality (hooks, 1994; McMurtry, 1998; Dhruvarajan, in press). Nevertheless, while efforts to convert the dominant groups must continue, focus must be on marginalized groups forging alliances and mounting strong resistance to convince the dominant groups that the maintenance of their dominant position is not viable. We can never be certain about the future, but we know that the cause is the right one morally, ethically and spiritually, in addition to being economically and politically viable. A commitment to the cause should inspire us to become activists in transforming this world to become a just and caring place for all.

References

Appadurai, Arjun. (1999). "Dead Certainty: Ethnic Violence in the Era of Globalization". In Peter Geschiere and Brigit Meyer (eds), *Globalization and Identity: Dialectics Of Flow and Closure*. Oxford: Blackwell Publishers

Appadurai, Arjun. (1996). *Modernity at Large*. Minneapolis: University of Minnesota Press.

Barnet, Richard and John Cavanagh. (1996). ""Electronic Money and the Casino Economy." In Jerry Mander and Edward Goldsmith (eds) *The Case against the Global Economy: and for a turn toward the local*. San Francisco: Sierra Club Books

Bakker, Isabella, (ed.). (1994). *The Strategic Silence: Gender and Economic Policy*. London: Zed Books.

Barndt, Deborah (ed.). (1999). *Women Working the NAFTA Food Chain: Women, Food & Globalization*. Toronto: Second Story Press.

Chomsky, Noam. (1997). *Perspectives on Power: Reflections on Human Nature and the Social Order*. London: Black Rose Books.

Chossudovsky, Michel (1997). *The Globalisation of Poverty*. London: Zed Books.

Cohen, Marjorie G. (1999). "Globalization: Some Implications & Strategies for Women." Address delivered at the 1999 NAC National Conference and the AGM.

Dhruvarajan, Vanaja (in Press). "Feminism and Social Transformation." In Vanaja Dhruvarajan and Jill Vickers (eds.), *Thinking Through Difference: A Global Perspective*. Toronto: University of Toronto Press.

Friedman, Thomas L. (2000). *The Lexus and the Olive Tree*. New York: Anchor Books.

Goldsmith, Alexander. (1996). "Seeds of Exploitation." In Jerry Mander and Edward Goldsmith (eds) *The Case against the Global Economy: and for a turn toward the local*. San Francisco: Sierra Club Books

Gramsci, A. (1987). "Class, Culture and Hegemony." In T. Bennett et al. (ed). *Culture, Ideology And Social Process*. London: Open University Press.

Gross, Rita N. (1996). *Feminism and Religion*. Boston: Beacon Press.

Grossman, Richard L. and Frank T. Adams. 1996. "Exercising Power Over Corporations Through State Charters." In Jerry Mander And Edward Goldsmith (eds) *The Case against the Global Economy: and for a turn toward the local*. San Francisco: Sierra Club Books

Hahnel, Robin (1999). *Panic Rules*. Cambridge, Ma: South End Press.

hooks, bell (1994). *Outlaw Cultures: Resisting Representations*. London: Routledge.

Kaplan, Caren and Inderpal Grewal. (1999). "Transnational Feminist Cultural Studies: Beyond the Marxism/Poststructuralism/Feminism Divides." In Kaplan, Caren et al. (eds). *Between Women and Nation: Nationalism, Transnational Feminism and the State*. London: Duke University Press.

Kerr, Joanna. (1996). "Transnational Resistance: Strategies to Alleviate the Impacts of Restructuring on Women". In Isabella Bakker (ed), *Rethinking Restructuring.* Toronto: University of Toronto Press.

Khor, Martin. (1996). "Global Economy and the Third World". In Jerry Mander and Edward Goldsmith (eds). *The Case against the Global Economy: and for a turn toward the local.* San Francisco: Sierra Club Books.

Kumar, Satish. (1996). "Gandhi's Swadeshi: The Economics of Permanence". In Jerry Mander and Edward Goldsmith (eds.) *The Case against the Global Economy: and for a turn toward the local.* San Francisco: Sierra Club Books

Lorde, Audre. (1984). *Sister Outsider.* Freedom Calif: The Freedom Press.

Mander, Jerry. (1996). "Facing the Rising Tide". In Jerry Mander and Edward Goldsmith (eds) *The Case against the Global Economy: and for a turn toward the local.* San Francisco: Sierra Club Books.

McMurtry, John (1998). *Unequal Freedoms: The Global Market as an Ethical System.* Toronto: Garamond Press.

Mies, Maria and Vandana Shiva. (1993). *Ecofeminism.* London: Zed Books.

Nader, Ralph and Lori Wallach. (1996). "GATT, NAFTA, and the subversion of the Democratic Process". In Jerry Mander and Edward Goldsmith (eds.), *The Case against the Global Economy: and for a turn toward the local.* San Francisco: Sierra Club Books.

Sen, Amartya. (2000). *Development as Freedom.* New York: Anchor Books.

Shiva, Vandana. (ed.) (1994). *Close to Home: Women Reconnect Ecology Health and Development Worldwide.* Philadelphia, PA: New Society Publishers.

Shiva, Vandana and Radha Holla-Bhar. (1996). "Piracy by Patent: The Case of the Neem Tree". In Jerry Mander and Edward Goldsmith (eds)*The Case against the Global Economy: and for a turn toward the local.* San Francisco: Sierra Club Books.

Sinclair, Scott. (2000). *GATS: How the World Trade Organization's New "Services" Negotiations Threaten Democracy.* Ottawa: Canadian Centre for Policy Alternatives.

Spivak, G. (1988). *In Other Worlds.* New York: Routledge, Chapman and Hall.

Teeple, Gary. (2000). *Globalization and the Decline of Social Reform.* Aurora, Ontario: Garamond Press.

Vickers, Jill (in press). "Methodologies for Women's Studies". In Vanaja Dhruvarajan and Jill Vickers (ed). *Thinking Through Difference: A Global Perspective.*

Waring, Marilyn. (1995). *If Women Counted: A New Feminist Economics.* San Francisco: Harper and Row.

Young, Kate. (1988). *Women and Economic Development.* Oxford: Berg Publishers Ltd.

Afterword

September 11 and the Reorganization of the World Economy

Yıldız Atasoy

The articles in this book have used the term globalization to refer to major political and economic transformations in the global system under the influence of what Polanyi called the "self-regulating market." Each chapter, in its own way, has illustrated the complexities and contradictions of the globalization process, and invited us to rethink globalization as a multifarious interplay between political-military, cultural-ideological and economic forces. This invitation has compelled us to illustrate how these complexities are organized into an aggregate whole in a way that the illusion is created that markets are self-regulating and globalization is inevitable. We have brought the conjunctural analysis to the forefront, and suggested that it is the actually existing historical processes of global shaping that must be examined. This requires us to conclude that globalization is not an inevitable process, but a deliberate political project designed by political and economic elites to integrate the world capitalist economy. Accordingly, we reconceptualize globalization as being simultaneously a response to economic crisis in the world economy *and* political-military crisis in the state system.

In order to illustrate this argument even further, I will now analyse the September 11 attacks on the World Trade Center and Pentagon, and the American declaration of war on al Qaeda and the Taliban regime in

Note: This is a revised version of a paper originally presented at the University of Michigan-Flint in September 2001 and published in *Canadian Dimension*, November 2001.

Afghanistan. I view these events as instances of the early 21st century of global shaping.

War on Global Terrorism

When the air strikes were declared on Afghanistan, we were told that this war was against global terrorism. Although no time has been spent trying to understand who these terrorists were and how to deal with the issue, Osama bin Laden was personified as evil and the Taliban was targeted for harbouring him. The Taliban collapsed immediately during the American military campaign. The war on "global terrorism" continues as the U.S. administration has developed an open-ended list of terrorists, including groups such as Hezbollah and Hamas, and states such as Iraq. Yet, this is a highly arbitrary list. Syria and Iran were listed as terrorist states before the September 11 attack, but now they are in the "loop" of coalition building against global terrorism. Syria was even elected as a new member of the UN security council on October 9, 2001. Iraq was defined as a terrorist state before its war with Iran. During the war it was taken off the list, and, after its invasion of Kuwait, Iraq was once again added to the list of terrorist states.

The patriotic passions of American citizens have been funnelled by the Bush administration into a drive for constant war against global terrorism. This resembles Captain Ahab's pursuit of Moby Dick. The Bush administration will not end its war although it could be quite devastating both for the U.S. and the rest of the world, as was the case with Captain Ahab and his crew. The war may soon expand to other Muslim countries, as we see in the current escalation of Israeli war in the West Bank and Gaza against the Palestinian authority and Hamas. If the Bush administration is Captain Ahab, who is Moby Dick?[1] Moby Dick is both the civil society and democratic-social terrain of the international system.

The war has increased the state's coercive power both domestically and internationally. At the domestic level, governments are enacting laws or executive orders that subordinate fundamental principles of democracy and human rights to the anti-terrorism measures. President Bush's Executive Order on military tribunals and the Canadian Bill C-36 are measures which show that governments are abandoning democracy's basic checks and balances. But, neither the American Congress nor Canadian Parliament have exhausted all available domestic legal remedies in their measures against terrorism. According to Human Rights Watch and Amnesty International, these hastily enacted anti-terrorist acts, especially President Bush's executive order, are bypassing international standards for a fair trial negotiated in 1966 within the International Covenant of Civil and Political Rights (ICCPR). The ICCPR was ratified in 1976 by the Canadian government and by the U.S. in 1992. With the violation and abandonment of international standards and national laws, both the U.S. and its close allies sacrifice fundamental human rights to liberty, security, and a fair trial. The anti-terrorism acts are legislated to expand the coercive sphere of state power in civil society.

At the international level, the political question facing the Bush administration is not how to punish and eradicate the political power of Islamist fanatics said to be responsible for the global terrorism, (although no credible evidence has yet been produced). What is at stake here is an image of the U.S. as the bulwark of stability, with the ability to govern the world capitalist economy in the face of rising challenges to its power. The U.S. has put its strategic-military visions of imperialist dominance at play by waging wars. The terrorist attacks have created opportunities for the U.S. to exploit. The issue for the U.S. government is to rearrange the political-military framework of the global economic system under its hegemonic power. If Osama bin Laden or al Qaeda did not exist, it would have been necessary to invent them.

This war is not against Islam or Islamists, nor it is a response to global terrorism. In his *The Grand Chessboard* (1997) Zbigniew Brzezinski, an American national security advisor, explains that U.S. governments were never interested in eradicating the political power of Islamists in certain Muslim countries. The issue is the form that political Islam, or any other nationalist movements in this regard, would take – whether it would cooperate or compete with the U.S. interests. This concern is intimately linked to the containment of Islamist groups or regimes, which involves reconstruction of new international political alliances favouring the enhancement of economic relations within a globalized world economy. I will examine this argument systematically from the American rise to global hegemony after passing through the Cold War challenges of the Soviet Union.

Cold War Oil Politics and Islam

In the immediate aftermath of WWII, the U.S. played a central role in organizing a multilateral open world economy. Its goal was to open up markets and displace the pre-war protectionist strategies of states (Block, 1977; van der Pijl, 1984). The goal was to link each state, and coordinate various aspects of production and finance, in order to evolve along complementary lines. What we call "globalization" today was attempted explicitly as an American imperial strategy at the end of WWII. It was within the conjuncture of the Cold War antagonisms that national projects were subordinated to the political-military framework of the respective military blocs.

The integration of various national economies into an open market economy required strengthening of pro-Western factions in the capitalist bloc. This explains why the U.S. has constantly been at war in many places since WWII, among them China (1945-46, 1950-53); Korea (1950-53); Guatemala (1954, 1967-69); Indonesia (1958); Cuba (1959-60); the Belgian Congo (1964); Peru (1965); Laos (1964-73); Vietnam (1961-73); Cambodia (1969-70); Grenada (1983); Libya (1986); El Salvador (1980s); Nicaragua (1980s); Panama (1989); Iraq (1991 -); Bosnia (1995); Sudan (1998); Yugoslavia (1999); and Afghanistan (2001 -). These places were highly important for American global interests. But, the existence of oil and its importance to Western economies underscored the eminence of the Middle East for the complex economic and geo-strategic conflict of interests between the Cold War military blocs (Venn, 1986).

The Soviet Union did not need Middle East oil, having control over large oil reserves in Russia, Caucasus and Central Asia. The Soviet Union's interest in the region was in restoring its status as a dominant Eurasian power, (once played out in the 19th century with the British Empire over the break-up of the Ottoman Empire and the revisions of the map of Europe, Middle East and Central Asia (Marriot, 1924).) It was against this "great power" legacy of Russia that the U.S. designed its Middle East oil politics to support conservative pro-American monarchical regimes in Saudi Arabia, Iran and Iraq (Stoff, 1980; Bromley, 1994). Especially after Nasser's rise to power in Egypt (Beattie, 1994), conservative regimes of the region became close allies of the U.S. (Gorst and Johnman, 1997). The CIA's involvement in the overthrow of the nationalist Mossadeq and restoration of the Shah of Iran into power is but one example.

One unintended consequence of the U.S. support for the conservative regimes was the rise of Islamic movements. In the period from the nationalization of the Suez Canal in 1956 until the fall of the Shah of Iran in 1978 and the Soviet invasion of Afghanistan in 1979, Islam emerged within the bipolar division of the Cold War state system as a nationalist project of independence and sovereignty. Islam was mobilized as a means to defeat "Western imperialism and Israeli aggression" in the region, and received its initial support from the Soviet Union.

I will not become immersed in the complex and ever-shifting sands of Soviet-Middle East relations, as they have been widely analysed in the relevant literature (See: Freedman, 1991; Golan, 1990; Dawisha and Dawisha, 1982). Suffice to say that, until the Suez crisis the Soviet Union was almost completely excluded from the Middle East. The Soviet Union achieved its greatest influence in the Muslim Middle East following the nationalization of the Suez Canal in 1956 until the Soviet invasion of Afghanistan in 1979. From the time of Khrushchev to the end of the

rezhnev era, the Soviet Union actively supported the Islamic movements
in the region (Bennigsen, et al., 1989).This was due to the fact that the
Soviet Union was unable to break oil-based economic ties between the
conservative regimes in the Middle East and the Western world (Bromley,
1994). The Soviet use of Islam was intensified during the Brezhnev era
(1964-1980)[2]. Within the context of the unfolding Arab-Israeli crises of the
Six-Day War (1967) and the Yom Kippur War (1973), Islam became a
strategic means used by the Soviet Union to unite Arabs against "Western
imperialism and Israeli aggression." The Soviet Muslim religious establishment and their functionaries from Central Asia and the Caucasus were the
main players in the Soviet Islamic strategy to establish Islamic solidarity in
the region (Bennigsen et al., 1989).

The U.S.-backed Shah of Iran was deposed by an Islamic revolution in
1978, and the Soviet Union invaded Afghanistan in December 1979.
Although these events created a major set-back in the Soviet Islamic
strategy, the call for Islamic unity against "Western imperialism and Israeli
aggression" contributed to the growth of an Islamic political movement. The
Islamic genie – once defined as a "tradition" to be subordinated to the
westernization projects of the secular political elite (Lerner, 1964) – was out
of the bottle.

The U.S. formulated a broader policy on Islam at this particular juncture
of the 1970s, shifting its earlier Cold War preoccupation with "modernization" of traditional societies (Escobar, 1995). The Islamic revolution in Iran
and events in Afghanistan had made the security of the Middle East and
Persian Gulf increasingly significant for American oil interests. In addition
to the possibility of a sharp rise in oil prices (Bromley, 1991), there was also
the possibility of radical Iranian-supported Shiite Islamist movements
generating even greater anti-western feelings and thus threatening American oil interests. The Carter administration required that vital U.S. oil
interests in the Gulf be defended by military force, thus undermining the
Nixon-Brezhnev detente of the early 1970s (Gaddis, 1982). This is often
referred to as "the second cold war" between the U.S. and the Soviet Union
(Halliday, 1984). Starting with President Carter in the late 1970s, and
expanding greatly under Reagan's "Star Wars" initiative in the 1980s, the
second cold war was sustained by American support of moderate Sunni
Islamist groups in Saudi Arabia, Pakistan, Afghanistan and Central Asia
(Rashid, 2000).

This promotion of Islam was a strategic alternative to U.S. failure to
build strong military alliances with Saudi Arabia, Iran or any other Middle
Eastern Muslim country (with the exception of Turkey), in order to secure
oil supplies. U.S. Islamic policy in Afghanistan had already sharpened
nationalism and weakened Soviet influence in the entire region (Rashid,

2000). While the CIA-aided Islamist groups eventually drove the Soviet out of Afghanistan, Islamist groups also increased their assertiveness and began stirring up national political alliances, demanding greater representation in national politics. Islamist demands of representation were often countered with an increase in the state's military and coercive powers over civil society. The military coup of 1980 and subsequent military interventions in Turkish politics are examples.

Another consequence of U.S. Islamic policy was felt at the international level. By backing Islamist movements in the region (Atasoy, 1998) the U.S. also created a force capable of embodying and mobilizing national resistance movements, not only against the Soviet Union but against the dominance of Western interests in the region. The September 11th attack is a "blowback" from this policy of fostering Islam as a strategic alternative[3] to the growth of Soviet influence and indigenous national independence movements.

Refashioning of the Global System After the Cold War

The Cold War helped the U.S. contain traditional national rivalries, suppress secular and indigenous oppositional movements, and integrate Islamist movements within a world capitalist economy. The rhetoric of a multilateral open world economy and the military arrangements of the period had bolstered an image of cohesion and stability for the U.S. and NATO.

The end of the Cold War destroyed this geopolitical ordering. A new era is emerging on the basis of the triumphal vision of a globalized capitalist economy, but its political structure is unknown. The Clinton administration tried multilateralism as a way to reconstitute the U.S. dominance in the world capitalist economy around the idea of global economic integration. The Clinton administration had defined a role for the U.S. in managing global economic issues with the help of the WTO while promoting peace and a policy of *strategic cooperation* and partnership with Russia, China, and North Korea. With the coming to power of George W. Bush this policy alternative has been shifted toward an aggressive unilateralism. Bush's unilateralism does not obliterate the trend towards an open market economy in favour of a policy of American national interests alone. Despite growing economic difficulties, the capitalist market economy is broadening and deepening in most parts of the world, including the Muslim world. The new rhetoric of George W. Bush was based on *international competition*. Initially this possibility was centred on the probability of a conflict with China over the Taiwan Strait, as evidenced by American arms sales to Taiwan. The Bush administration also distanced itself from Europe and Europe's Balkan problems in Macedonia, Kosovo and Bosnia. In addition, bringing e Arab-Israeli conflict to an end was not on the agenda. Moreover, Bush's ecision to pull out of the Kyoto Protocol, and hostility to the UN conference n racism, were among the policy initiatives designed to push the U.S. ational interest agenda forward. These examples were indicators of nilateralism under the Bush administration, an attempt to project U.S. orld supremacy.

But, there is no agreement on the political shaping of a globalized future. he U.S. is facing considerable challenges in trying to organize an ternational order around the globalization project. The destruction of the orld Trade Center in September, 2001 heightens the perception that the .S. no longer projects an image of stability and strength. There is no redible evidence to support the claim that the terrorists were motivated by heir hatred of freedoms enjoyed by Americans. What the attack clearly shows is that U.S. global power is not invincible and is vulnerable. In response, the sole world superpower, with the most powerful military hardware, is relying on its military/political assets to institute an open world economy. (This was already in the making as evidenced earlier by its wars against Iraq and Yugoslavia.) The war against Afghanistan also shows that the U.S. is resorting to its military power as the only strategy for integrating the world economy, by extending NATO over non-NATO areas through a grand international coalition with Britain and other NATO member states. This is not an act of multilateralism, as it does not involve the UN, but it is an attempt to legitimize American unilateralism. It is based on the highly fragile support of such states as Saudi Arabia, Pakistan and Russia, and may cause great political turmoil in some Muslim countries.

The U.S. wants to govern the post Cold War world economy order under its hegemony. By using the act of terrorism, the Bush administration is re-orienting U.S. dominance in the world. This was clearly stated by Tony Blair, Prime Minister of Britain, in his televised public statement that we must *"re-order the world around us."* The U.S. administration plans to wage a *permanent war* in order to reorient the world around its power. Bush initially called this war a *crusade*, with no understanding of what the term implies. He then called it operation *infinite justice*, which did not go down well either, as he conflated American military might with God's own divine justice. The Pentagon soon found another name to describe this war: *operation enduring freedom.* Tony Blair directed the world's attention to the necessity of this war. He said we either *"defeat it [terrorism] or be defeated by it."* George Bush is now trying to consolidate the world order by coercing other states into an arbitrary choice between those states that are with the U.S. and those against the U.S. The phrase used by President Bush *"you are either with us or against us"* is intended to maximize his unilateralism in re-ordering the post Cold War world order.

The re-alignment of the world would take place along an ideologic divide between *enemies of freedom*, as Bush has called it, and the f world of the U.S. and its allies. His attempts to forge a world-wide politi and military alliance is built on the assumption that non-alignment against *enemies of freedom* is immoral. This is reminiscent of the Cold War ordering of the world after WWII. During the Cold War it was also deeme immoral not to be allies of the free world against "communism". Today is immoral not to be allied against "terrorists" or the "enemies of freedom Another cold war has been forged.

Afghan War and Caspian Oil

This new cold war is designed to promote the rapid development of Caspia oil and natural gas fields by breaking Russian monopoly control over the transportation of oil from the region. The Caspian region consists of the states of the former Soviet Union in the Transcaucasus and Central Asia, which contain the world's largest and most undeveloped sources of oil and gas fields. Geo-strategic control of this region, stretching from the oil city Baku in Azerbaijan through the Central Asian states of Turkmenistan, Uzbekistan, Kazakhstan, Tajikistan and Kyrgyzstan, has a counterweight to the Persian Gulf oil fields. The Transcaspian has now become the most important area of contention between Russia and Western powers (Croissant and Aras, 1999: 250). This is reminiscent to the 19th century imperialist competition for the control of Central Eurasia. According to Brzezinsky (1997), the present day version of this competition involves the restructuring of U.S. hegemony and its relations with Russia and China.

Central Asia is now the most important location for U.S. dominance in the world economy. The energy fields of the Caspian region are landlocked, which requires building pipelines travelling thousands of kilometres over mountains and deserts. There is an intense competition over who will build the pipelines and where they will go. This question is the source of contention for the oil fields in the Caspian region and mediates new regional coalitions favouring or threatening the U.S. presence in Central Asia. Pipelines are expensive to build and vulnerable to sabotage. The initial U.S. support of the Taliban was based on the expectation that the Taliban could have brought stability to the region.

The U.S. and Pakistan had decided to install a stable regime in Afghanistan since 1994 – a regime that would end the civil war and ensure the safety of a possible oil pipelines linking Caspian oil to the Pakistan port of Karachi through Afghanistan. During the Afghan Civil War the Taliban received arms and funding in their struggle against the ethnically Tajik Northern Alliance, a close ally of both Russia and Iran (Rashid, 2000). But, the Taliban never succeeded in building a stable, pro-American Afghani-